D1826516

2nd in the Hitler Escape Series

"Hitler and the Secret Alliance!"

The Unknown Alliance between Germany and Argentina that facilitated the escape of thousands of the crumbled Third Reich to safety.

by MICHAEL IVINHEIM

Edited by **Harry Cooper**

Published by
Sharkhunters International
P. O. Box 1539 Hernando, FL 34441

www.sharkhunters.com

YOU can be published in our Sharkhunters Books

We welcome any factual stories and especially any wartime photographs you wish to send to us. Feel free to send to us at the address above and you will see your name in print in a subsequent Sharkhunters book.

MANY THANKS to:

- Translator **PETER STOCKNER**, Member #6894;
- Proofreader **JEFF CARSON**, Member #7228;
- Translator **GABRIELE DORR**, Member #7567.

This book is written by **Michael Ivinheim.** Editor **Harry Cooper** arranged the text and photos. This is a Sharkhunters book.

DEDICATION & THANKS

This book is dedicated to all who lost their lives in the Battle of the Atlantic as well as on all other seas and oceans during World War II. It seems impossible that another war of the magnitude of WW II could ever happen again and it is virtually impossible that the deeds of the individual combatants could ever again be experienced. Warfare is now more of a computer game than the man against man, ship against ship or plane against plane combat that was the norm for World War II.

While no sane person wants or enjoys war, we must remember those who did their part for their country and who fought honorably for their homeland. There was a spirit of camaraderie, friendship and fun at times while there was despair and terror at other times. It is only by the people who were there and who tell their stories that the real history and the actual '*flavor*' of the era can be saved for all time.

To our Sharkhunters Members who took the time and effort to send their memories by audiotape, videotape, typed or hand-written, we extend our heartfelt thanks. Their memories of the War at Sea will be permanently preserved in history for all time not as the deductions and assumptions of hobbyists or aficionados who never tasted battle – but rather as the first person memories of those who did; the warriors of World War II.

About Sharkhunters

Sharkhunters is the largest research center and publication in the world covering the history of the German U-Bootwaffe of the 2nd World War. In this history of the U-Bootwaffe we also unveil the secrets of their many trips to South America – primarily to a secluded bay in Argentina bringing spies in and out as well as bringing money and equipment in to support their espionage work in the southern hemisphere. Sharkhunters has opened hundreds of formerly classified files and made all that information available. That is revealed in our book "*Hitler in Argentina*". Here **Michael Ivinheim** writes another chapter in this incredible history.

About the Author
Michael Ivinheim

"Until his recent retirement, **Michael Ivinheim** worked as a professional translator specializing in German military and political history. His access to this wide range of literature led him to suspect a conspiracy of silence respecting Argentina in both world wars. In this book, the result of long research and much careful reflection, he sets out the reasons for his belief in the existence of a secret alliance between Argentina and Germany from 1908, an arrangement which benefited the Third Reich during the Second World War and later in exile in Argentina from the 1945 capitulation onwards."

Michael Ivinheim is just one of our network of S.E.I.G. Agents worldwide who contribute their research efforts and their information to this priceless history.

S.E.I.G. is an acronym for **S**harkhunters **E**aglehunters **I**ntelligence **G**roup.

EDITOR NOTE - The European conflict of World War Two ended in early May 1945. Those Germans in the Fatherland suffered incredible hardships as well as deliberate cruelty at the hands of the victorious Allies, not the least of which was wholesale rape, murder and plunder. Sadly, this is the fate of any and all who are vanquished.

Not all Germans remained to suffer their fate at the hands of the victorious Allies. The strong and patriotic cry of,

"We will fight to the last man!"

really meant they would fight to the last sergeant while high ranking men escaped south – far south!

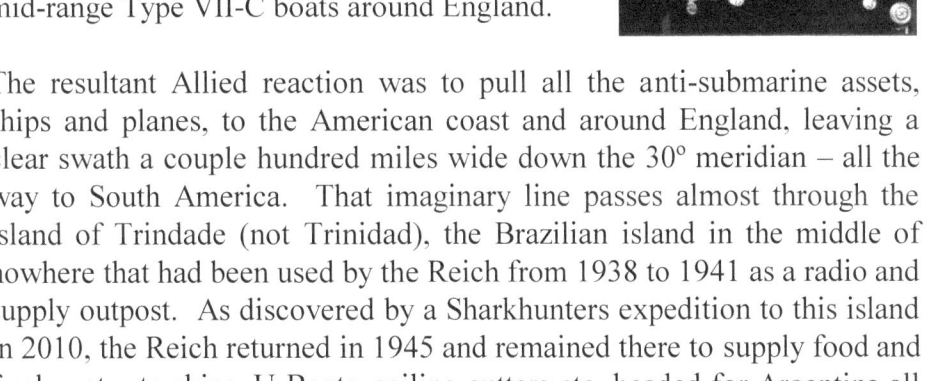

How was it possible for anyone to escape the vice of the Allies? Operation Mercator was put in place in late April 1945 as the final curtain was about to come down on the Reich. Großadmiral Karl Dönitz sent nearly two dozen long-range Type IX-C U-Boats to operate off the American east coast and almost 100 of the mid-range Type VII-C boats around England.

The resultant Allied reaction was to pull all the anti-submarine assets, ships and planes, to the American coast and around England, leaving a clear swath a couple hundred miles wide down the 30° meridian – all the way to South America. That imaginary line passes almost through the island of Trindade (not Trinidad), the Brazilian island in the middle of nowhere that had been used by the Reich from 1938 to 1941 as a radio and supply outpost. As discovered by a Sharkhunters expedition to this island in 2010, the Reich returned in 1945 and remained there to supply food and fresh water to ships, U-Boats, sailing cutters etc. headed for Argentina all the way until middle 1947 – two years **AFTER** the end of the war.

There are a great many stories of these exploits and in this book, Michael Ivinheim reveals what his research learned about a couple of these "*black boats*" that figure prominently into the history – not **OF** the end of the Third Reich, but rather of the relocation of it.

Preview from S.E.I.G. Agent **LUNAR**

"***Hitler and the Secret Alliance*** is a fantastic journey into the past and, to an extent, the present of the southern half of the Western Hemisphere. Almost everyone has been exposed to some aspects of World War I and II Germany and probably to a lesser extent, South America. However, only a few have delved deeply into the history of southern South America.

A few more will recall the brief war between England and Argentina where Argentina invaded and the British eventually retook the Falkland Islands/Islas Malvinas. The author briefly reviews the history behind the Falkland's importance to both countries. He gives some historical background on Argentina, Uruguay, Paraguay, Chile and the oceans bordering these countries.

The reader will more appreciate this book if he/she has some knowledge of the currently published history of this area and era, as he/she will be introduced to some amazing insights into history as one reads this book.

The secrets of governments (especially in wartime) are many times hidden from the world by subterfuge sometimes described as '*smoke and mirrors*'. No facts (truths) being clearly observable due to the '*smoke*' and never located where it seems, due to false reflections of the '*mirrors*'.

Winston Churchill is quoted as saying; '***In wartime, truth is so precious that she should always be attended by a bodyguard of lies.***' So, dissecting a government secret is like peeling an onion one thin layer at a time. First you peel away the layers of lies, one at a time, until you expose the truth. Then, you begin peeling away the layers of truth from the secret until it is no longer a secret!

Michael Ivinheim demonstrates, very effectively, this approach in this book. He applies logical perspective on known and verified incidents, geographical locations, participant's first person narratives, released government documents, media articles and what I call legends passed from person to person and generation to generation.

6

Ivinheim then adds his expertise and command of multiple languages from years of experience to his ability to seek out the nuances of language to assist him in '*reading between the lines*' of written sources with great accuracy. This reading between the lines ability of the author greatly enhances the reader's ability to see the underlying '*truth*' of any of the secrets being examined, thus assisting the process of identifying the lies, disinformation and just plain fantasy that are generally used to disguise '*secrets*'.

Readers having an interest in and/or working knowledge of this area of world history from current sources will be amazed how this book puts incidents in perspective and makes the gaps in this history suddenly apparent. For example, the presence of German nationals and representatives of the German government in South America has always been more or less obvious to the public. The extent of this presence in terms of land ownership, businesses and manufacturing enterprises and the influence on countries such as Argentina as illustrated in this book will amaze even the knowledgeable reader.

To delve into any specific examples of the author's work in this discussion would, I believe, simply help spoil the suspense of the book for the reader. Pick up this book with an open mind, as some of the content verges on the unbelievable, while at the same time remembering that a few short years ago, a man walking on the moon was considered science fiction, and aircraft with the ability to hide from radar was unheard of! In defense of the above statement I would like to quote a passage from the closing pages of **Ivinheim's** book;

> '*Once we have ruled out all the possibilities to explain a mystery, whatever remains, however improbable, must be the truth!*'"

Hitler & The Secret Alliance!

Comments about this particular segment of history from the Editor of this book and President of Sharkhunters, **Harry Cooper**.

"We had heard of these stories for decades but each time I tried to get information from official sources, I was blocked, so we put this project on the back burner. Then in about 1995 or so, I received a call from a retired Argentine Navy Officer who told me not to give up this search because these phantom U-Boats DO exist in reality and in official Argentine Navy files. This re-kindled our quest into the history of the relationship between Argentina and the Third Reich and so I wish to extend my sincere thanks to Lt. Cdr. **EDUARDO GERDING (6895-2004)**, Argentine Navy (Retired)"

A Special Thanks

To my wife Kay and to my kids, Sean and Meaghan. Their support while this book was underway was priceless. And to **Michael Ivinheim** – thanks for your incredible research into this part of history.

TABLE OF CONTENTS

TABLE OF CONTENTS (continued)

The previous pertain to the work of Michael Ivinheim. We now present excerpts from the KTB Magazine of Sharkhunters.

Here begins the story by Michael Ivinheim

THE SECRET ALLIANCE

The German Naval Presence in Argentine Waters from 1908

INTRODUCTION

"We shall never forget, nor be able to repay, the immense debt of gratitude we owe our comrades of the German Army."

Colonel Juan Domingo Perón, 4 April 1952; quoted in Silvano Santander: *Técnica de una traición*, Buenos Aires 1955.

Argentina became the destination for the wealth and advanced military technology of National Socialism at the end of the Second World War. Without the collaboration of Vice-President Perón it would not have been possible. For his debt of gratitude to remain valid in 1952, clearly whatever it was that the German Army had done to deserve it was truly colossal. The debt was the basis for the Secret Alliance between Germany and Argentina. The unheralded arrival of German U-Boats along the Argentine coast after the Second World War to unload passengers and cargo was an arrangement under the Secret Alliance. Nowadays it suits the political purposes of Argentina to know nothing of any such arrangement, and since the early 1990s it has been the aim of the Argentine Government to prove that there never was any such thing.

In May 1997, President Carlos Menem created the so-called Commission for the Clarification of Nazi Activities in Argentina (CEANA) by decree. Its express purpose was to "*come clean*" about collaboration between the Argentine Government and Nazism in the period 1933-1955, when Perón was overthrown. Menem said he was hoping to contribute to a "*greater transparency*" of Argentina's recent history, to build "*a new image*" and to "*intensify our carnal relationship with the United States.*" In view of the latter aim, any hope of a genuine impartial review of the facts was thus doomed from the start; the review was to be a whitewash.

The problem confronting historians and writers researching the naval wars in and around Argentina is that so few files have been declassified. Where the authorities have released genuinely sensitive material, it will generally have been only to Argentine nationals on a conditional basis. Therefore the world at large has to rely on what Argentine writers allege the material contains; an unsatisfactory state of affairs for the historian. In accepting the documentation for publication, the Argentine author will have to agree to publish only what he is told he may publish; he must not show the material to a third party and although he must report honestly what the material says, I know of at least one case where an item, a place-name, had to be misrepresented by the author to make it appear that the incident occurred in a neighbouring country to spare Argentina repercussions and embarrassment. (This is not exclusively an Argentine failing; Admiral Sturdee lied in his official report of March 1915 on the Battle of the Falklands, probably at the instigation of the British Admiralty, to hide from public view the presence of one particular German merchant ship, for reasons which will become clear in Part One of this volume).

Frederick Doveton Sturdee   Carlos Saùl Menem

A pro-Allied author, Uki Goñi, considered that CEANA provided excellent proof of the way Argentina continues to blur its wartime and postwar record:

*"I formed part of CEANA for three days in November 1998, resigning when it became evident that there were irreconcilable differences of criteria."***(1)**

First it may be asked what archives are open to the public in Argentina. The time limit on State documents is thirty years, and in 1992 by presidential decree all Nazi-related**(2)** records were supposed to be declassified. The observations of three authors throws light on what may be expected:

"In a blaze of publicity in 1992, the Government of Carlos Menem announced the opening of Argentina's Nazi files to researchers. The international Press descended on Buenos Aires, anxious to discover the truth behind the old rumours of Perón's secret dalliance with Hitler. But no such revelation was at hand. Instead, reporters and researchers found a batch of dog-eared "intelligence dossiers" containing mostly faded Press clippings but precious little new information....the dossiers proved hugely disappointing to journalists, while scholars inwardly cheered - the lack of evidence seemed to corroborate the growing consensus in academia that no Odessa had ever existed. In Buenos Aires, much of the vital documentation had reportedly been destroyed back in 1955, during the last days of Perón's Government, and again in 1996." (Uki Goñi).

A German author found:

*"In 2003, the new Government of Peronist Néstor Kirchner announced that it would permit access to archives which might contain information about the rat line - the flight of wanted Nazis to South America. Until then in the search for international documents it had been customary to be told: 'It cannot be found' or, 'It has been destroyed'"***(3)**.

Salinas and De Napoli discovered the following procedure to be in force when looking for naval archives from 1945:

> *"Holga Meding, author of* La ruta de los Nazis, *looked in Box 64 at the Naval General Archive for the report of base commander Mallea on the interrogations of Wermuth and Schäffer, and decree 19.160 transferring U-977 to the United States. After finding that this box contained only documents about the crew of* Admiral Graf Spee, *we were losing all hope of finding what we wanted...Midway through June 2002, when our book was practically finished, we applied without any great expectation of success - through the President of the Defence Committee of the Chamber of Deputies, Miguel Toma - to the Chief of the General Naval Staff, Admiral Joaquín Stella. He sent us to an even higher officer who, without too much red tape allowed us a brief look at the precious archives and gave us photocopies of the Spanish language translations of the interrogations of the two U-boat commanders, jealously guarded for the past 57 years. We suppose that the Navy took the decision in order to distance itself from the CEANA report of Professor Newton, in which it was not invited to participate.*(4)

Nestor Kirchner

One of the ten modules of the CEANA investigation ordered by President Menem in 1995 appeared in print in Spanish (in translation *Clandestine Activities of the German Navy in Argentine Waters)* by Professor Newton, a Canadian historian. He was given exclusive responsibility for furnishing a report on the naval aspects. Lacking any knowledge of U-Boats and their operations he was therefore not well qualified to author a report which made *"special reference to the surrender of the two German submarines at Mar del Plata in 1945."*

He had published a paper for the Argentinians in 1988 and thus the result of his endeavour in February 1998 was merely a rehash of what he had done ten years earlier(**5**).

When the Argentine Government appointed a scholar to review the classified material in its national archives with the primary objective of "*making a clean breast of it*", instead of opening the archive to the public, the last thing it wished to know was that an unknown number of German submarines actually did unload along its shores, and that even the two submarines it knew about did not come down to Argentina for the purpose everybody thought they did.

Professor Newton was not about to provide any unpopular revelations, however. Far from "*indulging the cheap fiction of the sensationalist Press*" as he said, he was firmly convinced that,

"Probably we shall never find an explanation for the inexplicable submarine sightings in 1945."

Police and naval witnesses were notoriously unreliable observers and could be discounted;

"Who knows what they saw?"

…..he demanded, and

"Nor is there any substantial evidence, no U-Boat wreck, no police dossier with photo or fingerprints, no death-bed testimony on the part of some German or Argentino-German participant, no discovery of identifiable human remains which would support an affirmative response to these enquiries."

What enquiries?

Professor Newton was not one to tarry with circumstantial evidence; even for the sake of denying the possibility out of hand he was not disposed to wonder about U-Boats taken off for use elsewhere or scrapped for their valuable parts and torpedoes. Apart from the two they knew about, the Argentine Government wanted no U-Boats and they got no U-Boats. In the midst of the tortuous labyrinth of lies, deceit and denials Professor Newton was cute enough to spot that four U-Boat crews had got home from Argentina and it was only known how two of these crews got to Argentina in order to be repatriated from there. To his credit he stated so and quoted his sources but split the information into two parts across different chapters so that the reader needed to be alert to spot it.

The German U-Boat Arm was formidable, he conceded, but it "*did not have much margin for manouevre in Argentine waters.*"

This was because the "*German espionage network was inept and unmindful of security. The local Buenos Aires Nazis were stupid.*"

He pointed to the conditions in which "*a lone U-Boat bound for Argentina would have had to face a clandestine group of German fugitives to organize the reception, the evasion of detection before, during and after the disembarkations, and the question of refueling and reprovisioning during the voyage.*"

This is a bogus argument. Large German U-boats could be provisioned and fuelled to make even the Far East non-stop, and Argentina is less than half the distance.

EDITOR NOTE – The Type IX-D2 boats had a range of more than 32,000 nautical miles. That is one and a half times around the world without refueling.

The Argentine Navy was recalled to port on 21 July 1945 leaving the 3000 kilometres of coast and river open to all callers after that date. The Lahusen network of "*stupid*" spies and the "*inept*" *Admiral Graf Spee* administrative office, which had arranged two hundred successful escapes from Argentina to Germany by officers and technical NCO's of the pocket battleship, 1/6 of the entire crew, handled the reception of the U-Boats.

All this is overlooked by Professor Newton, who ended his report with the First Commandment:
"*Two and only two U-boats came down to Argentina. Any other hypothesis is impossible.*"

It is now more than sixty-five years since the main body of events retold here drew the curtain over the seaborne activities of the German Navy in two world wars. There are many inconsistencies in the official histories, most of them deliberate, and I have attempted to set the record straight where I could. I dedicate my book to the memory of Fritz Berger, who knew the Great Secret of Tiahuanacu.

Michael Ivinheim
January 2011

Footnotes:
(1) Uki Goñi: *The Real Odessa*, Granta Books, 2003.
(2) For the sake of brevity and following the Argentine tradition I have generally shortened the term "*National Socialist*" to "*Nazi*" in the text. This is neither deprecatory nor has any political implication, it is simply a shortening of the term. See Heinrich Heim *Monologe im FHQ 1941-1944*, Orbis Verlag special edition 2000, discourse of 22 February 1942, p.293 in which Hitler uses "*Nazi*" similarly.
(3) Gaby Weber: *La Conexión Alemana*: Edhasa, Buenos Aires 2002, p.10
(4) Salinas/De Nápoli: *Ultramar Sur*, Ed. Norma, Buenos Aires, 2002, p.421
(5) Professor Newton is the author of *The Nazi Menace in Argentina 1931-1947*, Leland Stanford Junior University 1992; Spanish title *El cuarto lado del triángulo*, Panamericana, Buenos Aires 1995, a well researched scholarly volume covering all aspects of the Nazi penetration of Argentina but woefully short on naval knowledge and expertise.

CHAPTER ONE

From the Turn of the 19th Century to the Battle of the Falklands, 8 December 1914

The shoreline of Patagonia on the Atlantic side lies between 36°S and Cape Horn. It extends for 3000 kilometres. The Patagonia of Argentina is much greater in size than many European States but has one of the lowest densities of population in the world, in the 1930s only one person per five square kilometres. The scarcity of inhabitants is the direct consequence of the massacre of native aborigines practised towards the end of the 19th century and known as "*depopulation policy*".

In 1892 the Buenos Aires daily *El Día* proclaimed;
"The southern territories have their own future and are exclusively for the Northern European races: Germans, Austrians, British, Scandinavians, Russians and Danes must be the natural peoples of these immense areas. For that end to be achieved, Congress must contribute facilities towards encouraging immigration into those territories, the land to be split up in such a manner as to attract peoples as did North America."

In Patagonia the seeds of "*Germanism*" fell on fertile soil. Immigration was already under way from the mid to late 19th century. When the new century dawned, the new breed of conquistadores led by the Germans owned huge landed estates, many exceeding two million hectares. While Argentine officers received training in Berlin, German officers came to Patagonia to organize the Argentine forces in the classic Prussian style with German military discipline, German uniforms and German weapons.

In 1898 Germany had begun using its naval attachés at embassies and consulates abroad to set up a clandestine net of coastal stations. The idea was to unite representatives of shipping companies, chandlers and coal merchants into a rudimentary system for the replenishment of German warships in time of crisis.

Each station of the *Etappendienst* (literally *'service supporting the fighting front'*) was run by a naval officer controlling a number of spies (*'V-men'*) who gathered information and maintained contact with the net. Secrecy was essential, for the British secret service had a worldwide organization involving suppliers, ships' masters, consular officials and other intermediaries.

In 1908, Lt Wilhelm Canaris (photo left), commander's adjutant aboard the small cruiser **BREMEN**, became involved in a project to erect a network of V-men along the coasts of Argentina, Brazil and Chile.

One of the most important sheep-farming landowning families of Argentine Patagonia whom he contacted was the Lahusen dynasty from Bremen. Hardly a village in Patagonia did not have its Lahusen store and there was little about Patagonia that the Lahusen organisation did not know. Between the wars it was a standing joke in political circles that Hitler knew more about Patagonia than the Government in Buenos Aires did. When they bought the agency of the Hamburg-Südamerika shipping line in 1906, the Lahusens needed a coastal HQ as an operational base. They chose the town of San Antonio Oeste located in the north-west corner of the Gulf of San Matías.

First settled in 1905, it lacked paved roads, all work being concentrated on building a port facility to receive wool, leather and feathers from outlying farms for shipping to Buenos Aires. Most structures were shacks of sheet metal when the Lahusen Company arrived in 1908. Two years later the Argentine Government announced its intention to build a single track railroad from Viedma on the Atlantic coast through San Antonio Oeste to Bariloche near the Chilean border and from there across the Andes to Osorno, thus connecting the Atlantic to the Pacific and opening up the region.

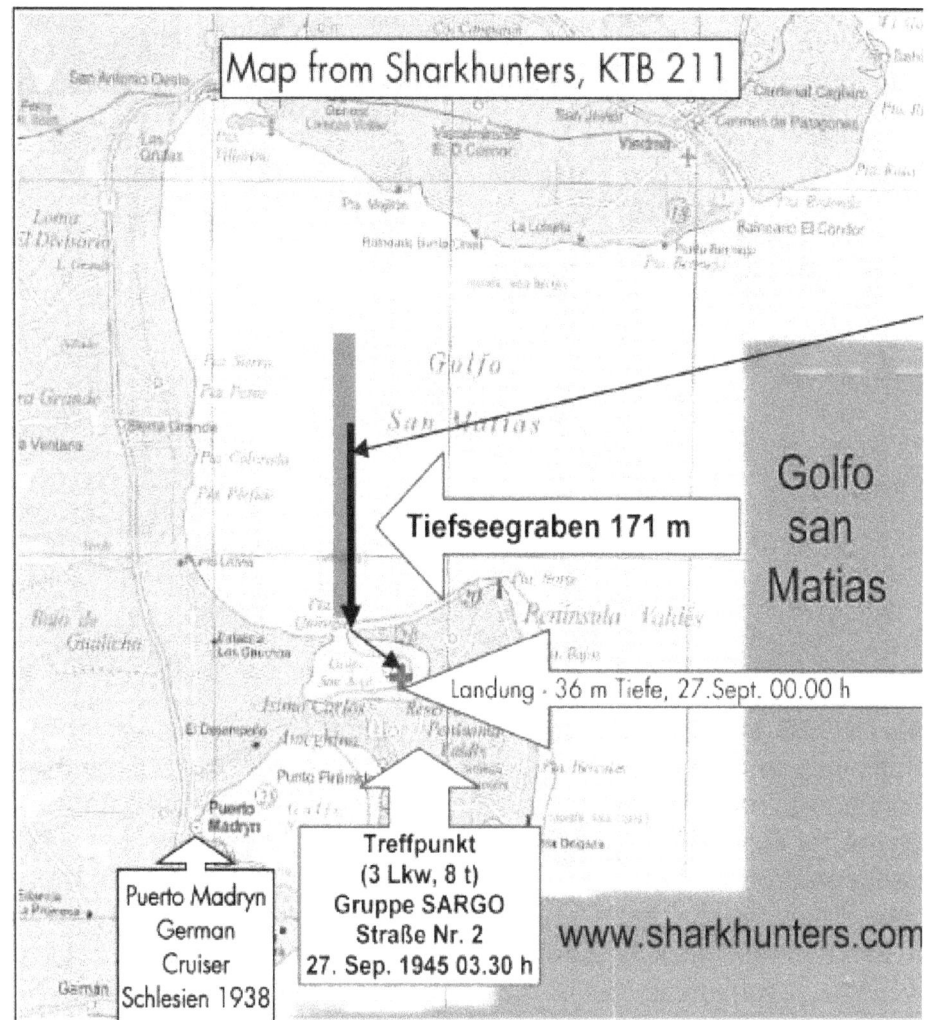

San Antonio Oeste is seen in the upper left of this map

Investors were not enthusiastic for political reasons, and eventually the line ran only from San Antonio Oeste westwards. When the money ran out, the railroad finished at the hamlet of Ingeniero Jacobacci in the middle of nowhere and 100 miles short of Bariloche and there it remains intact to this very day as though that was all that was ever intended. At the outbreak of war in August 1914, San Antonio Oeste was a small town with a dock, a couple of schools and the HQ building of the Lahusen wool empire. This building was centre of German naval espionage in Argentina.

AUTHORS NOTE – This pretty little bungalow in the seaport of San Antonio Oeste, Gulf of San Mathias, was built in 1905 by the Lahusen Wool Enterprise. In both World Wars it served as the centre for German espionage in Patagonia. So efficient was the Lahusen organization that it became a standing joke in Berlin that Hitler knew more about Patagonia than Buenos Aires did.

On 21 July 1908 in a Letters Patent, the British Government declared sovereignty over a huge area of the South Atlantic Ocean region based on their occupation of the Falklands Islands. At the time a nation of rapacious, bellicose racists upon whose great empire the sun never set, these Letters Patent laid claim to the territories of Chile and Argentina south of the line 50°S. Argentine had had experience of British invasions of Buenos Aires province in the previous hundred years, all of which had been beaten off, but invading Patagonia from the Falklands would be something the British had not tried before. In its claim was inherent the threat that Britain would eventually attempt to enforce sovereignty over the region by force of arms and it was this fear which led to the Secret Alliance between Germany and Argentina in the world wars and subsequently.

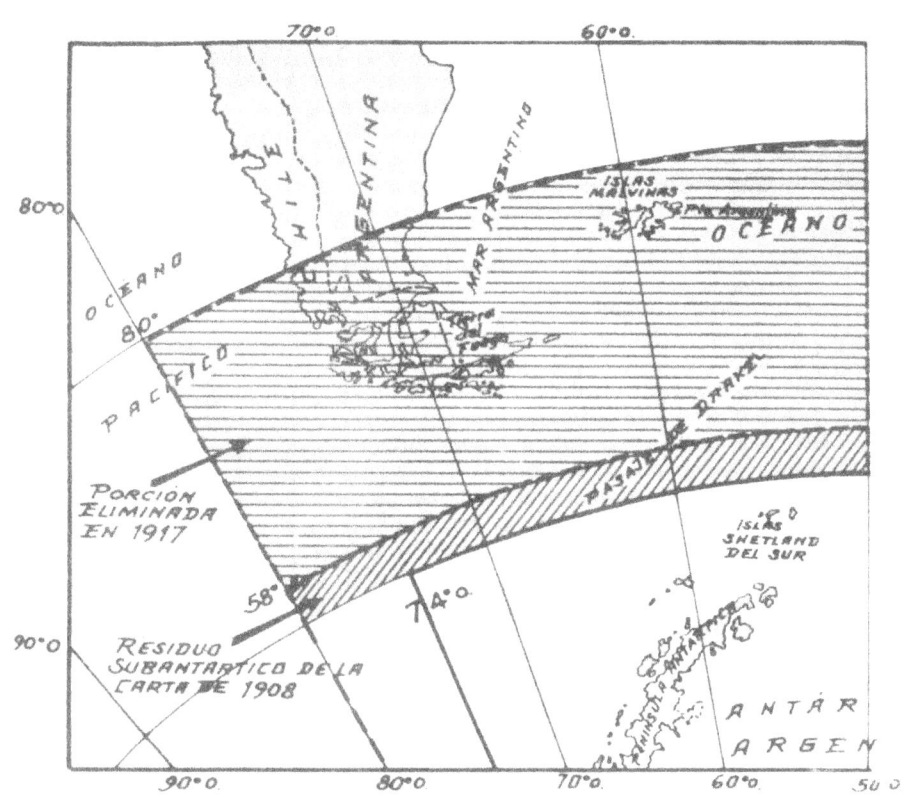

The area over which Great Britain proposed dominance.

SMS Dresden from Brazil to Easter Island

4 August 1914 the small cruiser **DRESDEN** (Fregettenkapitän Lüdecke) began commerce warfare against Entente shipping. While re-coaling in rough seas at Trindade Island off the coast of Brazil she received hull and structural damage. Being unable to coal satisfactorily, Lüdecke decided to find some remote Patagonian bay to coal up and repair.

Photo of Trindade taken by the Editor in 2009

On 8 August the cruiser was seen off Camocin by a British merchant vessel and reported to the British authorities in Brazil. Seven days later off Pernambuco, **DRESDEN** sank the British freighter **HYADES**. Her crew was put aboard the supply ship **PRUSSIA**, which landed them at Rio. This was an error which confirmed the presence of the German cruiser in Brazilian waters and her direction of travel. The British Admiralty now ordered Rear-Admiral Christopher Cradock to hunt for **DRESDEN** with his squadron of three cruisers and an AMC.

Argentina was neutral and friendly towards Germany and did not enforce the rules of neutrality strictly in areas of low population. ***DRESDEN*** re-coaled at several locations once in the waters of Chubut province. Lt Wilhelm Canaris, fifth officer of the cruiser who spoke good Spanish, used these re-coaling stops to make enquiries of the local inhabitants and noted for later valuable information about coves and bays along the coast.

EDITOR NOTE – These were called U-Plätze meaning hidden place. Canaris made detailed notes about these hidden coves and in 1938, an old German line ship retraced the route laid out by Canaris and further updated these charts for use in World War Two. One of these charts is shown here. Sharkhunters has many such charts

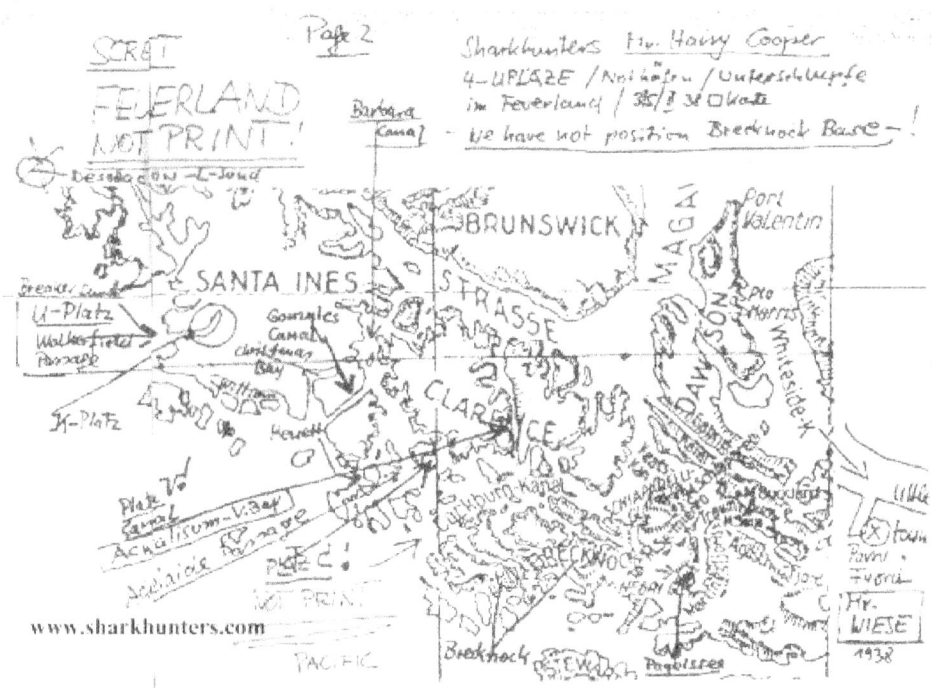

Chart supplied by Sharkhunters S.E.I.G. Agent **PIZZARRO**

On 2 September 1914 ***DRESDEN*** and her supply ship ***BADEN*** arrived at Hoste Island near False Cape Horn and here they spent the next ten days repairing the cruiser. A second supply ship, ***SANTA ISABEL*** was sent to Punta Arenas to communicate with Berlin, and on 11 September Lt.

Neiling brought news that the armoured cruisers **GOOD HOPE** (flagship of Admiral Cradock) plus **MONMOUTH**, and the light cruiser **GLASGOW** were operating east of the Straits of Magellan presumably in search of **DRESDEN**. This information was false. Cradock was at Montevideo with no knowledge of the whereabouts of the German cruiser, but to be on the safe side the German Admiralty recommended that Lüdecke join forces with the small cruiser **LEIPZIG** off the coast of western Chile.

SMS DRESDEN

On 25 September Berlin informed Lüdecke that Admiral Graf von Spee's East Asia Squadron was heading for Easter Island, and on 27th **SANTA ISABEL** brought news that Cradock's squadron was at Punta Arenas and that the British had halted all their merchant sailings along the west coast of Chile. The supply ship was then ordered to Valparaiso to expand Canaris' espionage system and arrange for the resupply of the East Asia Squadron. During this period Canaris had been busy. Ships of Norddeutscher Lloyd, HAPAG and the local German-owned Kosmos Line which were equipped with radio-telegraphy were asked to call in at Corall, Coronel, Talcahuano and Valparaiso under cover of darkness to collect telegrams and transmit the encoded contents. Later this system of spies and spy-ships would be found very useful by Admiral Spee. On the night of 30 September, learning that Admiral Cradock's four ships were making for the Chilean west coast, **DRESDEN** and **LEIPZIG** headed for Easter Island, where **DRESDEN** arrived alone on 11 October.

At sea on 4 October **DRESDEN** had established radio contact for the first time with von Spee's flagship **SCHARNHORST**. The latter advised that the German squadron was intending to reach the coast of southern Chile, at which **DRESDEN** in her reply warned of the presence of Cradock's squadron at Punta Arenas. This signal was intercepted, decoded in London and sent to Cradock, who had meanwhile reversed course from Punta Arenas for the Falklands.

SMS SCHARNHORST

The East Asia Squadron from
Tsingtau to Easter Island

On 20 June 1914 the armoured cruiser ***GNEISENAU*** left the German

Admiral Maximilian
Graf von Spee

colony of Tsingtau on the coast of China to collect cables from Berlin at Nagasaki for Admiral von Spee's East Asia Squadron, and on 7 July she joined with her sister ship ***SCHARNHORST*** at Truk in the Carolinas. The two 11,000-tonne armoured cruisers, the small cruiser ***LEIPZIG*** and a large retinue of supply ships and colliers now headed for the Eastern Pacific. Once war broke out, more than eighty Allied warships and many units of the Japanese Fleet searched for them in the Indian Ocean and Western Pacific.

SMS GNEISENAU

On 14 September, Admiral von Spee betrayed his whereabouts by showing the flag off the German colony of Samoa following its occupation by a New Zealand Expeditionary Force under Vice-Admiral Patey aboard his flagship *AUSTRALIA* and French Vice-Admiral de Kerilly aboard the cruiser *MONTCALM*. During the invasion and occupation, the German Governor had been kidnapped and maltreated, a serious breach of diplomatic protocol, and deported to Fiji with his staff.

Pochhammer describes it thus:

> *"At 0900 hrs on 15 September 1914 we approached the strait of Apolimas which separates the two large islands of the Samoan group. At the extreme west of Upola, a white launch came out from the coast wearing a black-white-red ensign. SCHARNHORST headed for it and took aboard two German plantation owners. They reported that on 30 August a powerful fleet had appeared off Apia led by the battle cruiser HMAS AUSTRALIA. There were a large number of Australian and New Zealand warships and troop transports. After the surrender of the islands (no resistance was offered, there being no fighting troops, only German and native police) the German Governor was taken aboard AUSTRALIA where he was brutally maltreated, and on 31 August deported with some of his staff to Suva, Fiji. An English officer was appointed to administer the islands."*

This event was the reason behind the intended German attack on the Falklands Islands at the end of 1914.

A few days after the Samoan visit, the squadron was seen off Bora-Bora in Polynesia and on 21 September bombarded the French island of Tahiti. The Allies now knew roughly where von Spee was and in what direction he was heading (the Atlantic) by virtue of their having the German naval code. On 12 October 1914, the squadron reached Easter Island to rest and re-coal.

From Easter Island to the Battle of Coronel

The surprise of the Easter Island inhabitants, who received the visit of one Chilean training cruiser twice yearly, was complete on 12 October 1914 with the appearance at the western end of their islands of no less than four large light-grey warships. The British administrator of a large estate, Mr. Henry Percival Edmunds, went aboard **SCHARNHORST** with the Chilean harbourmaster. Neither knew that war had broken out, and von Spee negotiated the purchase of cattle and sheep for the ships' butchers while the natives brought poultry, eggs and fruit. Mr. Edmunds was unable to determine the names of the four warships. The day was spent coaling inshore.

On 14 October the small cruiser **LEIPZIG** appeared from the north in company with three Kosmos Line steamers, and now Admiral von Spee had his full squadron of two armoured and three small cruisers: **SCHARNHORST** and **GNEISENAU, NÜRNBERG, DRESDEN** and **LEIPZIG.**

After hearing the reports of Lüdecke and Haun, commander of **LEIPZIG**, Spee recognized that the strategy of commerce warfare could not be pursued under the circumstances:

> *"The presence of strong enemy forces along the coast renders it impossible for the time being to carry out the original task, war on merchant shipping. In its place it is necessary to destroy the enemy squadron."*

Thus he decided he must go on the offensive, fearing that the British might bring up reinforcements. Accordingly he informed his commanders that he had to break through into the Atlantic before the enemy became too strong.

SCHARNHORST and **GNEISENAU** had sailed ten thousand miles without suffering damage or serious mechanical failure, and were well provisioned. After completing re-coaling, on 18 October the German squadron left Easter Island for Juan Fernández Island west of Valparaiso to complete the preparations for the voyage around Cape Horn into the South Atlantic.

Admiral Craddock in the Falklands had drawn a conclusion initially that it was important to intercept the German squadron in the Pacific. His thinking led him to mark his chart at Chonos south of Chiloé on the Chilean coast as his base for sorties. The British Admiralty was confident that his two 1899-built armoured cruisers *GOOD HOPE* and *MONMOUTH*, and the small cruiser *GLASGOW*, were enough to destroy the German squadron. Following a more sober appraisal of the respective strengths and weaknesses, however, he had begun to doubt he could overcome the five German ships together, since he would be outgunned and probably outranged. The German crews were also all regular navy men while he had many reservists. Now he proposed basing the centre of attack to radiate from the Falklands. In this he was overruled, and obliged to sail on 22 October for Chonos, where he arrived in his flagship *GOOD HOPE* five days later to find *MONMOUTH*, *GLASGOW* and the armed passenger ship *OTRANTO* awaiting him.

HMS GOOD HOPE

The Battle of Coronel

On 1 November 1914, Admiral Craddock formed a line four abreast with twenty miles between each ship proceeding at ten knots on a north-westerly heading off Concepción. At 1620 hrs when the line had fully extended, smoke was seen to the east and soon afterwards *GLASGOW* reported,

"Two armoured cruisers with four funnels, and a small cruiser with three funnels, in sight."

At 1700 Craddock had his battle line *GOOD HOPE-MONMOUTH-GLASGOW-OTRANTO* in place and at 1758 hrs he turned his squadron to run a course parallel to the German ships. von Spee declined combat and held his distance at 14 kilometers because the setting sun blinded his gunnery officers.

During the brief period when he had this advantage, Craddock had to consider whether he should engage the enemy this evening having regard to the heavy sea running and his disadvantage in gunnery. The respective broadsides were 1952 kilos as against his 1316 kilos. Only the two 9.2 inch guns aboard *GOOD HOPE* could inflict serious damage on the German armoured cruisers but his own gunners were mainly reservists.

Possibly he would have been mindful of the accusations of cowardice leveled at Rear-Admiral Sir Ernest Troubridge for not intercepting the German battle cruiser *GOEBEN* and the small cruiser *BRESLAU* in the Mediterranean in August 1914 on the grounds that they amounted to a superior force. At 1808 hrs his advantage dissolved and at 1818 hrs he obeyed his orders to the letter and ordered his squadron to 17 knots. *OTRANTO* being without armour was to drop back.

The opposing squadrons were as follows:

East Asia Squadron

- *SCHARNHORST*, (flagship) launched 1906, 11616 tonnes, 22.5 knots, eight x 8.2-inch in two twin turrets and four single casemates: six x 5.9-inch in single mountings;
- *GNEISENAU*, sister ship, all details similar;
- *NÜRNBERG*, launched 1906, 3469 tonnes, 23 knots, ten x 4.1-inch in single turrets;

Not involved in battle until closing stages:

- *LEIPZIG*, launched 1905, 3278 tonnes, 22 knots, armament as *NÜRNBERG*;
- *DRESDEN*, launched 1907, 3364 tonnes, 24 knots, armament as *NÜRNBERG.*

Admiral Craddock's Squadron

- *GOOD HOPE* (flagship), launched 1899, 14,100 tonnes, 23 knots, two 9.2-inch and sixteen x 6-inch in single casemates;
- *MONMOUTH*, launched 1901, 9800 tonnes, 23.5 knots, fourteen x 6-inch in two twin turrets and ten casemates;
- *OTRANTO,* armed merchant cruiser, not involved in line of battle;
- *GLASGOW*, launched 1909, 4820 tonnes, 26.3 knots, two x 6-inch and six 4-inch in single mounts.

The German squadron was steaming south between Craddock's line and the coast. This made the German ships difficult to pick out against the overcast and dark backdrop of the Andes Mountains whereas the British ships were highlighted against the lighter horizon.

At 1834 hrs *SCHARNHORST* opened fire at *GOOD HOPE* from a range of 10.3 kilometers. The third salvo destroyed one of the two 9.2-inch turrets. *MONMOUTH*, under fire from *GNEISENAU*, was hit by her third salvo forward, one of her 6-inch batteries being knocked out.

Already the big disadvantage was obvious to Craddock. *SCHARNHORST* and *GNEISENAU* were firing 8.2-inch salvoes every twenty seconds. *GOOD HOPE* had only one big gun left, while *MONMOUTH* could bring only seven of her six-inch guns to bear at any one time. The Germans were firing from the limit of their range and this was 300 meters longer than the British range. Driven by Force 6 winds heavy seas were flooding the lower casemates, rendering the inferior British optics unserviceable. If ever there was a time to honourably disengage, this was it.

By 1914 hrs *MONMOUTH* had taken enough punishment and pulled out of the line to starboard to escape the German fire and follow the flagship. Both British armoured cruisers were enveloped in flames and smoke and unable to avoid being hit repeatedly. Meanwhile *LEIPZIG* and *GLASGOW* fought out a duel in very high seas while *DRESDEN* pursued *OTRANTO*. *GOOD HOPE* had been hit at least thirty-five times by 8.2 inch shells and had suffered severe damage to the forward part of the ship. She was ablaze in the interior and this fire could not be extinguished. At 1953 hrs a terrible explosion resulted between the foremast and the leading funnel, flames reaching a height of 180 feet. Afire, hull blackened and sinking slowly, the flagship sought her grave in the darkness.

SCHARNHORST now concentrated fire on *MONMOUTH*, which had been hit thirty times by *GNEISENAU* and was listing to port but managing to fire sporadically. Around 2005 hrs *MONMOUTH* and *GLASGOW* ceased firing because the German gunners were aiming at the muzzle flashes in the darkness. In the final phase of the action the three German small cruisers prepared their torpedoes. At 2020 hrs the fastest ship present, *GLASGOW*, ran for safety.

NÜRNBERG found *MONMOUTH*, which had unsuccessfully tried to run ashore, and since she would not strike her flag, pumped shells into her at short range until she turned turtle and sank. Because of the high seas running and the uncertainty where *GLASGOW* was, Fregettenkapitän Schönberg of *NÜRNBERG* decided he could not risk lowering his boats to search for survivors. *LEIPZIG* found wreckage where *GOOD HOPE* was thought to have gone down, but none of her crew could be found.

It was the worst naval defeat suffered by the Royal Navy for over a century. Both armoured cruisers had been lost with all hands. *GLASGOW* and *OTRANTO* escaped.

On the German side *GNEISENAU* had received one 6-inch hit from *MONMOUTH* which penetrated the belt armour, injuring one man slightly and causing a fire in the clothing store.

At 1000 hrs on 3 November 1914 the Curaumilla lighthouse off Valparaiso reported the approach of several warships. At 1100 hrs a pilot vessel indicated to *SCHARNHORST* where she should anchor before receiving protocol salutes from three Chilean cruisers.

At Valparaiso for Orders (1)

On 3 November 1914 *SCHARNHORST, GNEISENAU* and *NÜRNBERG* entered the roadstead at Valparaiso to receive the adulation of the large Chilean-German colony. The German Minister, von Erckert, and the Consul-General, Dr Gumprecht, came aboard the flagship to provide Admiral von Spee with an update on the progress of the war and the situation in the Atlantic. At three in the afternoon Spee went to the German consulate to receive his orders and cabled a preliminary report on the Battle of Coronel to Berlin. He spent the rest of the afternoon closeted with von Erckert and Gumprecht studying the movements of British warships in the Atlantic and the possibilities of recoaling and reprovisioning there.

In the evening Admiral Spee attended a banquet at the Club Alemán which he left in sour mood after hearing an insult to the memory of Vice-Admiral Craddock. Upon leaving an embassy official, and a good friend of his, wished him *Auf wiedersehen.*

   "No," Spee replied, *"not auf wiedersehen, but adieu."*

This French word, used in the German language, has the terminal and tragic sense of *'Goodbye for ever'*. Spee added,
   "I know the British will destroy me just as I have destroyed them."

On the way to the naval pinnace he made a remark in similar vein upon being presented with a bouquet of roses. He accepted them with the solemn assurance that "*they would look very nice on his tomb*".

From the morose nature of his demeanour at Valparaiso it would appear that it was there on 3 November that he received his secret orders to attack the Falklands and he knew this would mean his death. No archive document has ever come to light in Germany ordering the attack and to the official report of the disaster furnished by the senior surviving officer Commander Pochhammer, the Kaiser appended the following manuscript note;
   "It remains a mystery what made Spee attack the Falkland Islands. See Mahan's Naval Strategy."(**2**)

Therefore, if it can be believed that neither the German Naval High Command nor the Kaiser ordered it, and it is clear that Admiral von Spee was not happy about doing it, the order must have come from the Foreign Ministry with a warning that it remain clandestine and it would been relayed to von Spee by von Erckert and Gumprecht. If that is the case, the connivance of the Argentine and Chilean Governments must be suspected, although there is not the least iota of proof of it.

Valparaiso was the mobilisation centre for German reservists and volunteers in South America. During the early morning of 4 November interviews were held to fill the 127 vacancies in the squadron. Those rejected were advised that a second opportunity would follow during the fortnight. The German squadron then sailed that morning for the island of Mas-a-Fuera where it arrived early on 6 November. It will be remembered that the British claim of sovereignty over all Patagonia below 50°S extended to Chile as well as Argentina and this may help explain the extreme leniency afforded the Germans during 1914 by the Chileans along their coasts and off their islands.

At Mas-a-Fuera a few days later in a "*council of war*", it was the opinion of the commanders that sooner or later the squadron would run into a superior British force without any hope of overcoming it. If the German ships dispersed, they would have a better chance of escaping the ring and carrying out a destructive campaign against British merchant shipping. Von Spee turned this idea down and, brushing aside the advice of his officers, ordered the formation to prepare for the Atlantic.

Naval historians have been content to pass off the attack by the East Asia Squadron as simply an attempt to destroy the wireless station at Port Stanley. To do this, expecting no opposition, the tactic should have been planned for one armoured cruiser and one small cruiser while the remainder of the squadron waited several hundred miles back and safely out of sight.

In the Falklands operation an unexpected superior force was lying in wait and the Germans, instead of losing two cruisers lost four cruisers and two supply ships while one cruiser and an auxiliary escaped because of the incompetence of the British admiral.

All eight ships of the squadron had been either approaching the Falklands or were actually moored amidst the islands, a proceeding which suggests that far from just aiming to destroy the wireless station, the squadron was intending to invade and occupy the Falklands.

There were eight German ships present. Historians admit the presence of seven ships but discount the eighth on the basis of Admiral Sturdee's falsified report to the Admiralty of 19 December 1914(**3**). The maxim is, because it does not appear in the official reports, it cannot be, which is the same maxim governing the existence of German U-Boats unloading in Argentina after the Second World War. It is this eighth ship, the 1903-built Norddeutscher Lloyd passenger liner *SEYDLITZ*, 7942 gross tons, which provides the clue as to what Spee had been ordered to do.

SEYDLITZ

The day prior to the outbreak of war, *SEYDLITZ* had sailed from Sydney for South America and laid up at Bahía Blanca near the Argentine main naval base awaiting instructions. Following the arrival of the German squadron at Valparaiso on 3 November, *SEYDLITZ* was ordered to make the long voyage through the Straits of Magellan to the Chilean port which was, as has been mentioned previously, the mobilization centre for German reservists and volunteers in South America and there to ship her requirements in personnel. Having accomplished this, she set back for San Quintín Bay in the Gulf of Penas and waited for the other seven ships of the squadron.

SMS LEIPZIG

On 13 November 1914 *LEIPZIG* and *DRESDEN* loaded provisions at Valparaiso while Baron von Erckert and Consul Gumprecht went aboard *DRESDEN* for a conference, the two commanders being given fresh instructions from Berlin for Admiral Spee.

On 15 November the squadron left Mas-a-Fuera and headed south for the Gulf of Penas at eight knots. Next day von Spee received a message from Berlin re-transmitted through Valparaiso asking his intentions and the state of his munitions. He replied that his plan was to break through the British blockade and reach Germany with his squadron. After pooling their ammunition, his armoured cruisers had four hundred forty-five 8.2

inch and one thousand one hundred 5.9 inch shells each while the small cruisers had one thousand eight hundred sixty 4.1 inch shells each.

On 18 November *DRESDEN* and *LEIPZIG* rejoined the squadron in the open sea carrying the cables from Berlin re-transmitted from Washington to the German Consul in Valparaiso. In one of these dated before the Battle of Coronel, the German Admiralty had suggested his leaving the Pacific to pursue cruiser warfare in the Atlantic, maintaining the squadron in two strong groups. Heavy units of the High Seas Fleet were promised for the last stage of the voyage home. The texts also mentioned the probable sailings from the Mediterranean of the British battle-cruisers *INVINCIBLE, INFLEXIBLE* and *INDOMITABLE*, but Spee doubted that the Royal Navy would send its most modern capital ships to the South Atlantic to look for him. This false assumption and a cable sent on 15 November by German agents at Punta Arenas confirming no warships due at Port Stanley, presented Spee with a very different picture from the reality.

On 21 November the squadron entered San Quintín Bay to coal, and found *SEYDLITZ* waiting for them there. The squadron was now in the formation which would attack Port Stanley seventeen days later: the cruisers *SCHARNHORST* and *GNEISENAU*, *NÜRNBERG*, *LEIPZIG* and *DRESDEN*, the HAPAG collier *BADEN*, 1913-built, 7676 gross tons, and the Hamburg-South America 1914-built *SANTA ISABEL*, 5199 gross tons, and the auxiliary passenger ship *SEYDLITZ*.

Pochhammer, Executive officer of *GNEISENAU*, was curious about *SEYDLITZ*. She was supposed to be a hospital ship, but had no Red Cross markings. There were twelve surgeons distributed between the five cruisers but no surgeons or nurses from *SEYDLITZ* was ever seen. She was armed but was not a troopship. From minor observations elsewhere in his book it is obvious he knew more about *SEYDLITZ* than he cared to say, but he leaves us to deduce her real purpose.

On 4 November, the British Naval Staff had sent three cables: one to Admiral Stoddart off Montevideo with the cruisers *CARNARVON, CORNWALL* and *DEFENCE*, ordering him to await the arrival of *CANOPUS, GLASGOW, OTRANTO* and *KENT*.

The Falkland Islands Governor received the second cable, warning of the possible arrival of the German squadron in which case he was to conceal his auxiliaries in remote ports or bays, prevent the destruction of all useful supplies and hide all code books should the German ships be sighted.

The third cable to Admiral Jellicoe, Commander-in-Chief, Grand Fleet, ordered him to send the modern battle-cruisers **INFLEXIBLE** and **INVINCIBLE** to Devonport to reprovision and complete working-up ready to leave for the Americas under Vice-Admiral Sturdee on Friday 13 November 1914. The First Sea Lord, Fisher, requested this date be amended to Wednesday 11 November for superstitious reasons.

From St Quintín Bay to Cape Horn

In St Quintín Bay, a rocky cove backed by snow-capped mountains, the squadron coaled. Colliers of the Kosmos Line - **AMASIS, MEMPHIS** and **LUXOR** - shuttled in coal from Punta Arenas, Coronel and El Callao.

"The frequent coaling operations made us more efficient at solving the difficulties of the work,"
Pochhammer wrote;

"Now we used cargo nets with a canvas lining. One of them was so large that in calm waters it would take a ton and a half of coal. We also had briquettes which we could stow below as ballast. Because of all the dust whirling around it was unpleasant work which required the use of goggles.

"Once the bunkers were crammed full we started piling coal on deck in unheard of quantities, for we had a long voyage ahead of us and nobody could tell how things would go on the Atlantic side. Both sides of the 'tween deck were bulging and we had to use stiffeners to stop the ship's sides flexing. Between the third and fourth funnels was coal and the oared pinnace. The potato store at the rear of the command bridge became a coal store. Any free area on the upper deck became a deposit for coal. As I have said, it was not pleasant to have coal everywhere above and below deck, for it prevented free movement, the dust got everywhere and I was not sure how we could engage the enemy in such a state. Possibly before that time came it would be all off the decks and down in the bunkers, but who could say?"

On 26 November the squadron set off for Cape Horn. The seas were occasionally whipped up by hurricane force winds, the two worst days being 27th and 30th. **SCHARNHORST** and **GNEISENAU** rode these well, but the three small cruisers were so top-heavy with all the coal on deck that their rails touched the sea and great crested seas swept over them. Recognizing the danger, von Spee authorised the coal on the decks of the small cruisers to be jettisoned.

By 2 December off the Horn the weather changed to misty and calm. The British full-rigged ship **DRUMMUIR** carrying 3,000 tons of English coal was stopped by **LEIPZIG** and taken prize. At 0500 hrs on the morning of 3 December the squadron anchored at the east end of Picton Island in the Beagle Channel. **DRUMMUIR** was sandwiched between **BADEN** and **SANTA ISABEL** while her coal was transferred to the small cruisers. Once empty her crew was put aboard **SEYDLITZ** and the sailing ship scuttled with explosives in deep waters at the three mile limit.

It is clear from the accumulation of great quantities of coal aboard all eight vessels of the squadron that it was not the intention to actually occupy the Falklands beyond that period of time necessary to complete the task which Admiral von Spee had been set. The Admiral had advised Berlin that he would be making for home and that appears to have been his ultimate aim.

At a meeting of the Admiral's Staff and commanders on 6 December, von Spee announced that the attack would begin early on 8 December 1914. It has puzzled naval historians why the Admiral allowed his crews three days to go hunting and exploring Picton Island, thus deliberately delaying his attack until 8 December. The probable answer is that just as the First Sea Lord Admiral Fisher requested from the British Admiralty permission to sail the battle-cruisers two days earlier than Friday 13 November for reasons of nautical superstition, it must be pointed out that Admiral von Spee was a devout Catholic and 8 December is a religious public holiday in Argentina (Ascension of the Virgin).

Possibly von Spee was hoping that his own endeavour would be favoured for the same kind of reason that Admiral Fisher sought to avoid disfavour by sailing on Friday 13th. Whether the Argentine Government was at all involved in choosing the date of 8 December is something we may guess at, but never know.

At the commanders' conference Pochhammer stated that the attack on Port Stanley appeared to have as its main purpose the destruction of the coal stocks and provisions warehouses, the ship repair facility and the radio-telegraphy complex plus anything else likely to be of use to the enemy in his prosecution of the war. **GNEISENAU** and **NÜRNBERG** would carry out the work of destruction while the others cruisers covered the operation *"hanging back"*.

At 0500 hrs on the morning of 8 December 1914, once the squadron had put to sea and was heading for the Falklands, the two appointed cruisers increased speed and detached from the main body. Repeating the impression that there is something about the operation which he prefers to keep secret, Pochhammer does not mention the departure of **BADEN**, **SANTA ISABEL** and **SEYDLITZ** from Picton Island on the early evening of 7 December. These three support ships must have left then in order to hide themselves inshore at Point Pleasant during the short hours of darkness that night and avoid being seen by the lookouts on the high ground before Port Stanley during their approach. It cannot have been any other way, for they emerged to everybody's surprise from under the coast late on the morning of 8 December to make a run for it.

Admiral Maximilian Graf von Spee

The Implications of the Battle of the Falklands

With regard to the narrative in this book it is only the intentions of the German Admiral with regard to the Falklands which interest us and not the encounter with British forces which resulted in the German naval disaster. Admiral Sturdee's Despatch to the British Admiralty(**3**) can be read on several Internet sites.

By 1030 hrs on Monday 7 December 1914 the main British force under Admiral Sturdee had arrived at Port Stanley, and began coaling. The British squadron consisted of the battle-cruisers *INVINCIBLE* and *INFLEXIBLE*, the cruisers *CARNARVON, CORNWALL, KENT, BRISTOL* and *GLASGOW*, and the armed merchant cruiser *MACEDONIA*.

It was a perfect late spring day - maximum visibility, a calm sea, bright sun, clear sky, light breeze and wind from the north-west. At 0800 next morning the lookouts on Sapper Hill reported the approach of *GNEISENAU* and *NÜRNBERG.* The smoke of other units was seen at a distance of about twenty miles twenty minutes later. At 0920 the beached monitor *CANOPUS* at Port Stanley opened fire from 11,000 yards, causing the two German cruisers to turn away, and at 0945 hrs when all but *BRISTOL* of the British squadron had weighed anchor and left harbour, the five German cruisers were visible hull down to the south east. At 1020 hrs the signal was given for a general chase.

Imaginative British Naval Accounting or How *Seydlitz* Became the Ship that Never Was

Sturdee's report states:

"*Information was received from **BRISTOL** at 1127 am that three enemy ships had appeared off Point Pleasant, probably colliers or transports. **BRISTOL** was therefore directed to take **MACEDONIA** under orders and destroy the transports.*"

At the foot of the Despatch, in the section headed *Action with the Enemy's Transports*, it is noted:

"***MACEDONIA** reports that only two ships, steamships **BADEN** and **SANTA ISABEL** were present. Both ships were sunk after removal of crew.*"

This is a false report. Three "*colliers or transports*" came out from under Point Pleasant, **BRISTOL** and **MACEDONIA** pursued **BADEN** and **SANTA ISABEL**, the third was let go. That is a fact which should have been reported in *Action with the Enemy's Transports*. The "*glorious victory*" at the Falklands looks less respectable when, against an overwhelmingly superior force with an equal number of ships, 25% of the German force escaped. Pochhammer(**4**) remarked:

"*The fast **SEYDLITZ** managed to escape. The officers of the armed merchant cruiser **HMS MACEDONIA** told me they thought she must be an auxiliary cruiser because of her speed.*"

SEYDLITZ put into San Antonio Oeste the day following the battle, and was immediately interned by the Argentines as a German auxiliary warship.

The Secret of the *SEYDLITZ*

Nowhere is there an explanation for the presence in the Falklands on 8 December 1914 of the Norddeutscher Lloyd liner **SEYDLITZ** which had accommodation for 2000 paying passengers in peacetime. The attack on the Falklands was a reprisal for the invasion and occupation of the German colony of Samoa on 29 August 1914 in which the Governor and his staff had been deported to Fiji. The only conceivable reason for the passenger ship **SEYDLITZ** to have been at the Falklands, and for all eight ships of Admiral von Spee's squadron to have gone there together to destroy the radio-telegraphy station and "*kidnap*" the Governor, was to round up not only the Governor and his staff for deportation to Germany, but also all the British military personnel and their helpers. The **SEYDLITZ** would also be available to accommodate any Entente merchant crews of ships sunk on the long way home.

Nowhere in the Historical Record of the Argentine Ministry of Foreign Affairs, nor in its archives, is there a mention of the Battle of the Falklands despite this being a zone to which the Argentines could not be indifferent. The presence of the German squadron at Picton in the Beagle Channel, an island then claimed by Argentina from Chile, provoked no reaction.   No report on the event seems to have been sent by the battleships **SAN MARTIN** and **PUEYRREDóN** which had been sent to the Beagle Channel "*to ensure Argentine neutrality was respected*", and Pochhammer does not mention having seen them there.

Even the newspapers appear to have been gagged. On 17 December 1914 a correspondent of *La Prensa* at Punta Arenas described an interview with members of the **DRESDEN** crew, whose declarations coincided with those from other sources:

> *"It would appear that the purpose of the German warships was to take possession of the Malvinas, destroying the radio-telegraphy station beforehand".*

But after that the shutters came down completely.

If Admiral von Spee's intentions were as outlined above, and had gone to plan, and his squadron had made off for Germany taking the population of the Falklands with them in the prison ship **SEYDLITZ**, how would the Argentine Government have reacted?   Were they involved in the diplomatic planning with the Germans in Valparaiso in November 1914?

There is good reason to suspect that they were. It is a remarkable fact that neither in the registries of the Argentina Ministry of Foreign Affairs nor in its archives is there any mention of the 1914 Battle of the Falklands. Yet the Argentina diplomat Josè Munoz Aspiri, eventually in his capacity as head of the Archive General of the Ministry of External Relations, compiled the 12 volume *'Historia de las Malvinas'* (Ed. Oriente, 1966) which include the following two references:

1. According to former Argentine Ambassador Cambioti, an Argentine Consul early in the first World War, the Germans showed him a special map indicating the British colonies to be given back *'to their rightful owners'*, and which included returning the Falkland Islands to Argentina.

2. A declaration signed by Argentine Consul Adolfo Blanc dated 4 July 1953 states, *"**According to statements I saw at that time here and in England, von Spee's squadron had received instructions from the Chancellery and German Admiralty to proclaim Argentine sovereignty over the archipelago once he had anchored at Port Stanley**."*

The arch enemy of Argentina has always been England or Great Britain. On 3 January 1833, Britain invaded and occupied the Falklands at a time when the Treaty of Friendship, Trade and Navigation was in force between both countries. This was the fifth time that the British had invaded Argentine territory since 1763, while the seventh attempt ensued in the blockades from 1845 to 1847. The uncomfortable feeling had therefore taken shape in Argentina that one day another British naval and military force assembled in the Falklands would suddenly arrive on the Argentine doorstep to grab what it wanted, and in 1908 all the Argentine fears and suspicions were justified.

"This year of 1908 is marked by an extremely important event in the history of the Falklands islands. On 21 July Letters Patent were stamped with the Great Seal, establishing 'The Falkland Islands Dependency." (5)

In an officially sponsored publication(**6**) at the time of the 1982 conflict, Rear-Admiral Laurio H. Destefani wrote of these Letters Patent:

"The most extraordinary thing about this unprecedented declaration of sovereignty is that it had been done so unscrupulously and included part of our territories of Tierra del Fuego and Santa Cruz, and the Chilean province of Magallanes."

In order to understand why the Argentine Government considered that these Letters Patent were an underhanded and fraudulent device used as a prelude to war it is necessary to look at the texts very closely.

The 1908 Letters Patent signed by H. M. King Edward VII under the Great Seal was the instrument used by the British authorities to claim as their dominions, various lands, islands and territorial waters in the South Atlantic. The claim of right to seize large areas of the Earth's surface was based solely on British occupation of the Falkland Islands.

The Letters Patent in this case had been prepared by highly competent cartographers who understood latitudes and longitudes on a map and could spell the names of territories. The text was created by the cleverest British lawyers trained to phrase their Government's intentions concisely and accurately in good English. And the whole thing was checked and rechecked for blemish and error before the King put his signature to it.

The 1908 Letters Patent were deliberately framed to be ambiguous and confusing as to their full purpose and intent. They designated the Governor of the groups of islands known as South Georgia, the South Orkneys, the South Shetlands and the Sandwich Islands *"and the territory known as Graham's Land situated in the South Atlantic Ocean to the south of the 50th parallel of South Latitude and lying between the 20th and 80th degrees of West Longitude".*

There is no such place as Graham's Land. There is a peninsula Graham Land in Antarctica whose position is accurately known and whose width is nowhere near 60 degrees of Latitude in extent. Furthermore it is south of the 58th parallel and not the 50th parallel, which places the enormous fictional 'Graham's Land' potentially in Patagonia. See map on page 23.

In 1917 the Argentine and Chilean ambassadors in London were summoned to be informed of an amendment to the 1908 Letters Patent in which sweeping changes had been made. The British now claimed as British dominions "all islands and territories whatsoever between the 20th degree of West Longitude situated south of the 50th parallel of South Latitude – *and all islands and territories whatsoever between the 50th parallel of West Longitude and the 80th degree of West Longitude which are situated south of the 58th parallel of South Latitude thus reaching the South Pole.*"

In order to clear up the ambiguity about Graham's Land, the 1917 amendment stated that:

"the territory known as Graham Land situated in the South Atlantic Ocean to the south of the 50th parallel South Latitude and lying between the 20th and 80th parallels of West Longitude, are part of our dominions…."

Graham Land is actually a small peninsula in the Antarctic between 50° W and 80° W and south of 58° S. Therefore it is a territory embraced by the 1917 amendment and there was no need to "clear up the ambiguity" because it was no longer relevant UNLESS it formed part of the secret plan to attack Argentina. That was why the statement about Graham Land needed to be made, retaining its northernmost extent as "south of the 50th parallel South", that is on the Argentine mainland, to remind Argentina that that part of Patagonia was claimed by Britain and up for grabs.

The purpose of the intended attack by Britain against Argentina when the time was ripe after 1908 had been to occupy the tip of South America and its islands near Cape Horn as a major naval base to control maritime traffic passing through Drake's Passage, particularly German shipping in the event of war.

From all this it can be seen that if the Falkland Islands had been proclaimed an Argentine dominion by their conqueror Admiral von Spee in December 1914 and fortified by the Germans and Argentines, the so-called "Falklands Islands Dependency" would have ceased to exist.

It is clear therefore that as late as 1917, Great Britain still intended to invade and occupy parts of Patagonia as part of the Falkland Islands Dependency. By 1918, however, in Flanders fields their terrible losses in men and materials had dampened their enthusiasm for more foreign empire-building adventures.

Remembering their poor performances in the Dardanelles, now they would have to attack Patagonia from the sea and be confronted by the fresh German-trained national armies of Argentina and Chile, stiffened by several hundred thousand young local men of German origins thirsting to avenge the defeat in the North and defending their own South American soil. And in six previous attempts to invade this or that part of the Argentine mainland, the British had always been defeated with heavy losses. Patagonia was too much to ask, for in Flanders fields the thug had already met his match.

It was in this sense that President Perón had spoken in 1952 when he said,

"We shall never forget, nor be able to repay, the immense debt of gratitude we owe to our comrades of the German Army."

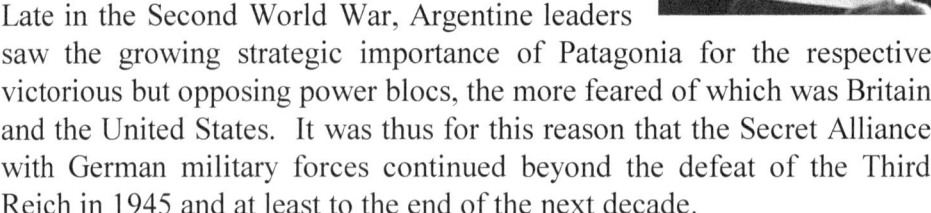

The Secret Alliance may have been signed in the month before the Battle of the Falklands in 1914, but was consolidated by the success of the German Army on the Western Front in the three years subsequently.

Late in the Second World War, Argentine leaders saw the growing strategic importance of Patagonia for the respective victorious but opposing power blocs, the more feared of which was Britain and the United States. It was thus for this reason that the Secret Alliance with German military forces continued beyond the defeat of the Third Reich in 1945 and at least to the end of the next decade.

Canaris

The cruiser **DRESDEN** escaped at the Battle of the Falklands by virtue of its one knot extra speed. She was pursued along the Chilean coast and through the coastal islands for the next three months and was eventually cornered at Germany's favourite recoaling venue, Mas-a-Fuera to be sunk by two British cruisers. Most of the crew survived and were interned on the small island of Quiriquina north of Coronel on 24 March 1915. Escapes, though rife, were all unsuccessful and frowned upon for fear of disturbing the relationship between Germany and Chile.

SMS DRESDEN

In August 1915, Lt Canaris obtained the approval of his commander to go after talks with von Erckert the German Minister and the local Consul, who made the arrangements. On 5 August 1915 he absconded. According to his personal file(7) he was provided with civilian clothes and a horse at Osorno and crossed the Andes (in mid-winter) into Argentina. The official Navy report states that "*from Neuquen he took the train to Buenos Aires*" but this seems unlikely, since there never has been a railway line between Neuquen and the capital. His biographer Abshagen(8) records that Canaris went to Bariloche to see Christian Lahusen, who arranged lodgings for him at a nearby farm. While there he made the acquaintance of a German aristocratic family, the Niebuhrs, of whom more later.

Resuming his journey on horseback to Ingeniero Jacobacci, he took the single track line to San Antonio Oeste, and while awaiting the steamer *CAMARONES* to take him to Buenos Aires, went aboard the interned *SEYDLITZ* to obtain information for Berlin. Canaris arrived in Buenos Aires on 21 August 1915, reported to the naval attaché and was provided with a false Chilean passport. He sailed for Amsterdam aboard the steamer *FRISIA* and disembarked in Rotterdam on 30 September. After debriefing and promotion to Kapitänleutnant, he transferred into the Admiralty Staff intelligence section and went to Spain to set up a supply system for U-Boats in the Mediterranean and create a network of informers to report enemy shipping movements(**9**)

Footnotes:

(**1**) For the progress of the East Asia Squadron in general I have relied primarily on the account provided by Korvettenkapitän Hans Pochhammer, senior surviving officer of the Squadron, in his *El Ultimo Viaje del Conde Spee*, transl. from the original German version by Captain Arturo Celery, Central Naval, Buenos Aires 1927: and Diego Lascano: *Graf Spee De China a Malvinas*, Stgo de Chile, 2002. Interesting supplementary information appears in Ernest de la Guardia: *La primera batalla de las Malvinas*, in: *Todo es Historia*, No. 335, Buenos Aires, June 1995.

(2) Captain von Rintelen: *The Dark Invader - Wartime Reminiscences of a German Naval Intelligence Officer*, Penguin Books, 1937 reprint (paperback), p.175.

(3) Admiral Sturdee's despatch dated 19 December 1914, published as supplement to the *London Gazette* No. 29087 3 March 1915.

(4) ibid, p.227

(5) For the full texts of the Letters Patent 1908 as amended see *The Falklands Gazette* on 1 September 1908 and 2 July 1917.

(6) Laurio H Destefani, Rear Admiral, *The Malvinas, the South Georgias and the South Sandwich Islands and the Conflict with Britain*, (official publication not to be offered for sale) Edipress SA, Buenos Aires, 1982.

(7) Aktenvermerk Admiralstab 5.10.1915 BA/MA RM 5/2228 Sheet 247

(8) Abshagen, Karl: *El almirante Canaris*, Buenos Aires 1952

(9) Müller, Michael: *Canaris*, Propyläen/Ullstein, 2006.

Hitler and the Secret Alliance

CHAPTER TWO

Between The Wars: The Naval Attachés; Moller and Niebuhr

The 18,710 gross ton **CAP TRAFALGAR** was a Hamburg-Süd passenger ship converted into a raider in August 1914 on the instructions of Korvettenkapitän August Moller, Imperial German Navy attaché for South America. He had his HQ in Buenos Aires. On 14 September 1914 before embarking upon her new career, **CAP TRAFALGAR** was surprised at Trindade Island off the coast of Brazil by the armed merchant cruiser **CARMANIA** and so badly damaged that she had to be scuttled. The surviving ten officers and 288 men were sent to Argentina for internment, where the majority spent the war on the island of Martin García in the River Plate. As time went by they gradually became forgotten.

In August 1919, an *"insolent Bolshevik clique"* of about sixty **CAP TRAFALGAR** men went to see Moller demanding back pay, clothing, lodging and a return ticket to Germany. He rejected their demands on the grounds that Berlin had sent him no instructions for their welfare. In his report to Berlin, Moller recommended that the disaffected men be *"sent back in small groups in separate ships"*, a request out of the question in 1919. Eventually most of the **CAP TRAFALGAR** men gave up the struggle to obtain anything from Social Democratic Germany, even its recognition of their existence, and the bulk of them remained in Argentina, either finding work at the gigantic German electrical plant in the port of Buenos Aires or wandering off into the provinces.

Moller was not sympathetic to the new Bolshevist spirit in the Fatherland. In 1920 when the German Admiralty ordered him to attend in Berlin to report orally on his activities since 1914, he refused *"on political grounds"*, said he was burning his files and that *"from 1 April 1920 he would not serve the present German Government in any sense whatsoever"* (this being heavily underlined in the original). He kept his word and once the stipulations of the Treaty of Versailles were enforced and Germany was not allowed to have naval attachés overseas, from then on he dedicated his life to making Argentina into a redoubt for those remaining loyal to Kaiser and Fatherland.

He attempted to attract German money to Argentina to consolidate control there by the German Right. He set up a propaganda organization, whipped up hostility to Weimar politicians and made public shows of rejecting the new black-red-gold German national flag. He helped make Argentina a refuge for *Freikorps* men. In 1921 he placed seventy-five of them in the Argentine police protecting the German communities. Moller was ably assisted by the Argentine Director of Immigration, Juan Ramos, a pro-German pamphleteer during the war. Ramos' specialty was blocking the entry into Argentina of German socialists and communists.

Moller reinstated the practice of appointing German military advisers to the Argentine Army. These were prohibited under the Treaty of Versailles

Oberstlt. Faupel.

but the Reichswehr *Truppenamt* was happy to engage in clandestine arrangements with Argentina (and also China and Bolivia). Their commander in Argentina was General Wilhelm Faupel, later Hitler's envoy to Spain. When he was replaced by Johannes Kretschmer in 1926 the Argentines rejoiced because they found him easier to get along with. Minister Gneist said in a letter to the German Foreign Ministry on 6 August 1928 that it was impossible to exaggerate the political and economic importance of his appointment;

"...the Argentine Army is friendly to Germany in the extreme in almost everything, and continues saturated in the German military spirit."

The key Argentinean in the restoration of the German military presence was Lt-General José Uriburu, Inspector-General of the Army, who had served in a German regiment. During the war he had worked as a propagandist for the German cause in Argentine military circles and in 1930 led the military coup which ended fourteen years of parliamentary democracy in Argentina.

German Influence in the Argentine Army

This is not the German army – this is the Argentine Army in 1941.

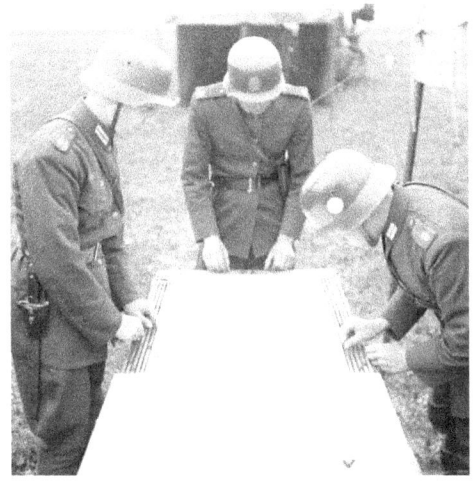

After the First World War, Argentina had become an attractive destination for emigrés from Germany who did not like the new Bolshevik inspired form of social democracy in vogue there.   By the early 1930s, *Reichsdeutsche* (persons with two German parents) numbered a quarter of a million.   *Volksdeutsche*, also known as the *Kreolertum*, persons of predominantly German blood who felt close ties of loyalty to Germany or Argentine citizens born of two German parents in Argentina who had not claimed German nationality at birth for the child, exceeded this number substantially.

The advent of National Socialism in Argentina occurred in 1931, mostly fostered by German seafarers in the port areas.   The doctrine was imported aboard Hamburg Süd and HAPAG-Lloyd ships from Hamburg, where the NSDAP had created an office especially to maintain contact with German expatriates.   It was tied to Gregor Strasser's left wing of the NSDAP, anti-capitalist and anti-elitist.   When he went in 1932 the activities of the office ceased, but once Hitler came to power the office was revived as the NSDAP *Auslandsorganisation* (AO) under Hitler devotee Erich Bohle.

Besides offering dockside help normally provided by the diplomatic service, AO workers distributed propaganda, spied on shipping and assisted the Gestapo to kidnap and ship back to the Third Reich all German opponents of Nazism.   The Argentine NSDAP was founded on 7 April 1931 with fifty-nine members.   The new Minister to Buenos Aires (Argentina did not have a German Embassy for several more years) Baron Edmund von Thermann disembarked on 10 December 1933 and made a brief speech from the gangplank wearing the uniform of an SS-Sturmführer, thus more or less setting the tone for the future as it applied to German circles in Argentina.

When the restrictions of the Treaty of Versailles were renounced by Hitler in 1935, Dietrich Niebuhr was appointed Naval/Luftwaffe attaché for South America.   Wilhelm Canaris, head of the Abwehr, had first met the Niebuhrs during his escape across Argentina in 1915.   Dietrich Niebuhr, born in 1888, had served in the Imperial German Navy from 1907 until his discharge after the Armistice, when he accepted a directorship with Coarico, a firm representing various German arms manufacturers.   In 1932 he rejoined the Reichmarine and was installed temporarily as naval attaché at the German Legation until called to Berlin for intensive training in naval intelligence. Returning to active duty in the rank of Kapitän zur See, he took over as head of the naval intelligence service at Kiel, where he met up with the old family friend, Canaris.

AUTHOR NOTE – Kapitän zur See Dietrich Niebuhr, German Naval attaché for Argentina and neighbouring coasts from 1938. He masterminded the **GRAF SPEE** escapes and organized the naval espionage organization until declared *persona non grata* by the Argentine Supreme Court and expelled from Argentina on 30 January 1943.

This reunion led to Niebuhr's recruitment into the Abwehr as director of its naval intelligence section, his office now being in Buenos Aires as Abwehr Resident. Under the terms of the agreement between the Abwehr and the Foreign Ministry worked out on 1 May 1935, his responsibility as Naval/Luftwaffe attaché extended to all Argentina, Brazil, Paraguay and (from the autumn of 1937) Chile, a huge area with thousands of miles of sea coast. Hitler had forbidden intelligence operations in the region,

Ortiz

however, and it was not until September 1938 that Niebuhr received orders to activate the espionage network in Argentina and Brazil and shift his headquarters to Rio de Janeiro.

On 20 March 1939, a militant anti-Nazi, Heinrich Jürgens, sent a batch of unsolicited documents to Argentine President Ortiz. The material suggested that the NSDAP in Germany wanted information about Argentina's military defences and economy. It was a crude forgery probably intended to wreck the forthcoming trade agreement between Argentina and Germany, and Ortiz knew this. On 30 March, however, *Noticias Gráficas*, a newspaper owned by an enemy of Ortiz, published the forgery as gospel, forcing Ortiz to act by appointing a commission of investigation.

The section of the forgery of most concern to Niebuhr as naval attaché were the accusations against "*Lahusen Cía*", the major German espionage organisation, and "*Antonio M. Delfino y Cía*", a subsidiary of the Hamburg Amerika Line and a family which had represented German interests in Buenos Aires as Etappendienst agents since the 1890s. Both companies were accused of being engaged in providing espionage reports on "*production, navigation, ports, railways, aerodromes and highways, and on climatic conditions.*" This publicity was unwelcome, for besides being true, the two companies were part of the network which Niebuhr had been building in compliance with the instructions of Etappendienst HQ in Berlin.

The commission of investigation did not delve too deeply into the Etappendienst, and went instead for the NSDAP organs in the cities. Since the mid-1930s, the Patagonian police authorities had been reporting on the expansion of Nazi cells and the spreading of Nazi propaganda throughout the region. The commission now noticed how, following the publication of the forged report, the network of Nazi spies, clandestine short-wave radio transmitters, suspected replenishment bases and support cells had "*begun to spring up*", thus confirming the police suspicions of earlier years.

Niebuhr turned his attentions to recruiting Germans working in the shipping industry around the port of Buenos Aires. He installed as his assistant a former Imperial Navy midshipman, Thilo Martens, a businessman who bought and sold ships and recruited spies as he went along. His office block was at Corrientes 323, still known today as "*the Martens Building*", as it proclaims over the doorway, and would have had in the 1930s and 1940s a wonderful view over the docks and warehouses from its top floor.

Controller of the Etappendienst in Germany was Kapitän zur See Werner Stophasius. At the end of the war he remarked that the major part of his work had been in Argentina "**where a good number of tankers were on hand for the purpose of refueling German raiders and U-Boats.**"(2)

When war came on 3 September 1939, the Argentine Government declared that it would adhere to the conventions respecting neutrality, and the following month accepted the Panamerican 300-mile exclusion zone off its coasts negotiated by the American republics at Panama. This nonsense lacked the force of international law and its futility was demonstrated by the ***ADMIRAL GRAF SPEE*** incident in December. As a result, on 19 April 1940 Argentina renounced it, the Minister for Foreign Relations even going so far as to suggest that Argentina would abandon neutrality in favour of "*non-belligerency*". Neither Germany nor the United States liked this idea, and Argentina remained neutral until coerced by the United States into making a declaration of war on paper against Germany in March 1945.

So far as Argentina was concerned, physical evidence of the war arrived on the Uruguayan bank of the River Plate on 13 December 1939, when the damaged pocket battleship ***ADMIRAL GRAF SPEE*** put into Montevideo and requested an unspecified period of time to repair.

Footnotes:
(1) Newton, Professor Ronald: *El Cuarto Lado del Triángulo*, p.39-40
(2) Salinas & De Napoli: *Ultramar Sur,* p.88
(3) Newton, ibid, p.53.

CHAPTER THREE

ADMIRAL GRAF SPEE and The Great Escape

The damage suffered by ***ADMIRAL GRAF SPEE*** in the Battle of the River Plate affected her ability to navigate. Her desalination plant had

Langmann

been destroyed and this meant that the diesels could only be run for a maximum of 24 hours. The Germans considered that they should be allowed a reasonable period of time to repair. The Uruguayans responded by offering 72 hours and would not discuss the matter until the Germans had accepted the 72 hours. In the opinion of Niebuhr and Minister Otto Langmann of the German Legation in Montevideo, this inflexibility put Uruguay in breach of its duty of strict neutrality and it was suggested to Kapitän zur See Langsdorf that he should turn his guns on the port installations

and then scuttle the ship across the harbour entrance(**1**).

Langsdorf rejected this idea. He was under the mistaken impression that a powerful British squadron was waiting off the estuary of the River Plate. To assist the British in maintaining this deception the Uruguayans had prohibited all flights beyond their territorial waters.

Accordingly Langsdorf saw his options as being reduced to an attempt to flee to the Argentine side. He had calculated that his ammunition would be exhausted after an exchange of fire lasting thirty minutes but the crossing would take two hours. On 16 December 1939 he signaled Berlin:

*"**RENOWN** and **ARK ROYAL**, cruisers and destroyers near Montevideo. Blockade closed at night. No prospect breakthrough for dash home. Propose sailing to limit of neutral waters. If can fight through to Buenos Aires shall*

attempt it. As enforced departure (17 December) might result in destruction of ship without opportunity of damaging enemy, request instructions whether I should then scuttle or intern."

The British vessels in the immediate vicinity were the two light cruisers *AJAX* and *ACHILLES*, and if he had gone at once for Buenos Aires he would have made it. In Berlin, Admiral Raeder decided to allow Langsdorf full freedom of action, except that the crew should under no circumstances be interned in Uruguay for fear that the Uruguayans would hand them over to the British in contravention of international law. The German ambassador to Argentina, Baron von Thermann, had advised that,

".....in Argentina there are sympathies for Germany and their Navy Minister Admiral León Scasso is a supporter of the Axis(2)".

The primary aim now was to avoid having the crew interned anywhere. If *ADMIRAL GRAF SPEE* could reach Buenos Aires, she could be sold to the Argentine Navy. The crossing would then be considered a "*delivery voyage*" and the crew could be repatriated to Germany by neutral ship. Failing that, there was one last, weak possibility, and this involved the steamer *TACOMA*.

Langsdorf eventually decided that in order to "*avoid unnecessary bloodshed*" he would sacrifice honour and scuttle his ship in international waters outside the port of Montevideo. Throughout 17 December, the crew, less the forty-three men needed to navigate the vessel and the fifty or so hospitalized in Montevideo, went aboard the steamer *TACOMA* surreptitiously in ones and twos so as not to attract the attention of the Uruguayan authorities. At six that evening when the *ADMIRAL GRAF SPEE* sailed, she was followed out by *TACOMA*. Six miles from the roadstead the vessels stopped and once the demolition charges aboard the pocket battleship had been set for 1940 hrs, the skeleton crew crossed to the *TACOMA*.

Following the plan engineered by the E-Dienst and the ambassadorial staff, once *ADMIRAL GRAF SPEE* had blown up the Argentine Flag tugs *COLOSO* and *GIGANTE* and the sand-dredger *CHIRIGUANA*, made for the scene, took the *GRAF SPEE* crew aboard from the

TACOMA and headed for Buenos Aires. Approaching the port they were met by a ferry bearing the ambassador, Baron von Thermann and members of the German colony in Argentina, who bore gifts of fruit, milk and other provisions.

On 18 December, Baron von Thermann put to the Argentine Government the case for the repatriation of the *ADMIRAL GRAF SPEE* crew based on his interpretation of international law. The crew was the "*shipwrecked survivors*" of the German warship who had been "*adrift in the River Plate*" when "*just by chance*" the two tugs and the dredger had come across them and "*in an act of mercy*" brought them to Buenos Aires. Clearly these men were entitled to be returned to Germany by neutral vessel.

The Argentine Government replied that the *ADMIRAL GRAF SPEE* was certainly a wreck, but had been reduced to that state by being scuttled with explosives on the orders of the ship's commander. The German crew could not be deemed "*shipwrecked*" because the term required some kind of maritime accident preceding the loss of the ship. Moreover the Argentine Government took into account that both tugs and the dredger were owned by the La Porteña shipping company, a subsidiary of the Hamburg-Süd Line, and they considered it too much of a coincidence that these three vessels "*just happened to be passing through*" that area of the river at the time.

On 19 December 1939 President Ortiz signed decree 50.826 ordering that,
*"the officers of the German cruiser **ADMIRAL GRAF SPEE** are to be interned in the city of Buenos Aires subject to the directions of the local police authorities, and are obliged to give their word of honour not to absent themselves without the special written permission of the said authorities."*

Under the Hague Convention 1046 crew members were interned, five medical staff were exempt. The crew was fingerprinted and photographed by the federal police and issued with identity cards before being lodged in the huge Hotel de los Inmigrantes (today the central immigration centre) along Avenida Antártida near the docks. German naval discipline was imposed. That same evening Kapitän zur See Langsdorf committed suicide by shooting himself with his service pistol after wrapping himself in the flag of Imperial Germany. Possibly he recognized that he had failed to live up to the standard of honour set by the man whose name his ship bore and was compelled to atone in the time-honoured manner. His grave is to be found in the German section of the Chacarita cemetery.

AUTHOR NOTE – A detachment of *GRAF SPEE* internees parade before the Hotel de los Immigrantes prior to relocation inland following the spate of escapes. Officers defected from the naval arsenal between the naval basin and the Hotel de los Immigrantes. The latter was and is a huge complex of three and four story buildings covering several acres and forming a quadrangle around central lawns. Nowadays it is the principal centre for the Department of Immigration and freely accessible.

Photo next page by kind permission of Diego Lascano

In order to prevent the possibility of hostile acts in the port areas, the Argentine Government decided to disperse the crew around the Northern provinces away from the sea. von Thermann and the Argentine Interior Minister Taboarda had agreed that the German Government was responsible for the upkeep of the men but the Argentines would pay the daily expenses. Under a ruling of the Inter-American Commission for Neutrality of 26 January 1940, internees were no longer subordinate to their military superiors and could work under police supervision. Thermann agreed to the men being transferred to the interior of the country but ordered embassy staff to search out jobs in the capital. By mid-February 1940, five hundred eighty-six (586) positions had been found in Buenos Aires together with lodgings with German families.

Crew of Graf Spee

At the beginning of internment, Fregettenkapitän Walter Kay, successor to Langsdorf, was allowed to open a small office to deal with administrative queries. The bureau was provided by the Banco Germánico de la América del Sur at No. 146, Avda 25 de Mayo, rooms 113 and 118 of the third floor. The plaque on the

Banco Germánica de la América del Sur

doors read: *"Graf Spee Administration and Personnel Office"*. The 19th century building, intact today, is a four story grey stone edifice in a gloomy narrow, traffic-clogged street and used today by the Argentine Interior Ministry. It is a five minute walk from the docks, which can be seen from the upper floors.

AUTHOR NOTE – During the Second World War, this gloomy Gothic structure in the narrow confines of Avda. 25 de Mayo housed the Banco Germánico de la América del Sur. From 1940 onwards the bank leased rooms 113 and 118 on the third floor for use as the

'*Graf Spee Administrative Office*' where four officers and a warrant officer worked hand in glove with Naval Attaché Dietrich Niebuhr to keep the escapes moving. Later the office liaised with the Lahusen Organization four blocks away for the reception of U-Boats unloading clandestinely along the coast of Argentina.

'***Through this office the internees remain subject to military discipline, and the internment is therefore purely illusory.***' The investigative commission CIAA complained in 1942. The building is now the Argentine Interior Ministry offices.

In mid-March the police arrived unannounced and ordered Kay to have one hundred men ready for transfer to Mendoza province by first light next morning. A few days later another two hundred were wanted, half for Córdoba province and the rest for Tucuman near the border with Bolivia. This latter was cancelled on the intervention of the Navy Minister, Admiral Scasso, because of a reported outbreak of "*swamp fever*" there, and so 150 went to Córdoba instead. In general the dispersal was chaotic and only in Córdoba province where the men were welcomed by the local authorities.

The fate of the **ADMIRAL GRAF SPEE** had been ignominious and represented a considerable loss to the Kriegsmarine, but it was past and what concerned Berlin most from the moment the survivors set foot in Argentina was to have the officers and veteran technical NCOs return to Germany as soon as possible. They had begun to escape almost immediately. The officers had been asked to give their word of honour not to proceed fifty kilometres beyond Buenos Aires city. All refused to swear unconditionally not to escape, but promised not to abscond on a twenty-four hour pass. They kept this promise, only making the arrangements to escape on the twenty-four hour pass and then fleeing alone or in pairs later.

The first to go, at the end of March 1940, was gunnery officer Fregettenkapitän Paul Ascher, taking with him the **ADMIRAL GRAF SPEE** war diary. He used a false passport to get to Brazil, took an LATI flight to Rome and reached Germany. Within a few days two more fled and on 7 April another eleven officers could not be found, including the chief engineer and navigating officer. Four months later they crossed from Bariloche into Chile assisted by one of Niebuhr's spies;

> *"As a result of the investigation by Bariloche police 'Report on Breach of Internment Decree 58.556 dated 16 March 1940', it has now been confirmed beyond doubt that at the beginning of August 1940, four German subjects, ex-officers of the* Admiral Graf Spee, *were led by a German from the El Bolsón neighbourhood, Francisco Woitschehofski, across the Puelo Pass from Chubut into the Republic of Chile..."*(**4**)

By the beginning of April 1940, fourteen officers, six midshipmen, thirty-one petty officers and five ratings had disappeared. Twenty-six members of the group were recaptured but none were officers. The escapes and refusals to give parole free of small print led to Government decree 59.459 of 8 April 1940 when President Ortiz ordered officers and warrant officers to be confined on the island of Martín Garcia in the River Plate off the Tigre Delta.

Warrant Officer Martin Wild escaped from Martín Garcia and went underground in Buenos Aires for four months, his final hiding place being the building site for the Faculty of Medicine under construction by the Siemens firm. He remained there with the complicity of the builders until Niebuhr was able to pair him with diesel mechanic warrant officer Johannes Fieber.

They were led by an E-Dienst guide to Catamarca province where an attempt to cross the Andes failed when the car broke down at 4,000 metres altitude. They returned to La Rioja province for the winter and used mules for the crossing into Chile when spring came. The pair then split up and Wild hid for six months at Osorno in the south of the country before being taken to Lima in Peru to ship aboard a Japanese freighter for Tokyo.

The German Embassy in Tokyo made arrangements with the Japanese Army for his onward journey through Korea to Manchuria, from where he crossed Siberia by train to Moscow, and caught the connection for Berlin. The odyssey lasted four hundred thirteen days, finishing a short while before Hitler's attack on the Soviet Union. Everywhere along the way Wild had German agents to offer him comfort and support(**5**).

AUTHOR NOTE-This impressive edifice at Paseo Colón 301 in Buenos Aires was the Lahusen HQ for their business and espionage activities throughout Argentina in both world wars. The company was never investigated by the authorities even though its purposes were an open secret. Still known as Edificio

Lahusen but owned by another company, the building is a mere five minute walk from the docks.

In February 1940, Niebuhr had been advised of an Abwehr sabotage operation codenamed *Südpol* against British shipping in Buenos Aires docks which he opposed on the grounds that it would interfere with the **GRAF SPEE** escapes. Nevertheless in June 1940 the operation went ahead, the freighter **GASCONY** being damaged in a bomb blast at pier 4 which killed the bomber. The police rounded up the usual suspects along the coast, causing uproar. Niebuhr had merchant marine Captain Wilhelm Lange brought before him to receive a savage rebuke, and Operation *Südpol* was abandoned.

In July 1940 when pro-British President Ortiz stepped down in favour of Vice-President Ramón Castillo, the situation took a turn for the better for Niebuhr's arrangements. Castillo was pro-German, his Navy Minister Scasso was pro-Axis and the commander of the corvette which patrolled the waters around Martín Garcia Island was Eduardo Aumann, a *Volksdeutscher*. Between 15 August and 5 September 1940, fifteen German officers disappeared from the island. The British Embassy staff submitted a report on the escape route and indicated where they thought the men were to be found, offering to join in the hunt. The Argentines advised the British that if their help was wanted they would ask for it. In any case, after investigating, Admiral Scasso could report that it was not possible "*to determine how the escapers got away since they left no discernable trail*". No Argentine could be blamed, although he promised to replace the commandant of Martín Garcia.

On 10 November 1940 when five German officers escaped, two were recaptured. They had left in a rubber boat wearing lifejackets and carrying a map of the Delta, compass, lanterns and food. The investigators were mystified as to where all this came from, but luckily no Argentine officer could be faulted. In similar frustrated escape attempts in February and March 1941 equipment was found but its origins could not be determined. On 11 March 1942 five officers went but three were recaptured. After five more disappeared on 10 April 1942, investigators found a tunnel to the water's edge, but no Argentinean could be blamed. On 4 May one man escaped but two others were discovered nailed into crates awaiting the ferry. This time - despite the most painstaking search and enquiries - no evidence was found as to the accomplices who helped.

The majority of the fugitives tried to reach Iberian ports aboard Spanish or Portuguese ships. In December 1942, eight **GRAF SPEE** men disembarked in Lisbon from the Portuguese ship **INHAMBANE**. The steward responsible for secreting them aboard received US$1,925 paid by Niebuhr. The Spanish Ybarra shipping company which operated the passenger ships **CABO de HORNOS** and **CABO de BUENA ESPERANZA** was notorious for the transport of agents, fugitives, contraband and messages. The cost of getting a **GRAF SPEE** man home was a worrying factor. For stowaways aboard Japanese, Spanish and Portuguese ships US$100 was paid for each, in those days a large sum, to which had to be added the cost of cross-country travel, safe houses and bribes. For that reason no simple jacktars were helped to return.

Another route involved traveling north across Argentina and Bolivia to the border with Peru at Talca, then back down to the Chilean port of Antofagasta to take a Japanese ship. In October 1940 four **GRAF SPEE** fugitives were taken off a Japanese ship searched at Valparaiso. To the scandal of the Chilean Press, they were found to be in possession of false papers supplied by the German Consul and were impersonating Chileans of German blood killed in the recent earthquake at Chilea.

A great deal of information was obtained from Alfons Haun, a man arrested by police in Buenos Aires on 15 November 1940 after he received a telephone call from Niebuhr requesting him to arrange passage for two officers, Reckhoff and Lang, aboard the ***GENERAL ARTIGAS*** for Brazil. Haun obtained false passports and admitted he had done the same for other escape groups. His practice was to escort the fugitives himself from safe house to safe house across Argentina, cross the Andes into Chile and hand the men over to the German Consul at Coquimbo before returning to Buenos Aires. In his statement to the Chamber of Deputies' board of enquiry CIAA in September 1942, Haun implicated the German Condor and Italian LATI airlines, ships of Japanese and Spanish register and consular and embassy staffs in the escapes. Robert Diers, manager of the Buenos Aires branch of Siemens Schuckert, even *"conveyed **GRAF SPEE** fugitives in his private car if the need arose".*

The CIAA - *Comisión de Actividades Anti-Argentinas* - was a radical congressional committee formed to investigate the ***GRAF SPEE*** disappearances. It delivered its report on 17 September 1942. The main outrage was the one hundred fifty-one known escapes at that date. The commission described in detail the escape routes to Europe and named six ***GRAF SPEE*** officers who were now commanding U-Boats(**6**).

By the time the CIAA report was published, the escapes had been stopped. When the Battle of the Atlantic became more important to Germany at the beginning of 1942 the Kriegsmarine asked for more volunteers for U-Boats, particularly engine-room men with diesel or electrical experience, and the *Graf Spee Aktion* had been revived. About thirty warrant officers machinists stepped forward. By September the reserve had practically dried up, but the Castillo administration was unable to prevent the CIAA investigation.

Up to September 1942, of one hundred fifty-one escapes confirmed, thirty-one had occurred before the Martín Garcia decree of April 1940, and one hundred twenty afterwards. Of the latter, fifty-eight men had gone from the naval arsenal or elsewhere in the capital, thirty from the island and thirty-two from the provinces. By September 1942 there were only six ***GRAF SPEE*** officers still in custody. The other thirty-two, together with the telegraphists, mechanics, master electricians and twenty-eight other specialists were either back in Europe or en route there. Beside these, at least twenty-nine ratings escaped subsequently, either to join the Nazi or Allied espionage networks or to settle beyond the long arm of the Kriegsmarine.

The CIAA was uncertain about the purpose of the *Graf Spee* administrative office in the city centre. Fregettenkapitän Kay was assisted by Kapitänleutnant Robert Höpfner, Kapitänleutnant Wilhelm Nahkotter, Leutnant zur See Herbert Drews and a warrant officer, A. Jerichow, all of whom were seconded there from Martín Garcia. The permission given to the Germans to have this office at all was tantamount to a tacit concession of extraterritoriality. Under the internment decree, the office had been set up to deal with minor enquiries, primarily problems of naval pay, yet for this purpose it had been considered necessary to install three officers of captain rank, a lieutenant and a warrant officer. Niebuhr used it as a discipline centre, deductions from pay being the main instrument of discipline although once he made a man stand to attention for three hours for marrying without permission. A complaint to the police by Kurt Ridzewski alleged that Niebuhr often threatened crewmen with reprisals against their families in Germany if they challenged naval discipline.

"Regarding the activities to which this strange office is devoted, the commission has discovered that since May 1941 it is visited daily by at least fifteen crew members to receive orders. This fact demonstrates that the internees are maintaining their own authorities in power, obey them and carry out their dictates even in those cases where to do so infringes or contravenes the rulings of the Government of this nation,"
the report complained. All five officers at the Office enjoyed free movement about the country and were contemptuous of Argentine supervision. Kay had had the effrontery to refuse to appear before the CIAA and Lieutenant zur See Drews had been jailed for four days for insolence to it. The commission therefore concluded:

"The internment is illusory and the internees remain subordinate to their officers through the Office, and the naval attaché at the German Embassy."

For this reason it was recommended that the Office should be closed down and the five officers returned to Martín Garcia, but this idea was ignored(**7**).

In conclusion the CIAA accused Niebuhr of obtaining false passports and papers for the escapers and recommended that he be declared *persona non grata*. At the end of December 1942 the Supreme Court ordered his detention. On 22 January 1943, the Uruguayan Emergency Consultative Committee for Political defence published a document denouncing Niebuhr as the head of an extensive and well-organized network of Nazi spies in Argentina. Foreign Minister von Ribbentrop (photo here) made a formal protest from Berlin and invoked Niebuhr's diplomatic immunity, but all was in vain.  Castillo's Government was forced to declare him *persona non grata* and expel him from Argentina on 30 January 1943. He went by neutral steamer; the British granting him safe conduct on the passage, so pleased were they to see him go.

Kapitän zur See Dietrich Niebuhr the naval attaché, his adjutant Oberleutnant zur See Martin Müller and second-in-command Thilo Martens organized the successful *Aktion*, but the German community in Argentina was indispensable in bringing it about. Although local Nazi Party members participated as individuals, the leaders were not involved. Niebuhr's successor as naval attaché and head of the Abwehr unit which worked from the same office was General Friedrich Wolf. Niebuhr's adjutant Müller continued to handle shipping intelligence, operate the various agents and oversaw the *Graf Spee* discipline office.

Anticipating the CIAA report, President Castillo had ordered that the internees, with exceptions, were to be concentrated "*elsewhere than Martín Garcia*", and the Interior Ministry was asked to prepare the necessary assessments of supervisory requirements and logistics. In December 1942 groups of **GRAF SPEE** men were lodged at the Hotel

Sierra, "*an enormous Government white elephant*" in an upland holiday area at Sierra de la Ventana, 100 miles north of the Argentine main naval base at Bahia Blanca. The FBI legal attaché in Buenos Aires pointed out with alarm that the hotel was situated in a zone surrounded by many German-owned estates; "*San Carlos*" of Lahusen, "*Ramón Diaz*" and "*El Pantanoso*" of Staudt & Co., "*El Retiro*" of Diego Mayer and the vast Funke "*Strength through Joy*" property of 130,000 acres administered by the local Nazi Party. The Hotel Sierra, the Americans alleged, would be transformed into "*a Nazi HQ*". Here we leave the remnants of the **GRAF SPEE** crew, but we shall see them later at the end of the war.

Footnotes:
(1) Laurence, Ric.: *Desde Wilhelmshaven a Montevideo*, Montevideo 1996
(2) Bayer, Osvaldo: *El fin del último corsario*, magazine *Todo es Historia*, issue 6.
(3) Newton, Ronald: *El Cuarto Lado del Triángulo*, Sudamericana 1995.
(4) Letter to the Governor of Rio Negro province, quoted in Laurence, Ricardo, *Tripulantes del Graf Spee*, Rosario, 2000.
(5) Lascano, *op cit*: Newton, *ibid*.
(6) Eventually this number rose to eleven. Four fell at the front, seven survived. The eleven were (last U-Boat command only):
  Kummer, Heinz Alfred (1915-1943, *U-467*)
  Mumm, Friedrich (1915-1943, *U-594*)
  Rieckeberg, Wolfgang (1918-1945), *U-637*)
  Schwebke, Hans-Joachim (1918-1945, *U-714*)
  Diggins, Kurt (1913-2007, *U-458*)
       Diggins was a Sharkhunters Member until his death
  Kottmann, Hermann (1915-1955, *U-203*)
  Kuhn, Hans Joachim (1910-1983, *U-1233*)
  Reckhoff, Johann (1911-1985, *U-398*)
  Schauenburg, Rolf (1913-1990, *U-536*)
  Schiebusch, Günter (1909-1997, *U-262*)
  Wattenberg, Jürgen (1900-1995, *U-162*)
       Wattenberg was a Sharkhunters Member until his death.
Paul Ascher, first officer to escape from Argentina, was lost with the Admiral's Staff aboard **BISMARCK**, 27 May 1941.
(7) Camarasa, Jorge: Odessa al Sur, Buenos Aires 1995, Newton, ibid.

Kurt Diggins at the periscope of his boat, *U-458*.

Jürgen Wattenberg with a trophy he picked up on a Caribbean patrol.

- **KURT DIGGINS** was Member **3518-1994**
- **JURGEN WATTENBERG** was Member **154-1985**

Sharkhunters Members and their Membership Numbers are all UPPER CASE and **BOLD**. The first series of numbers is the Member's sequential Membership Number and the second is the year in which they joined.

CHAPTER FOUR

Etappendienst Stations on the Argentine Coast

Dietrich Niebuhr had been the organizer of a colossal espionage network which continued to expand even after his departure. In the three years between the loss of the *ADMIRAL GRAF SPEE* and his expulsion from Argentina, he piloted groups of fugitives the length and breadth of the country and from his office in the German Embassy coordinated the tasks of espionage undertaken by the Abwehr and SD in Argentina, Chile and southern Brazil.

Niebuhr on the left with Langsdorf putting pressure on a wound he received in the sea battle and **DIGGINS** to right.

The escape of nearly twenty percent of the *GRAF SPEE* crew had been his greatest achievement. Here the merit was not only returning the officers and senior ratings to Germany, but establishing in the interior of Argentina, principally in Patagonia, a team of men of proven loyalty who would be of use as "*stevedores*" thirty months later when the U-Boats arrived and unloaded passengers and cargo by night along the Argentine beaches. These four men were:

- mechanic Willi Brennecke (absconded naval arsenal, Feb. 1941);
- telegraphist Rudolf Dettelmann (absconded Santa Fe, April 1941);
- petty officer/officer aspirant Alfred Schultz (absconded Córdoba province June 1940, recaptured, escaped Martín Garcia Isl. 1941);
- and electrical technician Heinriche Berthe (absconded naval arsenal May 1940).

Some of the more important bases are known to have been these:

Astra

Astra was a petroleum company established with German capital in 1912. The plant was situated on the banks of the Gulf San Jorge, twenty kilometers north of Comodoro Rivadavia in Chubut province. Its five hundred employees were drawn from the German resident colony in the region. Astra ran a fleet of tankers. Before the war Adolf Hitler had presented the company with a glider to show his appreciation for its efforts. The coordinator of the Astra operation was a Lahusen employee, Schulz, from Nueva Lubeca, a village where the Lahusen estate neighboured the property of Thilo Martens, deputy head of the E-Dienst in Argentina(**1**).

In August 1942 a Brazilian Navy seaplane photographed the tanker *SANTA CRUZ* refueling a U-Boat between Santos and Montevideo(**2**).

Tierra del Fuego

On 19 February 1940, Niebuhr sent an encoded message to Berlin via Transradio proposing the creation of a secret U-Boat base in Patagonia(**3**). One of his trusted spies, "*Robert*", thought that a base could be easily disguised as a plant to process fish meal, blubber, oil and seal skins. He had a concession for such a plant. The E-Dienst would invest half the capital and the local German community the other half. A good location was suggested as being 44°15'S, Bahía Vera, a place described as "*off the beaten track and easy to conceal*". All four **GRAF SPEE** stevedores found work in that area after 1941. A similar installation of this type built by a Norwegian company was in operation on the coast of Chubut at Comodoro Rivadavia. The stores of fuel oil and lubricants would be easily explained if anybody asked.

All that remains of this facility

Naval Command in Berlin allegedly *"rejected the idea for fear of antagonizing the United States"* which was expecting all Panamerican nations to keep on enforcing its unenforceable 300-mile neutrality zone. In any case, Bahía Vera was too close to Astra.

During his investigations in the region, Camarasa(**4**) was provided with a report authored by Chilean Professor René Cárdenas of the University of Magallanes for the information of Horacio Lafuente regarding several small German naval bases in and near the archipelago. Oscar Zanola, historian and director of the Museo del Fin del Mundo, Ushuaia, told Camarasa that in Tierra del Fuego on the Argentine side there were two German bases in Thetis Bay in the extreme east and Aguirre Bay in the south. From early in 1940 a company processing sealion fat, Sadiscafe, produced grease which the Germans apparently needed for their heavy machinery in Europe.

Based on testimony by former workers, German U-Boats would call in occasionally to load drums of sealion fat and also refuel for the long voyage back to the Baltic. By virtue of their standing as historians, credence must be given to Cárdenas and Zanola, and some thought given to this essential sealion-fat-for-the-Reich business.

To spare valuable U-Boats for round trips from one end of the world to the other to load sealion fat cannot be taken seriously but as a cover story for refueling U-Boats on station in Patagonia, it makes sense. It would not have been a breach of Argentina's neutrality for an Argentine company to supply U-Boats with sealion fat and fuel if the U-Boats were being used as transports in the way suggested. The whole point of the operation of course was to refuel the U-Boats, but the whole thing was neatly done, was probably the result of Niebuhr's suggestion of 19 February 1940, and in 1998 during his "*investigations*", Professor Newton never suspected anything. The question of these U-Boats in Patagonia in 1940 and 1941 is considered further after a look into the next mysterious base, Golfo Nuevo.

Golfo Nuevo

In May 1941 an unidentified informer reported to the US Embassy at Santiago the location of two German U-Boat supply points in Patagonia. This spy, "*a customarily reliable source*", indicated that one of the bases was located on the Valdez Peninsula somewhere between the Lobería, on the isthmus between Golfo Nuevo and Golfo San José, and Punta Delgado on the coast outside Golfo Nuevo but near the entrance. Accordingly it seems very possible that from 1941 onwards, German U-Boats visited Golfo Nuevo in Chubut province for an unknown purpose but probably to refuel, although no such visit to Patagonia was ever mentioned in a KTB (a U-Boat War Diary).

On 7 March 1942, the commander, 3rd Destroyer Division, Argentine Navy, Capitán Ricardo Campos, informed the commander of the Destroyer Squadron that the torpedo boats **SAN JUAN**, **SAN LUIS** and **MISIONES** had detected hydrophonically and visually a submerged submarine at the 9-mile wide entrance to Golfo Nuevo:

"Sir, I would inform you that at 1730 hrs today whilst the Division was manouevring to enter Golfo Nuevo on the south side of the Valdez Peninsula, and the 2nd Division was in the process of joining up, San Juan signaled:

'Have seen wake and ripples on the surface, my hydrophones detected a submerged vessel on port beam 2000 meters, position 42°55' 64°01'W."

On 25 March 1942 Admiral Benito Sueyro forwarded this report to Navy Minister Fincati:

"...It is not the first time that reports of this nature have been received by the commander-in-chief, all in the same zone, but over an extended period of time. In some cases the information has originated from senior commanders who had no doubt they had seen a periscope at 500 metres. Being confronted with reports of this nature, this commander-in-chief is disposed, should Your Excellency not order to the contrary, that in future cases of suspected submarines, they should be depth-charged."(5)

Fincati had no objections and Admiral Sueyro issued the order, for on 13 April 1942 Vice-Admiral Guisasola, commander Sea Fleet, sent a note to Chancellor Guiñazú requesting "*that foreign Governments be notified that all submerged submarines in Argentine waters will be attacked.*" A few hours later the Argentine submarine fleet was ordered to accept escort by surface vessels while in Argentine waters "*in order to avoid being depth charged in error.*" Golfo Nuevo remained the centre of mysterious submarine activity long after the Second World War as will be described in the closing chapters.

The reports of German U-Boats loading sealion fat and fuel in Tierra del Fuego and the submerged submarines detected in and around Golfo Nuevo in the period 1940 or "*over an extended period of time*" going back from 1942, leads one to suspect that German U-Boats were stationed secretly along the Argentine coast throughout the war. The provenance of these boats is difficult to explain.

At the outbreak of war, Germany had fifty-seven U-Boats in commission. Over the year to 31 August 1940, twenty-nine boats were sunk less one raised and recommissioned, and twenty-eight new boats were added to the fleet giving a net gain of nil but a net loss of twelve because of the transfers to the training flotilla. The home situation was therefore desperate having regard to the importance of the Battle of the Atlantic.

By reason of the secrecy required, possibly one or two coastal boats were built "*off the books*" and sent down to the Argentine coast as "*maids of all work*" to operate under the instructions of German naval intelligence. As suggested ahead at "*Villa Gesell*", these boats would have been Type II coastal U-boats.

San Antonio Oeste

This small town on the north-west shore of the Gulf of San Matías, Rio Negro province continued to be the seat of the Lahusen espionage organisation in Patagonia during the Second World War.

Firm evidence of the infrastructure to unload U-Boats can be found for Buenos Aires province. Its beaches, some as desolate and deserted as the coves and bays of Patagonia, were attractive for their proximity to the Argentine capital while huge tracts of the province were owned by German companies.

Bahía Blanca

The main Argentine naval base was and is located at Bahía Blanca. At least one visit was made here by a German U-Boat during the war. The presence of this U-Boat in a backwater of the Rio Colorado has gone unexplained until this moment, and in order to understand its purpose in being there we must travel back many centuries in time and rely on the only authoritative source for the facts, archaeologist Jacques de Mahieu(**6**) Tiwanaku, probably built around 17,000 years ago, is situated at an elevation of 12,900 feet on a broad, open unprotected arid plain of the Bolivian Altiplano.

In days long gone it was a major sacred ceremonial centre with a huge temple complex and pyramid, and the civilization was possibly the oldest and most advanced in all the Americas, if it was not actually the capital of Atlantis itself. Its stones, both standing and fallen, are of great size.

Nowadays the town is positioned twelve miles from Lake Titicaca, although originally it was only a few hundred feet from the waterfront. The Jesuit chronicler Agnelio Oliva recorded an Inca quipu reader as saying that the real Tiwanaku was a vast subterranean city accessible only to the initiated. The archaeological evidence leaves no room for doubt that the Danelaw was present at Tiwanaku from the years 1000 to 1290 of the present era, although what they found to occupy themselves there for the best part of three hundred years is unknown. It will be recalled that the primary purpose of the Thule Society, the foundation underpinning National Socialism itself, was to contact beings in the parallel world with great occult powers. It was hoped that a pact could be established with such beings to obtain advanced technological knowledge from them and so create a world inhabited by the New Man.

The first explorer post-Columbus to cross South America from the Atlantic to the Andes was the Portuguese Alejo García in 1521. He had been told by natives on Santa Catalina Island, Brazil, of a fabulous white king far inland whose realm could be reached along an old track which began at the seaport known in modern times as Santos. García reported that the track was in perfect repair, but of the great white king there was no sign.

The Bavarian explorer Ulrich Schmidel completed an expedition in 1552, noting in his book subsequently the existence of various localities in Paraguay and Brazil along the old track whose names were not Spanish or Portuguese and had no meaning in the local native tongues, but were recognizably Nordic.

Leaving Santos on the Atlantic coast westwards to Ourinhos, the track forked. The northern branch crossed the River Paraná at **Ivinheim** ("*home of the Ivin*", a red wood, tough but flexible, used by the Nordics for their longbows, probably the palm *acrocomia tatai*), continued to the River Paraguay, beyond whose far bank was the hamlet of Weibingo (23°35', the turning point in the path north to Tiahuanacu, Norse *vej*way, path, *vinkekl*) and rose to Tiwanaku near Lake Titicaca in Bolivia.

Nothing further appears to have been noted or discovered about this old path until 1940.

Sudeten German Fritz Berger was a mechanical engineer in his fifties. During the Chaco War (1932-1935) he set up a workshop in Asunción to recondition captured Bolivian weapons for the Paraguayan Army. When the war ended he went away for five years, but returned in February 1940 to become involved in an organization known as AGA (*Agrupación Geológica y Arqueológica*) run by Major Samaniego of the Paraguayan Army.

The immediate interest of AGA was a ring of low mountains about thirty kilometers south-west of the town of Pedro Juan Caballero. To the northeast of these lies Cerro Itaguambypé, a ridge two kilometres in length and 100 metres high. The base of this mountain is natural but the walls are of three kinds - rocky, almost vertical but irregular; rocky faces engineered vertical, and then for the top ten metres numerous blocks of stone of unequal size which fit together perfectly to form a smooth surface. The crest is three metres wide and level, providing a 300-metre long path separated midway by an artificial opening into the interior of the mountain. At the southern extremity is a rounded platform five metres above the path giving a panoramic view over the entire region, hence the native name Itaguambypé, "*fortress*".

The archaeologists under De Mahieu concluded later that the fortress could not have formed like that naturally. The rock walls in particular were built in the manner employed by the pre-Incas of Bolivia and Peru to defend against earthquake. Paraguay does not have earthquakes and so the method was not a local practice. Since the Jesuits never built in this way and had not settled the region and the Guaraní Indians did not know how to work stone in the 13th century, the fortress builders must have come from the only place in the Americas where blocks of unequal size had been used in building work, the Altiplano. The fortification appears unfinished but is surrounded by a deep valley close to the River Aquidabán, which may have provided a natural moat seven hundred years ago.

A fortress of such size suggests a large Viking garrison in a hostile region protecting something of great importance. Numerous runic inscriptions;
- at Cerro Guazú, a small mountainous plateau fifty kilometers from Cerro Corá still not fully explored, is the largest runic collection in the world, of which seventy-one inscriptions had been deciphered by the 1970s;
- the fortress built in the pre-Inca style of the Altiplano where the South American Danelaw had their capital, the giant stone steps by the waterfall worked by metal tools for use by tall men over six feet in stature, which the local natives were not;
- the Nordic stone temple discovered below a farmer's field at Tacuati: nothing more is needed to establish for certain that Cerro Corá was a Viking military centre in a strategic position.

The runes are of mixed *futharks*, often including Anglo-Saxon, Latinized or other archaic usage, indicating the length of the Viking migration to the region. Some of these archaic runes were never used in Scandinavia and are local to continental Germany. It was deduced by De Mahieu's runeologist that the Vikings of the region were not pure Danes but came predominantly from Schleswig where the German influence was strong.

Identifying Danish and German words in the quiché-maya and quichua led the runeologist to conclude that an intermediate dialect between Norse and Old Low German was spoken in the region. Thus a dialect distinct from classic Norse evolved over the centuries under the influence of the native languages which the Danelaw was obliged to use in its relationships with the Indians. Apparently the natives were forbidden to learn the Viking language, as was the case with the Peruvian Incas.

Ten kilometers south-south-east of Cerro Corá is a natural plain surrounded by hills. Of the greatest interest to the AGA was a rock of two humps, of maximum elevation forty metres, having dense vegetation to half its height and so called by the indigenous peoples Yvytyruzú - "*Bald Mountain*". It was said to be a tumulus containing a subterranean palace built to house the burial chamber of the Great White King, Ipir.

In February 1940 Fritz Berger went directly to Bald Mountain followed by AGA, which set up a permanent camp with wooden huts for its Paraguayan Army detachment. In the depression between the two humps a shaft was sunk. Here some gold items and artifacts were discovered, some of a kind of stone or metal unknown to science, and these were seized by the Paraguayans as treasure trove.

Dynamite was requisitioned from Asunción to continue the excavation, and by the end of October 1941 the shaft had been sunk to eighteen metres but without special explosives and drilling equipment usually sent from Germany, the work could not proceed and was suspended indefinitely.

In the course of 1942 four tunnels said to be over one hundred kilometres in length were investigated. Berger made very detailed cross sections of the entrances to these tunnels, which had a maximum height of 1.47 metres and breadth of 0.75 metres and had therefore not been built for Vikings.

On a day in November 1942(**8**) three intriguing factors came together. At the main Argentine naval base of Bahía Blanca, Major Pablo Stagni,

Harry Cooper   *Hitler and the Secret Alliance*

commander-in-chief of the Paraguayan Air Force came on an official visit and a German U-Boat moored in the estuary of the Rio Colorado. The resident US spies could not determine why the U-Boat was there, nor could they divine what Major Stagni was doing there.

EDITOR NOTE – Major Pablo Stagni was well entrenched in the German Intelligence; his code name was '***Hermann***'.

The solution is simple. The U-Boat had been sent from Europe, at the height of the Battle of the Atlantic with a cargo which would be loaded on Major Stagni's aircraft and flown to Paraguay, allowing the excavations on Bald Mountain to be resumed that very same month after work had been suspended for nearly a year for lack of explosives and drilling equipment.

The work continued. At twenty-three metres depth calculated from the vertical, the soldiers encountered a kind of stone slab impossible to break. The bits of the drill broke one after another and the explosives were unable to scratch what Berger considered to be the "*roof*" of the palace. It was concluded that the tumulus was made of some unknown form of concrete. Soundings were taken which provided dimensions for the tumulus of two hundred metres by eighty metres, of hollow structure with perhaps eight hundred rooms. A third attempt was made in 1944 and another shaft sunk but it was found impossible to break the concrete. AGA was dissolved in 1945. Berger remained with the Army of Paraguay until the 1947 war, when he retired to Dourados in Brazil and died the following year.

Simply on the grounds of the enormous coincidence of having the commander-in-chief of the Paraguayan Air Force and a German U-Boat present together at the Argentine main naval base, the evidence points to a collaboration between Argentina, Paraguay and Germany. It also indicates the enormous significance to the Third Reich of the archaeological work being done on the mountain Cerro Yvyvty in Paraguay. It may well be for this reason, a secret the world must never know, that despite the overwhelming evidence to support it, no academic historian or archaeologist will ever admit that the Danelaw once came to South America.

84   www.sharkhunters.com

To continue northwards along the Argentine coast - other E-Dienst stations or help-posts on the shores of Buenos Aires province were:

Moromar

The entrance to the Lahusen estate "*Moromar*" lay directly behind the sand dunes on a beach a few miles east of the town of Necochea. The best evidenced unloading operation occurred here on 28 July 1945 as will be described further on.

Miramar

This beach was sixty miles down the coast from Mar del Plata, behind it was a ranch owned by German-Bolivian tin magnate Gustav Eickenberg which was also the E-Dienst station.

A U-Boat Aid Port Near Mar del Plata

Colonel Rómulo Horacio Bustos (b. Buenos Aires 15 November 1921) served in the coastal artillery early in his career and subsequently in military intelligence. A long account of his experiences in and around Mar del Plata appeared in the national daily *La Nación* of Sunday 23 March 2008.

> *"That winter (i.e. June-July 1945) at Mar del Plata I experienced several more than suggestive episodes regarding U-Boat landings. At that time I was the commander of an AA battery in the Camet Park area (i.e. ten kilometers east of Mar del Plata city). One afternoon in the first half of June, all AA battery commanders were called before the senior commander, Lt-Colonel Pedro Lagrenade, to hear the text of a signal sent by the Army commander-in-chief. We were all assigned to various sectors of the coast between Mar del Plata and the Mar Chiquita lagoon with live ammunition. Our objective was to prevent possible debarkations from U-Boats.*
>
> *My battery was positioned at the far end of the lagoon. We had nine light Oerlikons on a cliff, all loaded and ready to fire. One night was very dark with rain and high winds. After midnight I saw light signals with short intervals between each being flashed from the sea towards an adjacent stretch of coast. While a second batch was being sent, I informed Lt.*

Colonel Lagrenade. When he arrived at my command position I pointed out where the signals had come from, but by then they had ceased.

As my commanding officer was about to leave in his vehicle, the signals resumed. Lagrenade decided to bring the guns in the adjoining sector closer and ordered us to take as many people as possible prisoner if there were disembarkations. After about 0100 however the light signals became less regular and then stopped altogether. It was assumed this would be on account of the bad weather (choppy seas and strong crosswinds) which would make landings in rubber dinghies hazardous, or because the crew of the mysterious vessel had been warned from the shore of the military presence on the coast."

The signals were not repeated on subsequent nights and most of the batteries were stood down. Bustos stated that he sent a top secret report to the Army commander-in-chief, but this has never been declassified. Bustos remembered a second strange incident which occurred at the end of June 1945, perhaps ten days after the episode of the light signals:

"This time it was a sunny morning with a pleasant temperature. I had brought my unit down to the beach for target practice and weapons handling with both live and blank ammunition. The beach (ten metres wide in this sector) was limited by a rocky cliff about twenty-five metres high. We dismantled our Oerlikons and lowered them down by ropes. While resting from our exertions, one of my men wandered off and discovered a small cave going about three metres into the cliff. Inside three wooden tables had been set up about ten to twenty centimetres above the high tide mark. Piled on these tables were dozens of cans the size of beer cans, all unmarked save for an impregnated single letter. The first can we opened contained recently baked brown bread, another had chocolate bars. It was evident that others contained liquids and other foodstuffs. Naturally I connected the contents of this cave with the mysterious nocturnal signals which I had seen in the same sector a few nights before. Personally I had no doubt that this was a support point either

to reprovision German U-Boats moving through the zone or to provide refreshment for persons disembarking clandestinely at this place. When we informed our commanding officer of this find, he photographed the interior and exterior of the cave, removed the tables and cans and took a statement from myself and my officers. All this material was taken by Lt. Colonel Lagrenade to the Army commander-in-chief. My men drew my attention to the fact that none of this was reported in the local newspapers, and nothing has been heard of it since."

The second half of Colonel Bustos' report follows in Chapter 6, "*U-530*".

Villa Gesell

In 1931, Villa Gesell was simply a large parcel of land acquired for beach development. Its founder was Carlos Gesell, a German engineer. The location is halfway between the exterior limit of the River Plate at San Clemente del Tuyú, and the town of Mar del Plata. Carlos Gesell's first family house is now the municipal historical museum. In 1942 a German married couple, the Starck's neighbours, occupied a house built by Gesell *"which marked the beginnings of tourism"* as the modern guide book tells us. Anybody looking for evidence of German U-Boats here nowadays will find it an unrewarding search.

The FBI had a close eye on Villa Gesell immediately postwar in the search for Hitler. An FBI Radiogram released by the US Department of Justice on 1 August 1945 reads:

"Reports indicate provincial police department raided German colony located Villa Gesell looking for individuals who possibly entered Argentina clandestinely via submarine, and during search short-wave receiver and transmitter were found. Other premises along beach near same area searched by authorities but no arrests made."

There can be little doubt that Villa Gesell was equipped to refuel, repair and assist in disembarkations from U-Boats. This is confirmed by the later discovery of infrastructure, stores and strange constructions in the vicinity. At the end of the 1960s when the village was being developed into a major holiday resort, construction work on the beach near the street Buenos Aires uncovered a railway track leading from the sea into a fifty-metre long shed near the house of Carlos Gesell. According to architect Jorge Castro, at the end of this railway track lived a German mechanic who specialized in diesel engines. Castro thought that the remains discovered amounted to a kind of dry dock.

In his unpublished manuscript *The Treasure of the Third Reich in Argentina* journalist Martin Malharro mentioned that,

"...at the end of the 1960s when the location started to grow into one of Argentina's most popular holiday resorts, they shifted a sand dune and found a bunker with lubricant and submarine parts."(**9**)

Type II U-boats ranged between 40.9 metres and 43.9 metres in length overall, and the 50-metre long shed at the end of the short railway track from the sea would have been satisfactory for sort of a kind of dry dock for a U-Boat. In a later chapter will be recounted the story of the mysterious small submarine of German design trying to help a much larger submarine of German design aground for an hour less than three miles offshore at San Clemente del Tuyú in July 1945.

After Abwehr agent Ernst Hoppe was removed from the steamer ***MONTE ALBERTIA*** by British authorities at Gibraltar on 14 October 1943, he stated under interrogation he was traveling to Argentina to meet a U-Boat carrying crates of documentation and ten million Reichsmarks for property investment. He said it was not the first such delivery there. The U-Boat was due to unload on the night of 21 February 1944 near El Rancho, a farm owned by Emil Fuchs.

Acting on this information, during the last fortnight of 1943 Argentine intelligence and FBI agents waited in ambush a few miles from Miramar E-Dienst station. The operation was called off when Uruguayan President Amézaga gave details of a transfer at sea off La Plata of boxes and crates from a U-boat to two tugs of the Delfino Cía. Otto Reinbeck, Head of the Reich Ministry for External Affairs, Latin America office, stated that:

"We heard much later of SD plans to unload technical equipment and valuables in Argentina by U-Boat,"

and upon enquiring further,

"the SD told us that the success of the operation was guaranteed by Argentine official circles."

EDITOR NOTE – the SD refers to the Sicherheitsdienst, the secret security service of the SS.

According to Goñi(**10**) the U-Boat brought forty crates, a radio transmitter, a Mipu microdot apparatus and two passengers, one of whom was an expert in radio transmissions. The U-Boats returned to Europe with platinum, mica, industrial diamonds, crystallized insulin and specialties such as shark-liver extract, whose properties were said to improve vision for pilots.

On the night of 2 July 1944 the Abwehr lobster smack *SANTA BARBARA* disembarked two SD agents at Punta Mogotes near Mar del Plata, and took aboard an SD leader and two telegraphists(**11**).

The cargo consisted of radio and microdot equipment for the German *Bolívar* espionage network, secret ink, pharmaceuticals and US$100,000 in cash. *SANTA BARBARA* had an auxiliary motor, was twenty-two metres in length and five metres in the beam. Her captain Hans (Heinrich) Garbers of Hamburg had a crew of five.

Garbers and his spy ship

The boat left Arcachon in the Bay of Biscay on 16 April 1944 and made the voyage in seventy-five days. The cargo was confiscated by Argentine police in August, although some of the money was recovered by judicial order. *SANTA BARBARA* made the return voyage without problems and put into Vigo, Spain on 16 September 1944.

For months the British naval authorities and the FBI refused to accept that a slow fishing boat could have made a round trip from Europe to Argentina evading all Allied naval and air patrols, and insisted that she must have been a U-Boat. The voyages of the *SANTA BARBARA*, whether fishing smack or U-Boat, planted the growing certainty in Allied minds that in its death throes the Third Reich would be sending U-Boats to Argentina on missions of ominous importance.

In a memorandum issued by the Argentine counter-intelligence service Coordinación Federal sent to the Navy Ministry on 18 April 1945, it was reported that a German submarine had unloaded recently at San Clemente del Tuyú:

*"Through our agents monitoring the operations of Ludwig Freude, Third Reich agent, it is known that there have been numerous deposits made to various banks in the name of the well-known radio-theatrical actress María Eva Duarte Ibarguren(**12**). Freude told our agent "Natalio" that on 7 February last a U-Boat carried out transport no. 1.744 with treasure to Argentina to help rebuild the Nazi empire. Subsequent investigations have enabled us to establish that the bags disembarked, marked **Geheime Reichssache**, were consigned to the Lahusen ranch and arrived there in various lorries on the night of 28 February. The deposits were made to Banco Alemán, Banco Transatlántico Alemán, Banco Germánico and Banco Tornquist, all in the name of the aforementioned lady. The investigation is continuing. Signed: Nicéforo Alarcón, Principal Officer"(**13**).*

   EDITOR NOTE – "*Geheim Reichssache*" means Secret Reich Affairs.

Ludwig Freude, labeled "*The Number One Nazi in Argentina*" by the *New York Times*, was one of the wealthiest *Volksdeutsch* businessmen in Argentina. He conducted business with the Argentine State and was a personal friend of the Vice-President and Minister for War, Colonel Juan Domingo Perón.

EDITOR NOTE - Freude (arrow) was best friends with Juan Perón, seen here putting his hand kerchief into his pocket. When the Allies wanted Freude deported to stand trial, Perón more or less said that Freude was his good friend and he wasn't going anywhere.

Footnotes:
(1) Camarasa, Jorge, *Puerto Seguro*, Ed. Norma, Buenos Aires, 2006. This book has the best coverage of German activities along the Argentine coast.
(2) Newton, Ronald C: *Actividades Clandestinas de la Armada Alemana en Aguas Argentinas*, CEANA preliminary report, February 1998 at level of footnote 26: the report can be read in Spanish under this title on the Internet.
(3) Newton, ibid.
(4) Camarasa, *ibid*, p.98.
(5) Camarasa, *ibid*: also Salinas and De Napoli, *Ultramar Sur*. Professor Newton is obviously unaware of these sightings and reports in Tierra del

Fuego and Golfo Nuevo, since he never mentions them in his book nor in the CEANA bulletin which he authored.

(6) See Jacques de Mahieu: *El Rey Vikingo del Paraguay*, Hachette (Buenos Aires) 1979.   De Mahieu, a French anthropologist and archaeologist, served as an officer with 33. Waffen-SS Grenadier Regiment *Charlemagne* on the Eastern Front. He arrived in Argentina on 22 August 1946. Perón nominated him National Secretary of the Higher School of Peronist Leadership, and in the 1960s he headed a Peronist Party branch in the capital. De Mahieu was a convinced sun-swastika worshipper and spoke regularly at the pagan solstice celebrations (*Sonnenwendfeir*) in postwar Argentina. He died in 1990.

(7) Daim, Professor Wilfred: *Der Mann, der Hitler die Ideen gab*, Vienna 1985. This book is the biography of Lanz von Liebenfels, co-founder of the Thule Society.

(8) Newton, Professor Ronald: *Actividades Clandestinas*, located around fn.27 in the main text.

(9) Camarasa, *ibid*, p.164. A facsimile of the FBI Radiogram mentioned above appears in this book at p.265.

(10) Goñi. Uki: *The Real Odessa*.

(11) Newton, Professor Ronald: *El Cuarto Lado del Triángulo*.

(12) Later known as "Evita", or Eva Perón. The couple were married on 10 December 1945. Radical congressman Silvano Santander called her "The No.1 Nazi spy in Argentina".

(13) A facsimile of this document appears in Farrago Ladislas: *Aftermath*, Avon Books, New York, 1974.

CHAPTER FIVE

The Political Change in Argentina, 1943-1945: The German Miracle Weapon

President Ramón Castillo of pro-German sentiment had taken office in July 1940. At the end of 1941 he consolidated his position by using the Pearl Harbour crisis to cancel provincial elections and impose a state of emergency. At the beginning of 1942, together with the Minister for External Relationships, Ruiz-Guiñazú, he torpedoed the efforts of the United States in the ministerial conference at Rio aimed at creating a united all-American front against the Axis. From then on the United States campaigned to force Castillo to put into effect inter-American resolutions respecting the control of Axis citizens, communications and economic enterprises, and this tended to dominate the relationship between the Allies and Argentina.

In December 1942, under pressure from the British ambassador to investigate Nazi activities, Castillo had been forced to act and within days discovered an espionage ring. To his amazement agents of the Axis were operating from Argentine bases under orders from Berlin, using clandestine radio stations and transmitting their findings to Germany. A head had to roll, and naval attaché Niebuhr, already under suspicion, was declared *persona non grata* and expelled but even so, Castillo ratified Argentina's neutrality(**1**).

Throughout 1943 President Castillo found himself embattled. The public was hostile to him. There was subversion, and the German espionage organisation was almost open in its activities. The national Catholic groups sniped at him as did the anti-US faction and circles of military power within his own Party. Buenos Aires, like Madrid, Lisbon and Geneva, was a leading capital of international espionage. Nazi agents were virtually celebrities, particularly those of the *Federación de Círculos Alemanes de Beneficiencia y Cultura*, the Nazi Party under its new name since the CIAA investigation of 1939 and which, despite the efforts of pro-Allied Cabinet members, continued to prosper.

At this stage of the war the United States did not want neutrals. The US Navy and War Department had proposed an Armaments Treaty to Argentina provided the diplomatic posture changed. The US Treasury Department wanted a freezing of Argentine credits in Washington and the Commission for Economic Warfare had erased Buenos Aires from its list of approved ports for exports. None of this moved the Argentines.

In the quest for quick results, pressure fell on the British, who dominated the Stock Exchange in Argentina. Here the problem was that Argentina represented British interest in the Far East and was in contact with the Japanese Government in the hope of improving the treatment of British prisoners of war. Moreover, Britain received shipments of meat and cereals through the port of Buenos Aires, for which Britain had recently negotiated credit repayable postwar. The British Foreign Office did not see eye to eye with the United States on the Argentine situation.

Washington maintained that Argentina was laundering funds arriving from the Axis; the British had found nothing to support this allegation. Washington claimed that the local Nazi Party spy rings posed a threat to the Allies. British agents considered them inoffensive and sluggish. Washington insisted that South America should break off diplomatic relations with the Axis. Britain did not want this because its intelligence service was reading messages from the German espionage organisations before Berlin got them. Washington was worried that Argentina was trading with firms on its black list. Britain refused to intervene because the US black list was too long(**2**).

Of all his opponents, the most dangerous to President Castillo was GOU, a junta of nineteen military officers whose principal ideologist was Colonel Juan Perón. GOU - what this stood for is uncertain - was committed to *"the defence of Argentina against internal and external enemies."*

Pro-Soviet Communists were the arch-enemy and not far behind came supporters of the United States who maintained constant pressure on Argentina to enter the war against Germany. GOU felt special revulsion towards the Masonic establishment, which it accused of being;

- "a fearsome secret organisation of international character",
- "a Jewish creation",
- "an enemy of the State and of the Army *par excellence*",
- and which it characterized as "a Mafia on the grand scale" embodying "anti-Catholicism" and "by definition everything anti-Argentine". It was responsible for the French Revolution and the Spanish Civil War.

The Rotary Club was the other main object of GOU ire being "*a straightforward network of espionage and international Jewish propaganda in the service of the United States*"(**3**).

On 17 November 1942, President Castillo had appointed General Ramírez as Minister for War. This officer was a member of GOU. When the sympathies of Ramírez for the lodge were discovered by Castillo, Ramírez was sacked on 3 June 1943. Next day a column of ten thousand troops led by General Arturo Rawson marched on Buenos Aires and seized power after a skirmish. That same night Rawson, a pro-Axis nationalist, was invested as President and named his Cabinet but was forced out two days later in favour of General Ramírez (photo left).

"The new Argentine military leaders avoided allying the nation alongside the other American republics to prosecute the war on the Allied side, and abstained from any convincing moves against the Axis espionage and propaganda rings"(**4**).

This was the opinion of the GOU military formed by the United States, but when GOU did eventually speak out the North Americans thought it *"left some room for hope"*. GOU explained that Castillo had been

"overthrown to defend the Allied cause", a preposterous statement given a cloak of credibility by the appointment of Admiral Storni, a known friend of the Allies, who announced to the US ambassador Norman Armour that
   "Argentina would break off diplomatic relations with the Axis on 15 August 1943."

The United States now recognized the revolutionary Government of Ramírez but 15 August 1943 came and went, and more than five months later they were still waiting for the severing of diplomatic relations with the Axis. The fall of Ramírez was in the wind, however, and came about in the following manner.

Himmler

Canaris

Himmler and Abwehr head Admiral Canaris had agreed in May 1942 that the SD and Abwehr should collaborate in South America in a consortium know as the *Bolívar* network. The organization was based in Buenos Aires but extended throughout Argentina and into Uruguay, Bolivia and Paraguay. Head of the Abwehr section was Hans Harnisch.

Osmar Hellmuth was of three-quarters German blood but Argentine by birth. He carried an Argentine diplomatic passport and his credentials identified him as auxiliary Argentine Consul to Barcelona. Acting on information received from a German traitor in Buenos Aires, on 29 October 1943 at Trinidad, British West Indies, British passport control authorities arrested Hellmuth aboard the neutral Spanish passenger ship **CABO de HORNOS** proceeding from Buenos Aires to Bilbao. Upon his arrival at Plymouth, England, on 12 November 1943, the Argentine Government protested unsuccessfully at the kidnap of their official. Unaware of this and feeling that he had been abandoned, Hellmuth came clean about his mission. He said he had orders to assure Berlin that President Ramírez intended for Argentina to remain neutral in the war, that if Argentina declared war on Germany it should be interpreted as a mere gesture to keep the United States happy, and in the case of war he was to seek Hitler's assurance that Argentine shipping would not be attacked.

Unfortunately for him, Hellmuth had in his possession a letter signed by Hans Harnisch, Abwehr head in Argentina, addressed to a Hamburg optics firm stating that Hellmuth would give Germany instructions on how to ship contraband to Argentina. In the opinion of Crown lawyers, this proved that Hellmuth was acting in breach of contraband controls, which justified his detention.

On 22nd and 24 January 1944, the London *Times* denounced Hellmuth's mission, and on 26 January President Ramírez, without consulting his Cabinet, broke off diplomatic relations with Germany and Japan on the grounds that they had violated Argentine sovereignty. Convinced that Ramírez had caved in to Allied pressure and was on the verge of declaring war on Germany, GOU overthrew him in a bloodless coup on 14 February 1944 and replaced him by General Edelmiro Farrell (photo left) with Colonel Perón as Vice-President and Minister for War.

The Ramírez affair also marked the end for the Abwehr and Canaris. The German ambassador to Madrid, Hans Dietrich Dieckhoff, a brother-in-law of Foreign Minister von Ribbentrop, used the scandal to strike the lethal blow against the Abwehr, whose sabotage activities in Spain had long been a thorn in the side of both and had now given rise to fears that other neutrals such as Turkey, Portugal, Sweden and Switzerland might reconsider where they stood. Ribbentrop backed Dieckhoff wholeheartedly. Hitler instructed Himmler to relieve Canaris as head of the Abwehr and place the entire intelligence service in the hands of the Reichsführer-SS and on 12 April 1944 Hitler signed the order for a unified German secret intelligence service with Himmler as its head(5).

EDITOR NOTE – Admiral Canaris was more than relieved; he was tried for his part in the 1944 assassination attempt on Hitler in the Wolfsschanze (Wolf's Lair). Whether Canaris took an active part in the plot or merely knew about it and failed to report it, either way he was convicted in a kangaroo court. He was sent to Flossenberg Concentration Camp and two days before the Allies seized the camp, he was given the same treatment as the other conspirators. He had a piece of piano wire wrapped around his throat, was hoisted up and the wire loop put over a hook where he was left to dance and strangle slowly. He was treated even more harshly than the others in that he was stripped naked before hanging and his body was tossed in the snow.

The United States identified the new GOU Government as ultra-nationalist admirers of the Axis and announced they did not recognize it.

"All South America will go Fascist unless we root it out in Argentina,"

warned Treasury Secretary Morgenthau. The Farrell regime was basically totalitarian and hostile to US policy and thus a threat to the United States as they saw it. Washington had only two possible policies within reason:

1. to accept the situation and allow Argentine resources to contribute to the defeat of the Axis,
2. or impose more rigorous economic sanctions with the aim of precipitating the collapse of the GOU regime. Secretary Cordell Hull inclined to the latter(**6**).

Conscious of the looming disaster facing the Nazis, the Farrell Government began to make diplomatic approaches to the United States through Ambassador Armour. Washington insisted that Argentina declare war on the Axis right now while Buenos Aires wanted a reduction in the pressure on Argentina first and then they would see. As an immediate reaction, the British and US ambassadors were recalled. On 30 November 1944 Nelson Rockefeller took charge of the relationship with Buenos Aires as Coordinator for Interamerican Affairs, changing the tactics and achieving in three months what his belligerent predecessors had failed to achieve in three years.

In the same way that the United States overlooked the Soviets being Communist, Rockefeller ignored the Fascism of Perón and took note of his growing popularity amongst the Argentine masses, his presidential ambitions and, most importantly, his will to arrive at an agreement with the United States to save appearances. After direct consultation with Roosevelt, the Secretary offered military aid and the membership of the United Nations to Argentina in exchange for a declaration of war against the Axis and a rolling up of the German commercial interests in the country. After much secret negotiating, Perón gave in.

On 27 March 1945, five weeks before the unconditional surrender of Germany, Farrell and Perón called a Press conference to publish decree 69/45(**7**). With a thinly veiled allusion to all the grim pressure exerted on Argentina by the United States, the decree announced that "*for the purposes of identifying national policies with those of the other American republics, a state of war exists between the Republic of Argentina and the Empire of Japan.*" Lower down at paragraph (3) the decree went on: "*A state of war is also declared between the Republic of Argentina and Germany as the result of the latter being an ally of Japan.*"…..and for no other reason. Rarely can a declaration of war have been issued with so little enthusiasm. In his memoirs Perón recalled:

> *"Long before the war ended we were preparing for postwar. Germany was defeated, that we knew. The victors would attempt to take advantage of the enormous technical effort which Germany had made during the previous ten years. We could not avail ourselves of the machinery because it had been destroyed. All we could use was the men. We let the*

Germans know that we were declaring war on them to save thousands of lives. We exchanged messages with them through Salazar in Portugal and Franco in Spain. They understood our intention immediately and helped us. The Germans were in agreement(8)."

Who was Perón, and why did he feel this way towards the Nazis?
"On 17 February 1939 Perón left for Europe aboard an Italian passenger ship. The two years he spent away from Argentina left an enduring impression on him. The dossier indicates that between 1 July 1939 and 31 May 1940 he served in various Italian Army units and attended alpinism training. His instructors returned excellent reports on his aptitude. From June 1940 until his return to Argentina that December he served as an aide to the military attaché at the Argentine Embassy in Rome. Although the dossier does not confirm it, there are indications that he visited Budapest, Berlin, Albania and the Russo-German frontier during the period of the Hitler-Stalin pact. It is also possible that he visited France after her surrender to Germany. He was amongst the multitude on the Piazza Venecia in Rome to hear Mussolini declare Italy's alliance with Germany in the war....Perón found nothing morally repugnant in Nazi Germany or Fascist Italy. Seen under the prism of their military structure, many characteristics of both systems of Government were most admirable in his view(9)."

Many members of the GOU Cabinet wanted a "*solution to the Jewish problems of Argentina*", and in 1943 it was rumoured that concentration camps to hold ten thousand Jews were to be built by GOU in the Buenos Aires suburb of Morón, and another in the woods at Ezeiza (nowadays the location of the principal airport), but Perón ruled against it (**10**).

In his memoirs in 1960 he stated his beliefs on the Jewish question:
*"How do you think I should get involved in that mess when you know very well that Hitler with 100 million inhabitants could not solve it? How would I succeed with 25 million Argentines? If the Jews live here we can't kill them, and we can't deport them either. There is no solution but to put them to work inside the community, and preventing them from forming separate Zionist groups. (**11**)"*

The long-time personal friend of Perón was Ludwig Freude (born 1892), in Argentina since 1913. After Argentina broke off diplomatic relations with Germany in January 1944, Freude, one of the ten richest men in Argentina, was entrusted with the administration of the fund financing the Nazi intelligence service there. After the severance he acted as unofficial German ambassador, and was consulted on matters of importance by the Swiss Legation, which handled German diplomatic interests in Argentina. Freude had been associated with the Embassy since before the war and this new status was the natural continuation of his role in diplomacy. His mansion in the elegant Belgrano suburb of Buenos Aires was a frequent meeting place for GOU military officers and the Nazi leadership in Argentina. SD chief Walter Schellenberg, who ran Ausland-SD, reported that Freude worked for Ribbentrop's secret service Informationsstelle III(**12**).

After the German defeat, the United States and Britain put intense pressure on Buenos Aires to repatriate Ludwig Freude to Germany for interrogation. On 6 September 1945 Foreign Minister Juan Cooke promised the US ambassador that Freude would be repatriated and next day the four joint trustees of the Nazi espionage fund including Freude were arrested. Perón worked out a compromise for this "*leader of the German community in Argentina*" whereby he was detained under house arrest only.

On 11 September 1945 decree 21.284 was signed expelling Freude as an undesirable alien, but in anticipation of this move Perón obtained from a judge a forged letter of Argentine citizenship for Freude which trumped the decree.

Bearing all this in mind is it possible that if Freude had informed Perón of six U-Boats coming down to Argentina during the month to unload in quiet coves, Peron would have told him *'over my dead body'*?

EDITOR NOTE – In the middle 1980's we reported that four of the big long-range Type IX-D2 boats went to Argentina with a reported one hundred million dollars worth of gold. This was Operation Feuerland II.

The Third Reich in Exile in Argentina

Contrary to the official line, the Reich leadership saw the writing on the wall quite early on. At Strasbourg on 18 June 1944 the first of a series of conferences took place aimed at working out evacuation measures. Reichsleiter Martin Bormann headed the committee. The overall operation was codenamed *Regentröpfchen* (raindrop) and its main destinations were neutral countries, particularly Argentina. *Aktion 1 Wiking* was the planning to ship out the scientific elite to safe havens, *Aktion 2 Läufer* the financial elite and *Eichhörnschön* (squirrel) the aristocracy. These plans went into action immediately, and by the end of the war little of the really advanced technology, scientists and technical staff remained to be removed out of Europe.

EDITOR NOTE – The Soviet Union and the USA (Operation Paperclip) were trying to scoop up as many of Germany's scientific elite as well. Many German scientists, such as Kurt Tank (designer of the **FW 190** fighter pictured here) escaped over Denmark to Norway and from there to Argentina. Tank brought about fifty aeronautical engineers with him and he designed the **PULQUI** jet fighter for the Argentine Air Force. He later retired to the little town of San Carlos di Bariloche. This is the same little town where Dr. Ronald Richter erected the German atomic research facility in 1947 on a little island in the massive lake – right across from the Mountain Troop training facility Perón built for his army.

Beginning of October 1944, the US Embassy in Montevideo reported:
> *"The Argentine regime has no interest in sheltering overthrown leaders or Nazi military commanders, but is very anxious to facilitate the arrival of German engineers to help in the defence programme. At this moment they are making arrangements to this end. They will be spending around a billion dollars, however the Argentine regime is convinced that the money will not stretch, & engineers are indispensable(**12**)"*

Is it possible that if Freude had told Perón of six U-Boat loads of military engineers and technicians coming down during the month to unload in quiet coves, Perón would have told him '*over my dead body*'?

Above – Richter at the facility in 1947

Below – One of the remaining buildings today

The German Miracle Weapon

Resistance circles in Germany followed the development of the miracle weapon programme closely. Former ambassador Ulrich von Hassell mentioned the miracle weapon twice in his diaries. In the entry for 13 November 1942, after recording that he had met Professor Heisenberg, technical head of the atomic research project, at the latest Wednesday Club meeting, von Hassell (photo below right) stated that,

"Everybody is pinning their faith on a "new secret weapon" of whose "fearsome effectiveness".

He was convinced. In his entry for 9 June 1943 he describes it as being "*a rocket gun, which with one firing from a great distance can reduce whole districts of a city to rubble.*(**14**)"

Contrary to what academic historians are pleased to call "*modern history*", the Germans were close to victory in 1944. In his formal biennial report to the Secretary for War in October 1945(**15**), General George C Marshall, Chief of the US Army Staff, wrote:

"France had to be invaded in 1944 to shorten the war by facilitating the advance westwards of Soviet forces. At the same time, German technological advances such as the development of atomic explosives made it imperative that we attacked before these terrible weapons could be turned against us....At the close of the German War in Europe, our factories in the United States were just on the outer fringe of the range of fire from an enemy in Europe."

The term "*atomic explosives*" does not mean "*nuclear bombs*", as will be clarified shortly. In the *American Air Force Review* of mid-1947 at *Operazione Pelenilunio*, p.80-81 it was confirmed:

"...That the Allies won the war by a frighteningly small margin is now accepted by almost all military chiefs who have seen the most recent revelations of German technology."

This makes little sense until one realizes that what has been misunderstood all along by historians is the role of the V-2 rocket.

U. S. Major William Bromley, Assistant to the Chief of Special Mission V-2, James Harmill, knew all the details of the V-2 project, and oversaw the transfer of one hundred V-2 rockets from Nordhausen to the United States in the months following the end of the European war. He was at Nordhausen between 15th and 20 May 1945, when he stated to reporters that the mass production of a "*V-2 with a range of 3000 miles*" would have been possible within six months of VE-Day"(**16**).

Leo T Crowley, Foreign Economy Administrator who submitted twenty-nine reports on postwar Germany to a Senate Committee, declared that,
> *"if the Germans had been able to hold out for only another six months, New York would have been reduced to rubble by improved V-2s."*(**17**)

In the April 1946 *Intelligence Bulletin*, article *Guided Missiles - The Weapon of the Future* issued by the War Department, Washington DC, it was admitted that regular bombardment by the New York Rocket would have begun at the latest by February 1946.

All studies on the A9/10 two-stage America Rocket were terminated at the latest by 1942:
> *"The A9/10 was never more than a drawing board concept and was shelved in 1942."*(**18**),
….yet as commando leader and former Obersturmbannführer Otto Skorzeny revealed:
> *"At the end of March 1945 the America Rocket was practically ready and could have been being mass produced from June."*(**19**).

Therefore, the America Rocket was the V-2, and since it could fly 3000 miles, whereas the standard V-2 could only fly three hundred miles, the improved range can only have been achieved by increasing the efficiency of the fuel tenfold. This is beyond the bounds of fuel science and reason, yet on 20 October 1943, Waffen-SS General Dr (Ing) Kammler cabled Dr

Brandt, Himmler's scientific adviser, requesting him to inform the Reichsführer-SS that,

"this day an agreement has been reached to set up a subterranean testing area for the development of the America Rocket with the tenfold propulsive force (zehnfache Antriebsstärke)"(**20**).

SS General Hans Kammler

A fuel is also an explosive, and thus the same means of increasing the propulsive force of a fuel tenfold would also increase tenfold the explosive force of a conventional explosive. The *"atomic explosives"* mentioned by General Marshall above were conventional explosives capable of manifold enhancement at the time of detonation caused by a reagent. Since the reagent (**21**) could be mass-produced, Germany would soon have had hundreds of rocket warheads each with the killing force of a single Hiroshima atom bomb. The reagent had an atomic principle, which possibly justifies the expression *"atomic explosive"*.

The improved V-2 rocket, even with a range of 3000 miles, could not have made New York from Germany, and the extra six months would have been needed to extend the range of the fuel or alter the configuration of the rocket. The warhead was ready but in tests had proved unstable. According to a British intelligence report(**22**), before the end of the war the Germans had *"138 types of guided missile in production or development using every known kind of remote control or fuse, radio, radar, infrared, light beamed, magnetic, etc, etc"*. For the final stage of an attack on New York, for example, a U-Boat with a homing transmitter would be stationed in New York waters to regulate the approach course of the V-2.

As a stop-gap it was planned to fire smaller rockets with the atomic-type warhead at New York from the modified deck gun of U-Boats. In December 1944 and February 1945, Armaments Minister Speer had promised New Yorkers that U-Boats would strike at their city *"with U-1 and U-2 bombs.*"(**23**) Because nobody knew what a "*U-1*" or "*U-2*" bomb was, researchers and historians have assumed it was a misprint for the V-1 and V-2 rockets, and much weird and wonderful literature has ensued from their error.

By virtually forcing Argentina to declare war on Germany in March 1945, the United States was hoping to prevent all this advanced technology being brought by the Germans to Patagonia. Behind all the cover-ups and denials of German U-Boats unloading along the shores of the Argentine Republic lies this fact, and dread.

Footnotes:
(1) Petersen, Harald F: La Argentina y los Estados Unidos, 1810-1960, Buenos Aires 1985, Vol II.

(2) Bendaña, Alejandro: *Churchill, Roosevelt y la neutralidad Argentina*, in: *Todo es historia*, Buenos Aires, issue No. 113.

(3) Salinas and De Napoli: *Ultramar Sur*, Buenos Aires, p.160.

(4) Petersen, *ibid*.

(5) Mueller, Michael: *Canaris*, Propyläen, 2006, p.417.

(6) Petersen, *ibid*.

(7) Bendaña, *ibid*.

(8) Martínez, Tomás Eloy, in: *El periodista de Buenos Aires*, issues 48/49, August 1985.

(9) Page, Joseph A: *Perón*, Part I, 1895-1952, Buenos Aires 1984.

(10) Goñi, *ibid*, Perón, on the Jewish question, p.39-42.

(11) Torcuato Luca de Tena and others: *Yo, Juan Domingo Perón*, Sudamericana-Planeta, Buenos Aires 1986.

(12) Goñi, *ibid*, p.360, fn.167 for numerous archive references on this point.

(13) Newton, Professor Ronald: *El cuarto lado del triángulo*, p.421: fn 69 provides reference US Embassy, Montevideo 2 October 1944, RG 84 BAPR 1944, Box 47, archive 820.02(2).

(14) Ulrich von Hassell: *Die Ulrich von Hassell Tagebücher 1938-1944*, Siedler Verlag, 1988.

(15) Biennial Report of Chief of Staff, US Army, 1 July 1943-30 June 1945, reproduced in *New York Times* edition of 10 October 1945, p.S11, col.8.

(16) *Daily Mail*, edition of 14 June 1945.

(17) *Chicago Daily Tribune*, 27 June 1945, p.4.

(18) Neufeld, B.Michael: *The Rocket and the Reich*, Free Press 1995, p.283.

(19) Skorzeny, Otto: *Meine Kommando-Unternehmen*, Universitas 1993, p.156.

(20) Telegram CBA NS 10/Old 273: Speer, Albert: *Infiltration - How Heinrich Himmler schemed to build an SS Industrial Empire*, MacMillan 1981, p.354: Heinz Magenheimer: *Die Militärstrategie Deutschlands*, Herbig 2nd edition 1997, p.33-36, 136.

(21) The action of this reagent is described simply and inaccurately in the *New York Times* article of 22 October 1944 at page E5.

(22) CIOS Report XXXII-125

(23) ibiblio.org/hyperwar/ETO/Ultra/SRH-008/SRH008-12.html at item 7d.

CHAPTER SIX

The Odyssey of *U-530*

The Type IX-C40 boat *U-530* was the first of two German submarines to surrender to Argentina postwar. The suppression of the interrogation files until 2002 by the archives of former Allies led to the development of a number of bizarre theories in which *U-530* and *U-977* were suspected of spending time in the Antarctic in the two months from May 1945 "*helping with the Nazi UFO project*".

Despite automatic declassification rules whereby official documents are released after thirty years, the US archive retained the material for more than fifty years and everything has still not been released, indicating that it has been kept secret all these years "*in the interests of national defense or foreign policy pursuant to an executive order*"(**1**). To keep the documentation classified so long indicates that *U-530* had a mission which directly affected the security of the United States.

In June 2002, Admiral Stella, Chief of the Argentine General Staff, released Spanish language photocopies of the interrogation report of the commander of *U-530*, Oberleutnant zur See Otto Wermuth held at Mar del Plata naval base from 13-15 July 1945. The recipients of the documentation were authors Salinas and De Napoli, enabling them to include the material in their forthcoming book *Ultramar Sur*(**2**). Several years later the US archive declassified an intelligence report and enclosures submitted by the US Naval Attaché at Buenos Aires on 24 July 1945. This material covered the interrogations of three officers, two midshipmen and two warrant officers of *U-530*(**3**), and from these one may form at least an outline of the last voyage of *U-530* and propose a solution to the mystery surrounding it. From the US papers it is clear that the statements appearing in *Ultramar Sur* were reported honestly, as the Argentine authors were obliged to do under the terms of their license. Where there are discrepancies between the Argentine and the US versions it is assumed by this author that the US Naval Attaché was responsible for the deviancy.

"On 10 July 1945 we arrived in Argentina. We entered the port of Mar del Plata in the early hours. All the guns, torpedoes, machinery and important apparatus had been jettisoned. The diesels had been run without water and lubricant to make them unserviceable. We moored to a buoy inside the base. Our commander was taken to the harbourmaster's office. A party of about thirty Argentine sailors came aboard. They gave us a hearty welcome, embraced us in the Argentine manner and gave us gifts of cigarettes. Before leaving the boat we gave her a triple Hurra! and were then transferred to the coastguard ship Belgrano. *There we received an excellent breakfast with abundant tropical fruit, following which they took us to the barracks to be billeted. We felt very good, were well fed and even had a military band play us to the dining hall."*(4)

U-530 appeared to have survived some dreadful calamity. The great rusty hull, its paintwork shredded and peeling, contrasted vividly with the smart steely grey, small Argentine submarines at the base. The decking was very corroded and had been the seat of a major fire. The conning tower had cracked and was falling apart. The commander, described in the national newspapers as a *"tall young man with blond hair"* identified himself as Oberleutnant zur See Otto Wermuth aged 25 years. His fifty-three crewmen, most of them lacking identity documents, paraded on deck to receive a final address before the boat was surrendered officially to the Argentine authorities. Wermuth brought ashore a single item of baggage, an attaché case containing the war flag, which he presented to the harbourmaster, Capitán de Fragata Julio César Mallea.

Authors Professors Holgar Meding and Ronald Newton had something to say about all this. Suspecting, as did US and Brazilian naval observers, that there had been a mutiny aboard *U-530*, Newton stated in his CEANA report that Oberleutnant Wermuth had had difficulties maintaining discipline - an assumption, no sources quoted - while Meding considered that it was a disgrace to bring *U-530* into port in such a rusty and filthy state and he thought that Wermuth would certainly have faced disciplinary charges had the Kriegsmarine infrastructure still existed(**5**).

Looking over the available material, two facts about *U-530* overlooked by Newton and Meding are sufficiently unusual to attract attention. When the *U-530* left Germany, Oberleutnant Wermuth was of average height and swarthy, but when he sailed the boat into Mar del Plata he was tall and blond. What event during the voyage caused his appearance to change in this manner while keeping his name? Furthermore, *U-530* was the first German U-Boat in history to enter port with her provisions lockers full and half the crew down with scurvy. Clearly, something horrendous had overtaken *U-530* during her war patrol, something which had to be kept so secret that the commander preferred it to be thought that his crew had mutinied rather than that the truth of the voyage be told.

U-530 Voyage - Kiel to the Capitulation, 8 May 1945

After coming out of drydock, *U-530* was provisioned and sailed for Norway at 1800 hrs on 19 February 1945. One weeks supply of fresh provisions was shipped, including meat and bread, and seventeen weeks supply of special submarine foodstuffs, and "*at no time did U-530 receive further provisions.*"

In Oslo Fjord dive and schnorchel trials were carried out, and the boat was fuelled. Capacity existed for 245 tonnes of fuel but at the request of the chief engineer only 225 tonnes was shipped "*so as to assist stability*".

U-977 also shipped fuel of a quantity substantially less than her bunkers could take.

Whereas a Type IX-C40 boat commonly sailed with twenty-two torpedoes and Wermuth stated that his mission was "*to attack shipping*", *U-530* carried only fourteen torpedoes on this voyage, eight T-3 LUT and six T-5 FAT. These were distributed 3 LUT+1 FAT in the forward tubes, 1 LUT+1 FAT in the stern tubes, 1 LUT+1FAT above the floor plates forward, 1 LUT+1FAT above the floor plates aft, 2 LUT+2FAT below the floor plates forward. This would have left much free space in the torpedo storage holds above deck.

EDITOR NOTE – The *LUT* (L̲angen-u̲nabhängiger T̲orpedo) had a pre-set gyro-angle and zig-zag course. It would go a certain distance into a convoy then make a zig-zag run in anticipation of hitting anything. The *FAT* (f̲lächen̲absuchender T̲orpedo) had a pre-set course.

It is necessary to explain here the fact that *U-530* had two commanders during the voyage, both using the name Otto Wermuth. It is not known exactly where the change took place but probably occurred during the last two days of the voyage near Mar del Plata. To avoid confusion is the following explanation, Wermuth-1 took the boat out from Germany, and Wermuth-2 surrendered the boat at Mar del Plata. Both Wermuths were present together at Mar del Plata for a day or so from 12 July 1945. Wermuth-1 sat for the interrogation. From the photographic plates (q.v.) it has not been possible to identify Wermuth-2.

Wermuth 3rd from left   Wermuth Argentine photo

Special attention is drawn here to the question of the deck gun. It was rare for a U-Boat to carry a deck gun by 1945. The US Navy report fails to mention it at all, and neither it, nor its ammunition, is listed with the boat's other armaments. Wermuth-1 declared under interrogation that *U-530* had sailed from Germany leaving the deck gun ashore(6). This conflicted with the account given by naval harbourmaster Mallea to the Argentine Press in which he stated that Wermuth-2 had ordered the crew to jettison the 5-tonne 105-mm deck gun into the sea during the voyage(7). *U-530* crew members described the episode of ditching the deck gun as one of the memorable events of the voyage. Colonel Bustos, the Argentine AA battery officer who visited Mar del Plata to look over *U-530* after her surrender stated:

> *"The naval authorities told me how surprised they were that the deck gun had been unshipped and ditched at sea."*

All these contradictions highlight the importance of the deck gun and its ammunition to the *U-530* story.

For the purpose of this chapter, it has been necessary to construct a theory based on the available facts. This theory is able to explain all the events which overtook *U-530* during her four-month odyssey. In a search for the causes of all the calamities which befell *U-530* during her last voyage, the one factor never considered has been the installation upon which the official reports are strangely silent, the 105-mm deck gun.

On 8 January 1945, Admiral Jonas Ingham, commander-in-chief, US Navy Atlantic Fleet, warned that within the next sixty days the Germans would *"launch attacks against New York and Washington"*. The US Navy and USAAF had introduced a secret plan codenamed Operation *Bumblebee* (later *Teardrop*) to intercept German U-Boats bearing down on the US coast. Speer announced on Berlin Radio that "*U-1* and *U-2*" missiles would hit New York on 1 February 1945. The threat proved hollow. In late April 1945, a US anti-submarine task force operating near the Azores intercepted and sank four U-Boats from a pack of six proceeding in line towards the United States:

Kapitänleutnant Paul Just (photo left), taken prisoner from *U-564*, was brutally mishandled by the FBI once ashore to make him "*spill the beans about the rocket attacks*", but he was unable to oblige them since he knew nothing. It is known that the reagent was proving problematical in larger quantities after the explosion at Ohrdruf on 12 March 1945, but it is also possible that some agreement had been reached between Germany and the United States to the effect that Germany would forgo the attack on New York in exchange for a one hundred day-respite on the Western Front, enabling the best German troops there to be transferred to the Russian Front. There is evidence of both possibilities, but it is not the purpose of this chapter to go into details.

EDITOR NOTE – Both WERMUTH (1344-1990) and JUST (206-1986) were Members of Sharkhunters until their death.

The reagent could be produced in all sizes. A large rocket could destroy vast areas of a city, a small rocket or modified shell could reduce a ship to smithereens. Of interest to U-Boat Command would be reports describing the effect of small rocket attacks on enemy merchant ships and warships.

Wermuth-1 refused to state under interrogation whether *U-530* was alone or a member of a flotilla, but he did admit that he operated "*directly from Berlin*", which meant U-Boat Command. He was ordered to proceed to a combat area which he refused to describe, but which we now know was the waters off New York, and there attack enemy shipping. For this purpose he had fourteen torpedoes and the deck gun.

He said he left Christiansand on 3 March 1945 and went along the coast to Horten, Oslo Fjord, where he spent two days for an unexplained purpose. *U-530* therefore sailed for her area of operations on 6 March 1945. Wermuth was not familiar with the route chosen for him, "*north of Britain*" and he decided to remain submerged continuously at sixty metres for three weeks to avoid air attack, recharging his batteries by use of the schnorchel at night.

The 200-metre line was followed northwards standing thirty miles off the Norwegian coast, turning north-west above Bergen. At 65°N the boat bore south-west. Periodic meteorological reports were transmitted from 61°N 19°W. After passing longitude 25°W the boat remained surfaced all night. Once astride the 100-fathom mark off the Newfoundland Bank, Wermuth steered for 41°N 60°W and there received orders by radio to operate off New York.

U-530 carried two short-wave receivers, one all-wave receiver, one long-wave and one short-wave transmitter, and one fixed 600 metre-frequency portable transmitter to be used by rubber dinghies. Wermuth-1 thought that one of the short-wave receivers might be damaged but the rest of the equipment was in good order. While in his combat area he was to follow procedure and not report attacks made or received. The only messages he sent were the daily weather reports. The last contact he had had with "*his commanding officer in Berlin*" was on 26 April, a message concerning defensive measures he should take.

In his interrogation, Wermuth stated that he was still receiving short wave signals until the end of April, but from then on none of the radio equipment functioned.

That this state of affairs was local to his boat is clear from the details of the voyage of *U-234*(8) which was passing through the same area at the time:

"We broke through into the Atlantic on the same day that we learned of the death of the Führer and the accession of Admiral Dönitz to succeed him (1 May 1945)...on the evening of 4 May 1945 I copied down the order of U-Boat Command to cease fire from 0800 German time next morning...the commander noted these instructions...the last long-wave transmitter Goliath at Magdeburg had been destroyed on the approach of enemy land forces and telegraphists had to rely on short-wave senders....Fehler listened to English Language radio broadcasts from the United States and Canada...on 8 May 1945, U-Boats at sea received notification of Germany's capitulation...late that same evening FdU North at Bergen, Kapitän zur See Rösing, sent Fehler a signal in the Japan Cypher..."

FEHLER   **HIRSCHFELD**   **ROSING**

EDITOR NOTE – The Skipper of *U-234* (Fehler), the I.W.O. (Pagenstecher), the Cargo Officer (Pfaff) and the Chief Radioman (Hirschfeld) were all Members of Sharkhunters as was Hans-Rudolf Rösing.

Yet while *U-234* telegraphists received all these signals and instructions, *U-530* was in a mysterious radio dead zone where even the domestic shore stations could not be heard. On 28 April Wermuth's boat crossed the 200-metre line and remained south of Long Island inactive, once coming into US territorial waters. At Mar del Plata later the crew told reporters that they "*had been allowed to view New York through the periscope, and had seen very clearly skyscrapers, trains and cars, and dirigibles of the coastal defence overhead.*"(**9**), *and never once during all this sightseeing was there ever a fear that the periscope might be detected from ashore or by those dirigibles overhead whose only purpose was to scour the inshore waters looking for U-Boat periscopes.*

On 4 May 1945, all shipboard radios dead and without news of the war situation, *U-530* came across a convoy of ten to twenty ships. There was fog at the time, and this resulted in the scattering of convoy vessels. Wermuth fired a spread of three LUTs, one stuck in the tube when the battery exploded, the other two missed.

On 6 May a very large convoy was sighted. A spread of two LUTs both missed. One hour later a LUT was fired at a tanker and missed. Another hour went by and a FAT missed a straggler.

On 7 May two FATs were fired and missed targets in another large convoy. During this period two blimps and one aircraft were seen through the periscope and the boat was bombed.

The LUT torpedo was almost infallible. It ran loops either side of a mean course and also had an acoustic guidance system. The FAT was not equipped with the latter but was generally very effective.

Wermuth stated that at this point the remaining five torpedoes were jettisoned, "*being in a condition to explode*". The sixth with the damaged battery was left in the tube.

It must have been on 7 May that it finally occurred to the technicians aboard *U-530* that there could be a connection between the total failure of the radio system and the torpedo electronics. The reagent in the munitions for the deck gun, which I theorize was the cause, emitted a gas which was both radioactive and radiated an electro-magnetic field and whose purpose was to combine with explosives for a massive reaction. If there was a seepage of this gas, it would drift surreptitiously through the pressure hull from stem to stern. It might have combined with the battery of the defective torpedo which exploded in the tube and also affected the electronic system of the other torpedoes, eventually resulting in those still aboard "*be in a condition to explode*". It would have shut down all the radio receivers and transmitters.

Once the possibility of a seepage of gas from the reagent was suspected the commander had to act fast. Torpedoes, the deck gun, the flak, all the munitions, anything which might be tainted with a residual trace of explosive, had to be jettisoned immediately. If, as would be logical, the cylinders containing the munition were stored in the conning tower lockers or empty storage holds for the torpedoes, from where the gas had drifted into the pressure hull, the entire structure would have to be scrubbed repeatedly inside and out with the virulent corrosive cleaner which was no doubt aboard for just that purpose. The fact that the tower and decks were split and cracked, apparently due to corrosion, and the casing appeared to have been the seat of a major fire, was widely reported when the boat arrived at Mar del Plata, but like the deck gun is never mentioned in the interrogations.

If any crewmen had died as a result of ingesting a speck of reagent, this would explain why a great fire was set on the decking. At Ohrdruf on 12 March 1945 during a test of the reagent, the strength of the explosive reaction was underestimated. Four hundred concentration camp inmates and twenty SS guards at or near the test site had been immolated. The bodies were heaped together in a great pyre and cremated, after which the ashes were spread from aircraft the length and breadth of the Harz. This incident points to the necessity, for some reason unknown, to disperse the material from spillage of the reagent over a wide area. If there were fatalities aboard *U-530* these would have been covered over by destroying the identity documents of the surviving crew and shipping in their replacements clandestinely at Miramar. Most *U-530* crewmen arrived at Mar del Plata without personal documents and gave false names to the Argentines. No true crew list for the *U-530* final voyage exists.

From ENE of Puerto Rico to Mar del Plata

On 8 May Wermuth stated that he had received a signal on the regular frequency to cease hostilities "because the war was over". Later he said he had received it as a repeat on 10 May. This was the message to set navigation lights by night, fly the blue(*sic*) flag, travel surfaced and surrender to the nearest Allied port. Wermuth said he thought this signal was a ruse "*because the signature did not seem right*".

He headed south-east for a point "*about 1000 sea miles east-north-east of Puerto Rico*". Here the waters are very deep and it may have been in this reasonably remote area that the boat was cleaned and the necessary steps taken for the run to Argentina. Regarding the decision to go to Argentina, the usual nonsense was dreamed up for the interrogation process whereby the crew was supposedly involved as a democratic factor in the same decision-making process, as occurred aboard *U-977*. Wermuth opted for Argentina "*even though he did not know until he arrived at Mar del Plata that Argentina had declared war on Germany*." This ludicrous statement requires the reader to believe that since at least late March 1945 German U-Boat Command had ceased informing U-Boat commanders which flags had to be considered as enemy, even if the enemy was friendly.

U-530 headed south, passing between the Peter and Paul Rocks and Fernando Noronha to cross the Equator on 16 June 1945. It took the boat no less than twenty-three days to get from the Equator to Mar del Plata due to submerged travel at two knots except when recharging the batteries, when *U-530* picked up speed to 7.5 knots and after passing 20°S this increased to nine knots. From Bustos' statement reproduced below, it seems clear that this final leg of the voyage south from Puerto Rico must have been made submerged and when surfaced to recharge the batteries the hatch remained always closed. This would be explained by the fear that despite all the cleansing with the corrosive, the fire on deck and the progress submerged, the seepage of the gas could still persist. The merest speck ingested would be fatal.

The Fiasco at Mar del Plata

Oberleutnant zur See Wermuth-1 stated to his Argentine interrogators that he saw the Punta Mogotes light at 0300 hrs on 9 July 1945 from eighteen miles out and went beyond Mar del Plata because his original intention was to sight land at Miramar, where he arrived at 0600 hrs. He denied that he had disembarked any *passengers* (the word *crew* was not put to him) or goods at Miramar, the E-Dienst station of Gustav Eickenberg, and explained,

> "…..he just wanted to spend the night there before scouting the entrance to Mar del Plata base."

He went on:

> "At nightfall on 9 July I surfaced and made my way eastwards along the coast keeping three miles offshore until reaching the naval base where I drifted until the early hours."

He admitted that **U-530** had six rubber dinghies when she sailed and could not give a satisfactory account of why he now only had five.

The US Navy Report, although based on the Argentine Navy documents, puts this differently. The Americans say that Wermuth-1 told the Argentines of first sighting the Mogotes light at 0300 hrs on 10 July from 18 miles out. He had a bearing of 240° on the light. He then submerged and waited for dawn to view the port of Mar del Plata.

According to the US Navy report he never went anywhere near Miramar. At first light he approached Mar del Plata submarine base and waited three miles offshore for visibility to improve. At 0630 he lit his navigation lamps and entered the port. Since there is no mention here of the missing dinghy, and the Americans cannot have made all these mistakes in translation, it seems fair to assume that the US Navy was embarrassed by the 24 hours unaccounted for between 0300 hrs on 9 July and 0300 hrs on the 10th, and their Report has been falsified in this respect. The switch of Wermuth-2 for Wermuth-1 must have occurred somewhere, and most likely it was at Miramar that Wermuth-1 went ashore with the War Diary and the essential papers, and Wermuth-2, who had been well briefed, took the dinghy back. Since that does not explain the loss of the dinghy, crew members must have kept up a steady shuttle of embarkations and disembarkations, the last to go being the SS weapons specialists with their priceless technical knowledge. I do not know this for a fact, but consider it a reasonable assumption. The dinghy used to reach shore was thus abandoned to the surf, and washed up down the coast later.

EDITOR NOTE – During any correspondence we had with Otto Wermuth, he always referred to this last voyage as '*ein Reise*' (a journey) rather than '*ein Feindfahrt*' (a war patrol). He also stated all papers were thrown overboard but in 1947, Sharkhunters Member Peter Hansen (Abwehr agent) was sent to Argentina to translate these papers.....the papers that according to Wermuth did not exist. The Argentine navy showed me these papers when I visited Mar del Plata in January 2008.

www.sharkhunters.com   Photo by Harry Cooper

Just some of the papers aboard *U-530* and *U-977*

Irregularities upon Surrendering to the Argentines

A few hours after the arrival of **U-530** at Mar del Plata submarine base, Wermuth and the naval harbourmaster signed the document of surrender:

"At Mar del Plata this tenth day of the month of July 1945, before those present and the Commanding Officer, Submarine Division, Argentine Navy, capitán de fragata Julio C Mallea; the commander of the German submarine U-530, teniente de fragata Otto Wermuth surrenders his vessel, his command and his crew, the list of whose members is appended hereto, unconditionally. Teniente de Fragata Wermuth declares that the submarine U-530, from which all crew has disembarked, is in a safe condition, that the only explosive aboard is a torpedo warhead without detonator and that there is no element or device in place to sink or damage the boat."

Wermuth-2 stated on his arrival that he had had the diesels sabotaged just before entering port by cutting off the oil circulation, drawing the oil and racing the motors, then putting a nitric-sulfuric-hydrochloric acid mixture in the oil to circulate through the motors. All oil bunkers containing oil had also been contaminated with acid.

He also admitted having jettisoned the War Diary, fifty-three code books, the navigation charts, the unused torpedoes, the gyroscope and warhead-detonator of the useless torpedo, the UZO torpedo aiming apparatus, all the flak ammunition plus parts of the 37 mm gun, the scuttling charges, gauges, three Metox anti-radars and the Hohentwiel radar plus aerial. No mention of the deck gun and its ammunition was made at this stage, although he did refer to it later.

All but the most junior ratings had destroyed their identity documents, and so those crew members who had been aboard upon leaving Germany, and those who had come aboard at some time subsequently, were known only to the officers. As has been suggested, this tactic must have been created to conceal substitutions and deaths.

All *U-530* documentation had also been ditched, or so it was alleged. This was accepted by the Argentine authorities as true, since they had searched the boat from stem to stern and found nothing, yet in a mysterious way the Argentine Navy Ministry was able later to work out what courses *U-530* had sailed after leaving the Equator, a fact which suggests that what the Germans were anxious to cover up was the period in US waters in early May. The US Intelligence Report revealed that the "*submarine's documents examined*" had been thoroughly censored. This seems to confirm that the War Diary and other material was not jettisoned at sea, but probably went ashore with Wermuth-1 at Miramar on 9 July 1945, and after German naval intelligence had perused it, those parts approved for publication returned with Wermuth-1 for his mysterious appearance at Mar del Plata on 12 July.

Mallea's adjutant Azcueta expressed surprise that the boat had arrived with so little fuel, 6 tonnes - this would be explained by so much submerged travel, particularly on the last leg south from the Equator - but with the provisions lockers still well stocked. Only enough had been loaded in Norway 17 weeks previously for a 17-week patrol, yet they still had most of it aboard.

On the night of 11 July at a Press conference in Buenos Aires, Navy Minister Tessaire stated that the first job of the naval enquiry was "*to go over the navigation log, determine the route pursued by the boat up to its arrival at the Argentine port, and study the naval operations undertaken.*" This statement obviously cast doubt on the earlier assurance that all the documentation had been thrown overboard.

More of the paperwork that "*wasn't*" on board

Towards midnight on 13 July, a Navy Ministry bulletin reported that after the necessary investigations had been made, it could be stated categorically that:

(i)   *U-530* had not been involved in the sinking of the Brazilian cruiser *BAHIA* at the Equator on 4 July 1945

(ii) no civilians or military personnel not included in the boat's muster had been aboard;

(iii) that the fifty-four crew members now held prisoner were the crew of the submarine and

(iv) that before surrendering to the base authorities, no person had disembarked from the submarine on the Argentine coast.

Items (ii) and (iv) were false.

The crew of *U-530*

"Will the Real Otto Wermuth Please Stand Up?"

The naval interrogation of Oberleutnant zur See Otto Wermuth commenced at Mar del Plata on 13 July 1945. US Navy observers were present but only as onlookers. It was thought likely to be more productive if they refrained from taking part because Wermuth hated the Americans and British.

Otto Wermuth was born on 28 July 1920 at Aalen/Württemberg and entered the Kriegsmarine as a naval cadet with intake IX/1939. After receiving his commission he spent two months aboard new destroyer *Z-23* and joined the U-Boat Arm in September 1941. He served as IIWO and IWO with training boat *U-37* and between July 1942 and February 1944 completed four long patrols as IIWO and IWO with *U-103*. At the recommendation of Admiral von Friedeburg, Wermuth was given command of *U-853* for two months from July 1944 but completed no war patrols, and in September 1944 he joined *U-530* as IWO. He made no voyages with *U-530* until being given command in January 1945.

It will be seen from the annotated Argentine Federal Police photograph taken at Mar del Plata on 13 July 1945 that Wermuth had dark hair and was 5 feet 8 inches in height. He cannot therefore be called "*tall and blond*". On his uniform are seen the Iron Cross First Class and U-Boat Badge. He told the interrogators that he had been awarded the *Kriegsabzeichen*, a war medal, the *Frontabzeichen*, awarded to U-Boat men after one voyage, and the *Iron Cross First* and *Second Class*. These latter were awarded after two years' and four years' U-Boat service respectively and did not necessarily signify any heroic individual deeds.

From the photographs, the Otto Wermuth presented by the Argentine naval harbourmaster, capitán Mallea, as "*the commander of U-530*" in the first newspaper reports was of Nordic facial structure, tall and blond. Besides the *Frontabzeichen* and *Iron Cross*, this man wore the *Ubootfrontspange* which Otto Wermuth-1 lacked. During lunch on 11 July the "*tall blond*" Wermuth told *La Razón* and *Noticias Gráficas* reporters that he had won his *Iron Cross* as "*an officer of the surface fleet*". The real Otto Wermuth had spent only two months with the surface fleet serving aboard the new destroyer *Z-23* working up in the Baltic.

EDITOR NOTE – The *"Frontspange"* was the close combat badge, awarded to men who had seen heavy combat. It was awarded first in bronze and if a higher award was required, it was presented in silver. There was never a U-Boat-Frontspange in gold as the war ended before that award could be authorized.

At the opening of the interrogation, the US Report makes clear that the Argentines were not convinced that the Otto Wermuth seated before them had ever been in command of the boat, and asked if he had any proof of the fact. This was a stupid question, for had he not brought the boat into Mar del Plata submarine base and signed the instrument of surrender? It was not a stupid question, however, if an imposter had commanded the boat for those few days while he was ashore in conference with German naval intelligence, and this was obviously the case, as the Argentines well knew. The interrogation was therefore an utter farce, and in fact we will learn more about the circumstances of the last leg of the *U-530* voyage from the second part of the article by Colonel Bustos(**10**):

"On 10 July 1945 the town of Mar del Plata was in uproar over the surrender there of the German submarine U-530, a fact which made headlines worldwide the same day. I was an AA officer with a local coastal battery and went to the submarine base to see the boat and speak to the naval authorities. They were still bemused by the fact that the deck gun and two large caliber weapons had been thrown overboard.

When I was allowed aboard the U-boat on 12 July I noticed the vile, nauseating stench in the interior despite the boat having been aired for three days; secondly the presence of tins identical to those we had found in the cave on the beach at Mar Chiquita at the end of June.

The crew was surprisingly young (18 to 20 year olds) and gave a general impression of exhaustion and starvation. They wore their hair and beards long and unkempt. At the submarine base they received oranges and other citrus fruits as an anti-scorbutic as soon as they came ashore. The interior of the U-boat was very narrow and we had to proceed stooped, which was very uncomfortable. Even the commander's compartment was tiny and austere. We saw no Nazi symbols in the boat. Most of the crew slept in hammocks.

I spoke to the commander, Oberleutnant Wermuth, who spoke good English and French. He was kept on the coastguard ship General Belgrano while the crew lived in tents on a football pitch where they were fed boiled potatoes and lemons on doctor's orders. I remember that the German commander was very youthful and pleasant. The ordeal he had suffered had erased none of the boyishness from his features. He had started to cultivate a blond beard covering his chin and was sporting a fine elongated blond moustache. He was very grateful for the good treatment we had given him and his crew. He did not seem especially fanatical or Nazi. He just kept saying how much he missed his family."

If it had not been for Colonel Bustos we should have known nothing of the scurvy aboard *U-530*. Scurvy is the seaman's disease. It disables three men for every man it kills, which makes the actual situation aboard ship far worse than the statistics suggest. Living on a diet lacking the Vitamin C in fresh vegetables and fruit, a sailor would begin to notice the insidious onset of scurvy within five to six weeks - pimples on the gums, teeth loose and falling out, dark blotches on the skin, old sores reappearing and fatigue developing into profound lethargy. Untreated, scurvy is invariably fatal. It was the terrible scourge of the days of sail, and no less lethal in the 20th century aboard a German U-Boat.

It is an assumption that the pervasive gas from the reagent must have combined with the provisions to destroy at least the Vitamin C content and contaminate the food generally. Taking 28 April 1945 - the day when the radio system closed down inexplicably - as the first day when the seepage affected the Vitamin C in the provisions, the signs of scurvy probably manifested around mid-June when *U-530* was near the Equator. Apart from the proper diet in submarine provisions, the preventive measure for scurvy is a dose of lemon juice in a 10% alcohol solution.

Even if *U-530* had this aboard, it would not have been stocked in sufficient quantity to provide fifty-four men with a tablespoonful every day for eight weeks.

What a horror this voyage from the Equator to Argentina must have been. Virtually permanent submerged travel in an intolerably humid environment, moulds forming and deckheads dripping, always that same vile, disgusting stench, nothing to eat and nothing to drink but water from the desalination plant, the men haggard and weak and no safe port of call to unload the sick.

By the time *U-530* reached Miramar on 9 July 1945 for instructions and for Wermuth to make his report, a number of crewmen might well have been in a sufficiently dangerous medical state to warrant their immediate transfer ashore. The substitutions would have occurred for the sickness and to avoid awkward questions from the future captors as to why the crew had scurvy when the provisions lockers were full.

U-530 was in rough shape when she surrendered

U-530 and Her Crew Handed
Over to the United States

On 12 July 1945 when the Argentines hoisted their national flag at the ensign staff of *U-530* it was taken as a sign that they intended to appropriate the boat. Upon receipt of a demand the same day from the United States and Britain to hand over boat and crew, the Argentine President ordered a naval committee to consider the matter. The following day it was agreed that "*U-530 had either deliberately or involuntarily violated the agreement enshrined in the instrument of unconditional surrender signed at Rheims on 7 May 1945*" which obliged all U-Boats to "*surrender unconditionally*" to the Allies "*after surfacing and hoisting a black flag*". The Argentine committee therefore recommended that *U-530* "*be placed at the disposal of the United States and Great Britain together with the crew of fifty-four persons and the archive compiled by Argentine naval forces.*"

At the end of July 1945 in pursuance of presidential decree 16.162, the crew of *U-530* was flown out to Washington DC, and from there to a PoW camp at Fort Hunt, Virginia, where Wermuth and IWO Karl-Felix Schlüter were subject to long periods of grilling. The missing log, maps and War Diary created many suspicions about the activities of *U-530*, and the Western Allies had the uncomfortable feeling that their reluctant and pro-German if not pro-Nazi ally Argentina was not being completely forthright and honest about what they knew of the *U-530* voyage.

Footnotes:
(1) Title 552(a)(6)(b)(1)(A) USCA Title 5, 1-552, p.109.
(2) Salinas and De Napoli: *Ultramar Sur*, Ed. Norma, Buenos Aires, 2002.
(3) The US Navy report provides a commentary on the still classified interrogations of four U-530 officers (Schüller, Löffler, Lenz and Schlüter) and four warrant officers (Zicker, Petrasch, Krause and Schlitsch) who were held incommunicado on different vessels at Mar del Plata during the interrogations while the other forty-five crew were held on the prison island at Martín Garcia.

(4) Letter from U-530 crewman held as a prisoner of war in Belgium, 1947, quoted in: Kraft: *Submarinos alemanes en la Argentina*, Buenos Aires 1998.

(5) Newton, Professor Ronald: *Actividades clandestinas de la armada alemana en aguas argentinas*, CEANA 1998.

(6) Salinas, *ibid*, p.423

(7) Salinas, *ibid*, p.301

(8) Brooks/Hirschfeld: *Hirschfeld- The Story of U-boat NCO 1940-1946*, Pen & Sword Books/USNIP, 1997, p.207-208.

(9) Salinas and De Napoli, *ibid*, p.401: Kraft, Helmut, *Submarinos alemanes en la Argentina*, Buenos Aires, 1998.

(10) Bustos, Colonel Rómulo: Yo fuí testigo, *La Nación*, Buenos Aires 23 March 2008.

CHAPTER SEVEN
Mysterious Sinking of the Brazilian Cruiser *Bahía*

BAHIA

Juan Salinas and Carlos De Nápoli, authors of *Ultramar Sur*(1), researched this tragedy. As researchers they are first-class, but as authors they tend to allow their bias for the Allied cause, and their hatred for the Nazis, to cloud their objectivity, and they draw conclusions which are unwarranted on the facts they have uncovered. They simply *know* who sank the *BAHIA* and are so certain in their judgment that they dedicate their book to the victims of the disaster in terms which leave no room for doubt:

> *"Dedicated to the 336 sailors of the **BAHIA** - including the four last victims of the Nazis - whose murders are still being incomprehensibly denied."*

In their view it was Schäffer in *U-977*, on his way to Argentina, who was the guilty party.

The Official Version of How the *Bahía* Was Sunk

BAHIA was a clapped-out 3150-ton cruiser built in Britain in 1906 and now operating out of Recife. She had seen action in both world wars and was well known to the U-Boat Arm. Her commander was Capitán Pires Carvalho e Albuquerque, the son of a Brazilian Procurator-General. He had fought in France in World War I and after a period with the Brazilian naval staff had commanded a submarine until 1942. Following a stint as liaison officer to the US Naval Mission in Rio, in January 1945 at age forty-eight he was given command of the cruiser **BAHIA**.

In July 1945 an air bridge existed between Natal in Brazil and Dakar in Senegal. Its basic purpose was to provide a radio-communications path for aircraft flying between Brazil and West Africa. There were four warships strung out along the path, three supplied by the Royal Navy and one by the Brazilians. During the relevant period the Brazilian cruiser was on "*Station 13*", located at 30°W on the Equator, 600 miles from Natal.

At 0900 hrs on Wednesday 4 July 1945, the cruiser was exercising her Oerlikon crews. She had seven 20-mm guns of this type arranged on the after-deck. The cruiser had stopped to lower a target raft, and at 0910 hrs had just got under way again at slow ahead when a massive explosion destroyed the stern, sent up a huge column of water, knocked down the mainmast, killed or maimed half the crew and sowed pandemonium.

BAHIA began to founder so quickly that only seventeen of her rafts could be got away. Though equipped with a first aid kit, some medicaments and dehydrated rations, the rafts had no radio or flares, and very quickly the occupants allowed them to drift apart.

When the cruiser **RIO GRANDE do SUL** arrived at Station 13 on the morning of 7 July to relieve **BAHIA** she could not be found, and it was thought at first that she might have left her position to search for a US Navy aircraft missing since 5 July. At 0730 hrs on 8 July a cook aboard the British freighter **BALFE** heard cries, and seeing a raft 200 yards away carrying a man waving a white shirt, raised the alarm. During that morning, **BALFE** recovered seven rafts with thirty-three survivors, five of whom died shortly after rescue. The last survivor was found on 13 July, bringing the final tally to thirty-six out of a crew of 372. Amongst those lost were four American radio-telegraphists:

- William Joseph Eustace,
- Andrew Jackson Pendleton,
- Emmet Peter Salles and
- Frank Benjamin Sparks.

The official Brazilian history records the first reports as claiming that **BAHIA** had gone down within ten minutes of the explosion, and most survivors thought that the explosion was the result of a torpedo hit. On 9 July the Brazilian Navy Ministry issued a bulletin stating:

"North East Naval Command reports that the cruiser Bahía on active service near St Peter and Paul Rocks has sunk as the result of an explosion whose cause is as yet uncertain",

and on 18 July distributed an update to the effect that reports indicated their cruiser must have "*hit a drifting mine*".

The Brazilian Board of Enquiry Delivers its Verdict

By the end of October 1945 the Brazilian Navy Ministry had completed its deliberations into the loss of **BAHIA** and published its findings. Apparently, during a routine gunnery exercise, a stack of depth charges on the poop was hit by a burst of accidental machine gun fire and exploded. None of the gunners survived. It was a very notable fact that the board of enquiry discounted the evidence of all eye-witnesses and used only the deposition of the single officer survivor, Lt (Eng.) Torres Dias, who at the material time had been in the engine-room and saw nothing.

His deposition stated:

> *"A little before 0900 hrs I received the order to stop the ship briefly to allow a float to be lowered into the water for use in target practice by the 20-mm Oerlikon crews. About 0910 hrs I received the order to put the ship to slow ahead so that we would have about two kilometers between the ship and the float. At that moment, I heard No.7 Oerlikon situated well astern began to fire. I had counted off five rounds when a terrible explosion shook the ship.*
>
> *"The turbines stopped and the engine-room began to flood very quickly. I found the entire upper deck enveloped in a dense, acrid, chocolate-coloured smoke. The visible destruction extended to the forepeak. Companionways, boats, masts and all superstructure were badly damaged. I saw many men with fatal injuries from splinters and a large number of dead on the bridge. These men had no obvious injuries, but were bleeding from the nose and mouth, and their clothing had been torn off."*

The official report stated that the correct position for the Oerlikons when not in use was with the barrel pointing skywards. The depth-charges were correctly stowed in that position on the poop. It was believed that an accidental round from one of the Oerlikons hit a depth charge, causing it to explode. Oerlikons were fitted with traversing stops to prevent their firing projectiles into the standing superstructure during the heat of combat, and these stops were almost impossible to disengage without factory help, but allegedly they had been removed from the cruiser's Oerlikons. Although most survivors attributed the explosion to a torpedo attack because of their belief that they had seen a submarine minutes before the ship blew up, Torres Dias, from his position in the engine-room from where he could see nothing, was firmly convinced that the explosion resulted from "*the accidental firing of a weapon left cocked*", and his was the opinion which counted.

EDITOR NOTE – In 2010 we interviewed one of the remaining survivors of **U-977** (seen here in Mar del Plata) and we asked if that submarine had fired torpedoes at the cruiser **BAHIA**. He said that **U-977** definitely did not fire at any ship during the trip to Argentina. The reader must give that statement as much or as little credibility as they believe it warrants.

The Dissenting Views

In the magazine *O Navigador*, issue No.15, *O mistério do cruzador* Bahía, Admirals Martins and Saldanha da Gama recalled the service manual being adamant that the small charges of trotyl in the 20-mm projectiles could not detonate a depth charge. If that were possible, then warships with depth charges stacked on deck would run a permanent risk of blowing up whenever they came under fire from enemy aircraft.

To dispel all doubts, the Brazilian Navy ran tests firing a 20mm Oerlikon into a depth charge from three metres' range and "*to the surprise of the experts*" and "*contradicting the safety manuals*" the depth charge exploded. Since one depth charge could not have caused the terrible damage to the cruiser reported by Lt Torres Dias, the first depth charge must have detonated the other twenty-nine in the stack, but even then, taking into account that the charge was not directed, and ninety per cent of its force was dissipated upwards, "*the admirals were not convinced that that was how the disaster must have come about*".

An equally difficult thing for them to envisage was the event whereby the Oerlikon came to be fired. The gun crews were stood down for the ten minutes it took to lower the target raft into the water. Cocking the Oerlikon required great force to depress the spring manually to fire the first round. Thus the gun would have had to be left cocked after the previous exercise, which was a court-martial offence. Next it was necessary to accept a string of coincidences:
- the gun had been left unattended, loaded and cocked and pointing at the depth charges on the poop;
- The gun had had its safety stops removed;
- the depth charges supplied by a Detroit firm were defective and dangerous;
- and then an unauthorised sailor - "*The Drunken Sailor Theory*" the admirals called it - just happened along, took charge of the gun and pulled the trigger. And the gunners who knew if that were true or not were all dead.

Torres Dias concluded:

"The high tribute in lives was a consequence of various causes, but above all the failure to duly observe the necessary security precautions, and this originated the tragedy."

Thus the ship's commander, Albuquerque, was responsible for the loss of his ship through gross negligence. The official verdict was never accepted wholeheartedly by the Brazilian Navy. Admiral Saldanha da Gama expressed his suspicions that the United States pulled the strings of the enquiry. Allegedly nobody saw the fatal firing of the Oerlikon for no witnesses who had been on deck were called. When we see what they would have had to say, an entirely different picture forms of the circumstances of the tragedy.

The Evidence the Board of Enquiry Did Not Want

Surviving crewmen who had been on the starboard side of the ship all agreed that as the cruiser got under way at 0910 hrs, the commander saw a strange fishing vessel, which he suspected to be a disguised submarine. She was coming up on the starboard quarter on a parallel course several miles off. Albuquerque ordered a burst of fire ahead of the submarine's path to bring her to a stop. An Oerlikon on the stern fired five rounds and hit the turret of the submarine, as the survivors saw clearly.

The European War was over. The cruiser **BAHIA** had attacked an unidentified vessel without warning and obtained a hit. This was an act of piracy on the high seas, and **BAHIA** had clearly put herself in the wrong. The submarine would be German and proceeding to an Argentine port to surrender knowingly or involuntarily in breach of the Rheims agreement of 7 May 1945, but this was not a fact known to the commander of **BAHIA** until he enquired, and he could not fire at the submarine until he had fulfilled a number of procedures. If there was a drunken sailor at the Oerlikon gun, as the Brazilian board of enquiry was quite happy to concede, the other four rounds could have gone anywhere, including into the cruiser's depth charges. The submarine had the right to defend herself and according to witnesses responded with one or more rounds from a flak weapon on the platform abaft the tower. **BAHIA** then exploded astern.

Was This *U-977*?

As will be seen from Chapter 10, according to his charts and his written admission, Schäffer in *U-977* was about fifty miles away from **BAHIA** at the time she was sunk. All the nonsense about the world record 66-day voyage always submerged was a fiction designed to make it appear he was a thousand miles further north than his true position on 4 July 1945. In the unexpurgated version of his book *El Secreto del U-977* (Hismar, Buenos Aires, 2006) at pages 220-221, Schäffer described how *U-977* was disguised to look like a small steamer from a distance:

> *"We cut some linen and sailcloth into strips and hung them to give us the look of a freighter. We fashioned a sheet of tin-plate into a funnel and set it up on the conning tower. We dipped some rags in oil and set them alight to make smoke".*

The compressed air pump was used for a better blaze. From then on we never needed to avoid other vessels because our camouflage was excellent. Intense smoke and sparks rose to the skies from the "*funnel*" whenever necessary. Tomorrow we were to cross the Equator on the surface. We would celebrate crossing the Line. I would be Neptune...the celebrations had reached their high point when we heard the sound of aircraft. I connected up the anti-radar. Had we been discovered? The lookouts had not been very alert during the ceremony, but there was nothing in sight, we just kept hearing the aircraft noises. Should we dive? The flak guns were loaded. Thetis, daughter of Neptune, was at the 3.7cm. I warned the men we might have to dive. There we were, all dressed up in our picturesque costumes, *but ready to defend ourselves if attacked...*"

Theory One

If this mystery submarine was Schäffer's *U-977*, why was he there? He was surfaced with lookouts posted and his hydrophones should have given him warning of the Oerlikon practice aboard the slow moving cruiser long before he came up on her. The Germans knew all about the ships stationed along the Natal-Dakar path. He knew she was there and if he had wanted to avoid her Schäffer could have done so easily. He was very optimistic if he thought his "*small steamer*" disguise would have fooled a Brazilian cruiser. In *Theory One*, *U-977* was sailing parallel to the cruiser a few miles off. The cruiser fired and hit the "*funnel*" or the conning tower itself. Schäffer's 3.7-cm flak gun replied, and either by sheer unintended misfortune hit the defective Detroit depth charges on the poop, or the cruiser's Oerlikon did so, and the explosion resulted, solving his problem for him.

Theory Two

Schäffer was proceeding towards Argentina to surrender - in forty-four days' time. There can be no doubt that he had a significant cargo aboard (Chapter 10) and that he would "*defend himself if attacked*" as he promised in his book.

If it was Schäffer's boat which was seen and attacked by **BAHIA**, the question must be asked why he passed deliberately within the vision of the cruiser and what did he think he would achieve by returning fire with a 37mm flak gun - unless it had an unusually destructive effect, and he wanted to see its effect on a cruiser?

Unlike Wermuth in **U-530**, Schäffer surrendered at Mar del Plata with his issue of weapons intact - except for his flak munitions. He explained that he had none left because they had been "*expended in gunnery practice before the war ended and some were jettisoned when they got wet.*" Therefore it is not known whether his flak munitions were rounds of a special type.

If we look for motive, the date July 4th for the sinking may be significant. Furthermore, the fact may also be significant that between 11 December 1941 and 22 August 1942. Brazil had leased an airstrip at Natal to the US Naval Air Squadron enabling it to fly missions of reconnaissance and attack against U-Boats at sea, a clear breach of Brazil's neutrality by Brazil and the United States, and an undeclared state of war by Brazil on Germany. 4th July - Natal - Brazil - United States: these form a mere basis for speculation that a message was being sent and a score settled. Here for lack of any further information we must abandon the **BAHIA** mystery.

Footnotes:
(1) Salinas and De Nápoli: *Ultramar Sur*, Norma Ed., Buenos Aires, 2002. The official version of the *Bahía* tragedy is contained in, Almirante Saldanha da Gama: *A tragedia do Bahía*, Historia Naval Brasileira, Vol 5, Part II, Rio de Janeiro, 1985, p.412.
(2) Salinas, *ibid*, p.427.

CHAPTER EIGHT

Delivering the Goods

Tuesday 22 May 1945 Memorandum from Admiral Vernengo Lima, Chief of the Argentine Naval General Staff to Navy Minister Alberto Tessaire (photo right):

"I draw to the attention of Your Excellency that according to information received from the Ministry for Foreign Affairs, German submarines are present in the waters of the South Atlantic and intending to make for Japan."

The problem confronting the *"inept and incompetent"* German intelligence service in Argentina immediately postwar was how to lure away as much of the Argentine fleet as possible on a wild goose chase and thereby enable U-Boats arriving from Europe to disembark passengers and unload cargo safely on the sandy shores of Buenos Aires province.

In an informal conversation with General Lang, military attaché at the US Embassy, an unknown German source fed him the idea of *"German plans to route fugitive U-Boats around Cape Horn to disembark important passengers on the south coast of Chile."* The US naval attaché Captain Webb reported that *"the information was subsequently blown out of all proportion"* and by the time the Argentine Ministry of Foreign Affairs received it the U-Boats for Chile were believed to be actually on their way(1).

The Argentine Navy acted with alacrity. Vicealmirante Héctor Vernengo Lima, pro-Allied Chief of the Naval General Staff, was of the opinion that he ought to *"give the order to the commander-in-chief of the Sea Squadron to prevent the passage of German U-Boats from the Atlantic into the Pacific by establishing a patrol line in the far south until further orders,"* and he enclosed an encoded message to that effect for the approval of His Excellency the Navy Minister.

Tessaire was in favour, and next day the commander-in-chief of the Sea Squadron put the order into effect. On 25 May eight torpedo boats and all available minesweepers set off for Tierra del Fuego**(2)**, and on 29 May it was reported that an anti-submarine cordon had been established across the Straits of Magellan, and from Le Maire and the south-east of Isla de los Estados south to the region of the pack ice.

At the conclusion of the naval review at Buenos Aires on 9 July 1945 the destroyer squadron also headed south at full speed to join the cordon. Over the period ending 21 July 1945, the major part of the Argentine surface fleet drifted off Cape Horn looking for U-Boats and sighted nothing. On 13 July, in utter exasperation, the US Navy admitted to being *"unsure of the whereabouts of between four and six U-boats, although by 18 July the US Navy Department knew enough to issue a dispatch through UP that they thought it improbable that any of the four submarines whose whereabouts are unknown will be near the coast of Argentina, it being undoubtedly an error that Nazi submarines have been seen near that country,"* an assurance that set all minds at rest.

The Incidents at San Clemente del Tuyú and San Antonio Oeste, 17/18 July 1945

San Clemente was then a small village on the headland dividing the River Plate from the South Atlantic. Its location is 200 miles from Buenos Aires, to which it used to be linked only by dirt roads often impassable due to heavy rainfall. The inhabitants were mainly of German origin. U-Boats were reported to have unloaded on several occasions in Samborombón Bay, formed by a huge tract of uninhabited marshy terrain on the River Plate side of the headland. The headland was dominated by the 1892-built lighthouse providing an excellent panorama of coast and sea, the light and living quarters being set atop a 58-metre tall metal tripod on the edge of the village.

Tuesday 17 July 1945 at San Clemente del Tuyú dawned misty with a calm sea. Just after 0800 hrs as the haze lifted, around twenty villagers saw two submarines of different sizes heading south along the coast about three miles offshore. Agent Longhi at the Mar de Ajó police office was informed by telephone, the witnesses adding that the larger submarine had the number "*124*" painted on the conning tower(**3**).

EDITOR NOTE – the actual *U-124*, known as the '*Edelweißboot*', was sunk in combat on 2 April 1943. Also, it was forbidden to have the actual numbers on the conning tower after the war began in September 1939 so this must have had another meaning.

When Longhi arrived with a local official, Mariano González, he found the villagers in a "*state of excitement*", many being on the roofs of their dwellings or on the terraces of the two hotels looking out to sea. Longhi was told that the two submarines had headed south-east and submerged. The persons who spoke to Longhi were described as "*upright members of the community*".

> *"To: C-in-C River Squadron and C-in-C Sea Squadron: Today 17 July 0900 civilians saw submarine three kms off San Clemente beach submerging on approach of aircraft. Seen again at 1000, more to south, submerging. Lima, Chief of Naval General Staff."*

Towards ten that morning, González and Longhi saw a submarine appear towards the San Antonio lighthouse. According to Newton, the trained observers in the San Antonio lighthouse saw nothing on the waters at any time during the entire day of 17 July despite their dominating vantage point and since none ever wrote his memoirs, we shall never know what they actually did see. Officer Longhi now found two ladies of German origin on the beach signaling out to sea with a lamp and arrested them.

At two in the afternoon, Longhi spoke to Capitán Isaac Rosas, adjutant to vicealmirante Lima, and reported having seen "a vessel close to San Antonio light but difficult to make out clearly due to the mist. Later when the sun broke through he had seen that the vessel was a submarine, nothing like an Argentine submarine and very similar to the published photographs of *U-530*. It had stopped two miles offshore. He saw cables running from the conning tower, one to the bow, the other to the stern. It had no chimney. When an aircraft approached it submerged. Later, at about ten, he and other persons saw it a little further south, heading towards Mar del Plata. The sea was calm. He did not see it after it submerged the second time(**4**)".

The sightings were announced on local radio stations and the people of Mar del Ajó claimed to have seen the submarines from the seawall, according to the national newspaper *La Nación*. The article went on to say that not only Longhi and his neighbours had seen the vessels. The correspondent of *El Tribuno,* who happened to be in the town of Dolores, reported that the smaller of the two submarines had grounded on a sandbank and had been held fast for five minutes "*before reversing off*".

At 1500 on 17 July the Navy Ministry received information as to the intentions of these submarines and advised that part of the Torpedo Boat Squadron not drifting off Antarctica:

> *"Another submarine is expected to enter port or disembark passengers on our coast before 2200 hrs. River Squadron aerial search down to Necochea and surface vessels search from Necochea to Cabo Blanco. General Plan: this force will bring pressure on submarine and prevent possibility of disembarkation crew or passengers, capturing them between Querandí and Cabo Blanco. Attack if they resist..."*

Agent Longhi had informed his superiors at La Plata, capital of Buenos Aires province, and the Chief of Police told the Navy Ministry. The Naval General Staff met during the day and were in constant contact with San Clemente for reports. Around eleven that night the provincial Government reported that a submarine was aground "*on a sandy shoal five miles south of the village two hundred metres out*". Coastal naval forces were ordered to attend, but so few were available because of the Cape Horn fiasco that the first did not arrive until two days later.

The conference at Naval General Staff continued into the early hours of 18 July. Land and coastal patrols were ordered in cooperation with the local naval prefecture and police forces. The Sub-prefect of La Plata, Emilio Cabrera, set out from la Plata at 0130 that morning and drove to San Clemente del Tuyú to interview witnesses. José Casibe described the U-Boat conning tower, which he could identify from naval knowledge gained in the First World War.

Roy Gibson of Los Yngleses ranch said the same(**5**), having watched the submarines through a telescope from the top of a sand dune. Domingo Talpone, "*well acquainted with Argentine submarines from having been aboard them at Mar del Plata*" and nine other men also made statements. All twelve witnesses concurred that after one of the submarines submerged, a light aircraft had approached and circled the other one "*signalling with a handkerchief or something similar until boat were lost to sight in the coastal mists*".

On 19 July 1945 Agent Longhi was dismissed from the police for making two false arrests. It was not an arrestable offence to signal seawards with a lamp from a beach unless the recipient vessel was suspected of being engaged in customs offences or was an enemy of Argentina, i.e. Japanese. The number "*124*" painted on the conning tower of the larger submarine must have served as a coded message for German helpers ashore. It was undoubtedly the role of the two German ladies on the beach to instruct "*U-124*" what to do next, and this was probably to proceed to waters off Necochea and await further orders regarding unloading. The nature of the smaller submarine cannot be determined on the evidence available but may have been a Type II or an early post WWI submarine built in one of the yards outside Germany during the clandestine U-Boat resurrection programme of the 1920s.

EDITOR NOTE – This clandestine resurgence program of the submarine design, engineering, testing and building is reported in detail in our book "*The Rise and Fall of the U-Bootwaffe*" available from Sharkhunters.

The naval vessel of most concern to the Hitlerists in Argentina was the torpedo boat *MENDOZA* at Bahía Blanca naval base within a few hours' sailing time of Necochea beaches where the U-Boats were to unload. Now there came information of a U-Boat seen at Caleta de los Loros, three hundred miles to the south of Bahía Blanca, and late on the night of 17 July *MENDOZA* sailed for the Golfo San Matías to the south to search for the intruder. This rid the coast of the main threat for the intended unloading at Necochea. To what extent there was collaboration between Perón, Tessaire and the German intelligence fraternity at this time can only be guessed at, but the urgency of the situation was relieved within a few days following a political development in Argentina.

Vicealmirante Héctor Vernengo Lima was a pro-Allied veteran of the First World War. He had served with the US Navy then and had been awarded the Victory Medal in Washington in 1939. As principal of the Argentine Naval Academy in 1938 he had clashed with the then Colonel Perón at a lecture when Perón was speaking about the occupation of the Baltic States during the First World War. Lima had humiliated him by making continual interruptions to correct errors and Lima became his bitter enemy. By July 1945 Lima was Chief of the Naval General Staff while Perón was Vice-President and Minister for War.

The political orders which Lima received came directly from Navy Secretary Alberto Tessaire, a personal friend of Perón. As Chief of the Naval General Staff, Limas could propose plans of action but the decision had always to be taken at the higher level. It had been his own idea to send the greater part of the Argentine fleet to Antarctica in May to block the passage of U-Boats into the Pacific, and now he had come up with the idea of attacking all submarines without warning. Somebody convinced Minister Tessaire that this was going too far(**6**) and on 21 July 1945 Lima was obliged to issue this remarkable order:

"To Commanders-in-Chief Sea and River Squadrons
Call off the coastal patrols.
Signed: Vicealmirante Lma, Chief of Naval General Staff.

With this signal Argentina threw open all four thousand kilometers of its sea and river coasts to the remnants of the German U-Boat Arm.

The *MENDOZA* Incident, 18 July 1945

After sailing post haste from Bahía Blanca on the night of 17 July, the torpedo boat *MENDOZA* arrived in Golfo San Matías just after eight next morning and headed for Caleta de los Loros on the north coast of the gulf about halfway between San Antonio Oeste and Viedma. She closed to within two miles of the shore and searched the waters assisted by a Corsair naval aircraft. Having found nothing, *MENDOZA* continued west towards San Antonio Oeste which, it will be recalled, was the Patagonian HQ of the German naval and military intelligence organisation, the Lahusen wool empire.

In the roadstead *MENDOZA* had more luck and saw with perfect clarity the periscope of a submarine trailing a long wake:

"1730 hrs sighted submarine periscope, clear grey tube followed by long wake with tumescence, Av 140 exterior anchorage San Antonio Oeste, heading 160°. Gave submarine alarm, maximum speed 23 knots, headed for indicated position, dropped eight depth charges, patrolled zone one hour forty minutes. Left area dusk."

Lacking any kind of search force, or support other than aircraft, *MENDOZA* spent the next two days patrolling the northern coastline of Golfo San Matías in vain searching for the mysterious U-Boat. This particular coastline will loom larger as a region of interest in the closing chapter of this book.

The Copetonas Beach Sighting, 23 July 1945

Copetonas beach is located roughly halfway between the Bahía Blanca naval base and Necochea. High dunes near the village of Reta inshore provide an excellent vantage point to look out to sea. At sunset on 23 July 1945, fishing vessel owner José Alfaro was examining the horizon from the crest of one such sand dune when he saw "*a submarine 70 metres in length with a central turret lacking identification, painted grey, which surfaced facing south and then submerged again.*" He estimated the distance offshore as seven miles. Visibility was excellent and the witness well qualified, since he had been master of one of his own boats for many years and was versed in vessel recognition, estimating size at a distance and calculating positions at sea with reference to the coast.

Sr. Alfaro made a statement both to police and at the Prefecture. Sub-Prefect Vergara informed the main naval base 100 miles away, describing the witness as "*a professional fisherman, well known to this maritime authority.*" The sighting was also confirmed by the three-man crew of **ALFARO II**, who were ashore at the time. On the afternoon of 24 July, the Prefect-General, contraalmirante Clarizza, informed the Navy Minister of the facts, and the Chief of the Naval General Staff ordered his adjutant, capitán Rojas, to prepare a report.

As at San Clemente del Tuyú, the Navy delegated the investigation to the Prefercture, and on 25 July, forty hours after the sighting, Vergara arrived at Copetonas to interview the witnesses. In his report of 26 July to Rojas, Vergara stated that,

> *"It seems certain to have been a submarine because the sighting was supported by three of his crew members who confirmed having seen the incident from start to finish."*

The Navy mobilized a naval aircraft and minesweeper to scour the zone, and a torpedo boat at Bahía Blanca was held at readiness with steam up, but by now three days had passed and, hardly surprisingly, nothing was found. Salinas(**7**) mentions that there is a note in the top margin of Rojas' memorandum reporting the Brazilian ship ***OESTELOIDES*** acting in a suspicious manner in the area.

This submarine could well have been Heinz Schäffer's ***U-977*** (see Chapter 10). The whereabouts of his boat with heavy cargo since crossing the Equator on 4 July 1945 remain unknown, and his main periscope was damaged beyond repair. In order to establish his position he would have needed to surface to take bearings on shore marks during the hours of daylight.

EDITOR NOTE – If the submarine sighted were approximately 70 meters in length (approximately 225 feet) that would be about right for a Type VII-C German U-Boat and since ***U-977*** was a Type VII-C, this theory is possible.

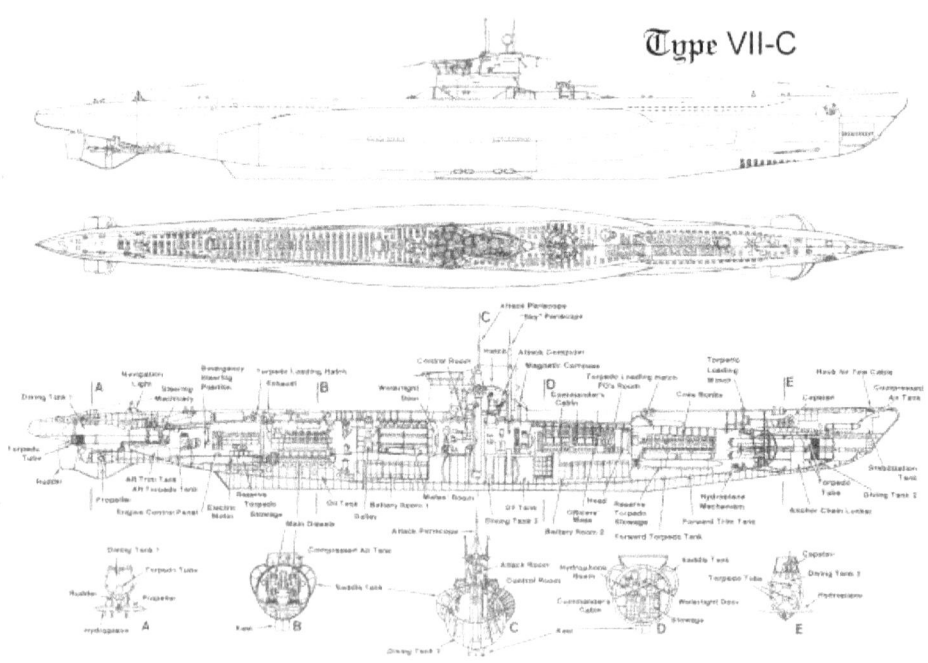

𝕿𝖞𝖕𝖊 VII-C

The Moromar Incident, 28 July 1945

The presence of German U-Boats around Necochea, a town on the southern coast of Buenos Aires province, is the best documented anywhere. In a UP despatch from London on 18 July 1945 a report was made of "*several men coming ashore in a rubber dinghy 160 kms south of Mar del Plata, the place indicated being between two resorts, Las Grutas and Los Ángelese, about thirty kilometers out of Necochea at Punta Negra.*"

> *"Memorandum: To Navy Minister from Maritime Prefecture-General   Buenos Aires 30 July 1945*
> *Attached hereto Prefecture Zone River Plate respecting report of submarine appearing in Necochea jurisdiction.*
> *Signed, Clarizza, contraalmirante.*

The information is signed by capitán de fragata Matías López, Prefect of River Plate District and the Port of Buenos Aires.:

> *"For the information of the Prefect-General transcribed herewith is Note N No.2-R dated 28 July 1945, received on that date and originating from the Sub-Prefecture of Quequén with a report on the presence of an alleged submarine.*
>
> *The signatory, together with the police chief of Necochea, don Luis Marriotti, proceeded to Punta Negra for the purpose of assessing the accuracy of the information which the police station received yesterday afternoon from agent Ricardo Montero, badge number 9179, on duty at the coast and close to the location stated. The officer as aforesaid states that yesterday morning, 27 July 1945 at 0930 hrs, he saw at a distance which he estimates at four kilometers a black shape which seemed to him to be the conning tower of a submarine. It remained surfaced for a period of thirty minutes and then disappeared. He reported this information to the desk sergeant at Necochea yesterday afternoon when his shift ended."*

The remainder of the document relates the interrogation of officer Montero by López and Marriotti, the officer eventually being broken and recanting, his inquisitors reporting with satisfaction:

*"We deduce that the officer misidentified a fishing boat as a submarine's conning tower, given that the majority of the fishing vessels which put out to fish yesterday headed south and saw nothing abnormal(**8**)."*

The abnormal thing here was for a police officer to think that a fishing boat, of which he saw numerous examples going out to sea daily, and which he watched from a mere four kilometers for a period of half an hour, was a U-Boat. However, the purpose of the enquiry was not to investigate his fitness to continue as a policeman but to extract from him a statement denying his report. It was on that very evening that two U-Boats unloaded at Necochea, as is evidenced by the following. In 1992, an open letter was published in the newspaper *Clarín*. The author preferred to remain anonymous for reasons which will be apparent from it.

"In the year 1945 I was eighteen years old, and the son of a police officer attached to Necochea police station. At about six on the evening of 27 July 1945 a police sergeant called at our house to inform my father that the Superintendent needed to see him urgently.

My father went at once and returned an hour later to change his clothes, telling my mother not to expect him for dinner because information had been received that a vessel (he did not know if it was a submarine or surface ship, given the onset of darkness) was sending Morse signals to the beach at Necochea, and somebody was replying.

Having overheard this I insisted that my father took me with him, to which he agreed. We went to the beach in three private cars and detected that the signals were being sent at intervals. The officers spread out along the foreshore and after several hours a man was found signaling out to sea. He was a German artisan who made souvenirs for tourists. After an "exhaustive" investigation at the police station, at which of course I was not present, the man confessed that the vessel was a submarine which had been damaged and needed to find a secure spot on the coast to disembark.

By now it was close to dawn, and the Superintendent and my father planned a sweep over several miles of beach either side of Necochea. Eventually my father, together with two police corporals and four agents, came across a place on the coast with a huge number of tracks from the waterline across the beach (made by boats and rubber dinghies) and which led to the tree-shrouded entrance of a big ranch with many tamarinds. It was called Moromar*, and its owners at that time were Germans.*

Finding this important proof, and noting the impressions of cases which had been dragged to lorries (identified by their tyre tracks), my father sent for the Superintendent, and once he arrived they entered the property. The farm building lay behind some hills, and after driving a mile or so towards the house we were stopped and forced to leave by four Germans armed with sub-machine guns. Seeing that the possibilities of entry were remote, lacking as they did a search warrant, the squad returned to Necochea without leaving a guard at the entrance, discretion being called for.

*At the police station the Superintendent made a telephone call immediately to the Chief of Police at La Plata. It was two hours before he could be found, and he ordered the Superintendent to abandon the search for illegal German immigrants and stay clear of the Moromar ranch(***9***). The spy who had been detained for questioning was sent to La Plata but no charges were preferred and he was soon back on the beach."*

In 1952 a congressional committee led by radical Silvano Santander investigated Nazi activities in Argentina in the period during and after the war. Called to give sworn evidence were three former ***ADMIRAL GRAF SPEE*** crewmen who had returned to Argentina as immigrants, Alfred Schulz, Walter Dettelmann and Willi Brennecke. The trio had escaped from internment and remained at liberty in Argentina during the war under the direction of Fregettenkapitän Walter Kay, who found them work and held them at readiness as "*stevedores*" for jobs which would need doing when the time came.

They gave evidence to the committee that on a date between 23rd and 29 July 1945 they assisted at the unloading of two U-Boats on the Argentine coast. Their verbatim testimony in shorthand, like much else of a sensitive historical importance in Argentina, has not survived the passage of time, but a synopsis is extant in the chronicles of the committee of enquiry. The stevedores did not remember exactly where the place was, but all agreed it was a Lahusen ranch(**10**). Shortly after their arrival at the ranch,

> *"Two U-Boats unloaded a huge number of heavy crates which were then shuttled to the house on the estate in eight lorries. Eighty persons - whether crew or passengers is not stated; disembarked in rubber dinghies. It was alleged that the cargo was "some of the treasure of the SS-RSHA" and* **"documentation pertaining to the technical science of the secret weaponry**".

Footnotes:

(1) Newton, Professor Ronald: *Actividades clandestinas*, text and footnotes 44/46.

(2) Camarasa, Jorge, *Puerto Seguro*, Ed. Norma, 2006, p.118.

(3) Moyano, Miguel Ángel, *Submarinos alemanes in Mar del Plata*, in: *Todo es Historia*, Buenos Aires No. 72: Newton, *ibid*, Camarasa, *ibid*. Newton provides the redundant information that it was not the practice of the Kriegsmarine to paint running numbers on U-boat conning towers during wartime, (17 July 1945 being "peacetime"), while Camarasa points out that the "real *U-124*" was sunk off Oporto in 1943.

(4) Rojas, Capitán Isaac, Report 17 July 1945, Archive General, Naval General Staff.

(5) It is not clear if they were saying that one of the submarines was a German U-Boat design of the First World War. No sketch or photograph of the submarines involved in all these incidents has ever been made public.

(6) Camarasa, *ibid*, quoting *Memorias del almirante Isaac F Rojas*, Planeta, Buenos Aires, 1993: and González Crespo, *El coronel*, Ediciones Ayer y Hoy, Buenos Aires, 1998.

(7) Salinas and De Nápoli, *Ultramar Sur*, p.314.

(8) Per Camarasa, Jorge, *ibid*, Archivo General memorandum NS No. 246, 30 July 1945.

(9) Moromar has changed hands several times since 1945 and today is a model holiday complex administered by a limited company.

(10) Although at the time one of the principal German conglomerates in Argentina, with a seven-storey building on Boulevard Colón in central Buenos Aires, 100,000 hectares of property in Patagonia and a thousand employees, Lahusen S.A., notorious as the central organisation of German espionage in the First World War, was exempted from a list of firms investigated by the commission overseeing enemy property created by the Argentine Government after the declaration of war in March 1945.

CHAPTER NINE
Black Boat *U-235*: Getting *Black Boat* Crews Home to Germany

Besides *U-530* and *U-977* there is a third U-boat which is mentioned in an Argentine declassified document from 1952 as having discharged at least one passenger at Mar del Plata while en route to Patagonia after the war. This was a "***Black Boat***" known only by its number "*U-235*"(**1**).

EDITOR NOTE – Again, this would be a false number inasmuch as the actual *U-235* was sunk in error by a German torpedo boat in the closing moments of the war.

A "***Black Boat***" was a German U-Boat in use but not in commission and for which it has proved impossible to find a document trail relating to its origins.   We pick up the story as told by Oberfunkmeister Wolfgang Hirschfeld (photo right), senior radio operator of Type X-B submarine *U-234*, bound for Tokyo(**2**):

"One morning in February 1945 on the quayside at Kiel I saw Japanese Air Force Colonel Genzo Shosi and naval Captain Hideo Tomonaga, a submarine designer, seated on a crate on the forecasing of my boat U-234. They were engaged in painting "U-235" in black characters on the wrapping paper gummed around each of a large number of containers of uniform size. Once each container was ready, it would be stowed aboard U-234. I asked Captain Tomonaga what the packages contained and he said,

"It is the cargo from U-235. That boat is no longer going to Japan."

When I enquired at 5th U-Flotilla Office, they told me that U-235 was a Type VII training boat which had never been scheduled for operations outside the Baltic, and so I knew that Tomonaga had lied to me."

German naval historian Professor Jürgen Rohwer confirmed from the first *Magic* signal decrypts for 1943 and 1944/1945 that Japan had requested from Germany a quantity of uranium oxide in connection with atomic research into fissile isotopes. Two one-tonne lots of uranium oxide were to have been sent, one tonne each aboard *U-234*, and the "***Black Boat***" known as *U-235*. When Captain Hideo Tomonaga told Hirschfeld at Kiel that *U-235* would now not be going to Japan, he already knew that both one-tonne lots were being shipped to Japan aboard *U-234*, and Hirschfeld actually saw this being done(**3**).

There was another witness to these events. Kunihiko Kigoshi was a chemist who worked for Dr. Nishina, head of the Japanese Army atomic project. He was also the brother of Yasukazu Kigoshi, the Japanese military attaché to Germany in 1945. Yasukazu told his brother that he had attended at Kiel twice to watch uranium being loaded aboard *U-234*. He knew that there had been a second submarine due to go to Japan, but that it "*would not be reaching that far*"(**4**).

It would appear that *U-235* was actually replaced. The Type IX-D2 boat *U-876* (Kapitänleutnant Rolf Bahn) was on stand-by to take passengers and cargo for Japan at least as late as 25 April 1945, but never sailed(**5**).

This proves that the primary intention was to withdraw the "***Black Boat***" *U-235* from circulation, and not to reduce the number of boats potentially bound for Japan from Kiel from two to one.

When we look more closely at the reason why Captain Hideo Tomonaga came to Europe, it is possible to discern why he and black boat *U-235* must be considered together. Tomonaga had arrived in German-occupied France aboard *U-180* with a substantial quantity of gold of so enormous a weight that the *U-180* chief engineer used it to trim the boat. The gold was said to be payment for German technology. Tomonaga was a submarine designer and came to Germany to inform himself about U-Boat developments(**6**).

EDITOR NOTE – This boat, *U-180*, was one of only two very rare Type IX-D1 submarines that originally used six fast running Mercedes built diesel engines. Constant mechanical problems forced the U-Bootwaffe to replace these with the normal two dependable M.A.N. diesels. This boat, like most of the very large cargo boats, was attached to the 12th U-Bootflottille based at Bordeaux, France about twelve miles up the Gironde River. On 22 August 1944 *U-180* struck a mine in the Gironde estuary and was destroyed.

The cargo of *U-234* for Japan included many blueprints and plans for advanced weaponry and aircraft. By February 1945 the Japanese knew all there was to know about obsolete Type VII and Type IX U-boats. Their interest was now directed to the new breed of U-boat such as Type XXI. Since *U-235* was a *"Black Boat"* given that number merely for convenience, we assume that it was a new Type XXI not intended to enter Kriegsmarine service. Almost certainly the idea was that it should make a delivery voyage to Japan and be handed over there to the Japanese Navy, either as a gift, or the proceeds of a sale contract.

When the military situation began to deteriorate rapidly for both Japan and Germany in February 1945, the Germans must have decided to cancel the arrangement with Japan and send *U-235* to Argentina where under the Secret Alliance they would be able to continue clandestine naval activities after the defeat.

Therefore when Captain Tomonaga was asked by Hirschfeld on the quayside at Kiel about the contents of the small heavy containers, Captain Tomonaga's full reply would have been, had he been at liberty to express it:

*"It is the cargo from **U-235**. That boat is no longer going to Japan. It is going to Argentina."*

The Memorandum

"Coordinación Federal DAE 568
To: Chief of Division of Foreigners' Affairs
From: Chief of Córdoba Delegation
14 October 1952
Movement of Foreigners
I bring to your attention that our agents have detected at Ascochinga, Córdoba province, mountainous zone, a property located on Cerro Negro which has been acquired by an ex-officer who disembarked at Mar del Plata submarine base from U-235, which together with other German submarines arrived at Patagonia from Germany at the end of the war..."(**7**)

This Argentine archive document provides the evidence that ***U-235*** and a number of other German U-boats besides ***U-530*** and ***U-977*** arrived in Patagonia after the war and did so with the knowledge and acquiescence of the Argentine authorities. Of that there can be no doubt. But how did those crews get home, those men who preferred not to make a new life at Nuevo Wewelsburgo or wherever, and not spend the rest of their lives working at some secret U-Boat base in a forlorn corner of Patagonia?

Getting Black Boat Crews Home to Germany

In an earlier chapter it was demonstrated how Admiral Sturdee's report on the Battle of the Falklands in 1914 was doctored to show only two German transports present in the Falklands when there were three. This is how history is falsified. Many such documents turned out by the armed services of a nation and linked Government agencies contain disinformation of a similar nature. Over the course of time historians come to treat the material as gospel, resisting all challenges as to the correctness of the contents, and in that way, academic historians serve humanity by manufacturing a false view of history.

Early in 1946, the American authorities in the River Plate region were confronted with a very difficult problem which they needed to explain for political reasons and could not. In principle the problem was caused by Argentine bureaucracy and the manner in which the Argentine authorities occasionally get round it.

First it is necessary to show the prevailing situation. When *U-530* surrendered at Mar del Plata on 10 July 1945, the document authorizing the presence of the crew on Argentine soil was the instrument of surrender listing the names of the crew. This instrument was signed by the boat's commander and counter-signed by the commander of the Mar del Plata naval base who accepted the surrender of the submarine. The document evidenced the legal right of the *U-530* crew to be present in Argentina in the status of prisoners of war.

On 17 July 1945 President Farrell and Vice-President Perón signed presidential decree 16.162 expelling the *U-530* crew from Argentina and into the custody of the United States. The men were flown out to Washington DC, and from there ended up in a PoW camp at Fort Hunt, Virginia. The crew of *U-977* went through the same experience one month later.

At that time, negotiations were being conducted in Washington between the OSS and former Abwehr leader General Reinhard Gehlen (photo right). As a result, in November 1945 the crews of *U-530* and *U-977* were released and put on a ship at New York for Germany. British intelligence was not satisfied that all had been extracted from these men which could be extracted, and accordingly they were taken off the ship at Antwerp and brought to London for further grilling. Schäffer and Wermuth were released in mid-1946 but the crews remained prisoner until 1947. So sensitive is the material which the British obtained from these interrogations that it cannot be declassified until the year 2020; seventy-five years later. As this book has insinuated, the real purposes of *U-530* and *U-977* at the end of the Second World War has yet to be revealed officially.

At all stages of their captivity in Argentina, the presence of the crews of *U-530* and *U-977* was authorized by an official document in the form of a presidential decree or document assimilated to one. This is important to bear in mind as the story progresses.

At the beginning of 1946 when it was decided to repatriate the remnants of the **ADMIRAL GRAF SPEE** crew to Germany, the United States forced the Argentine and Uruguayan Governments to repatriate all of them irrespective or whether or not they were married to local women(**9**). The men and their families were brought to Campo de Mayo outside Buenos Aires on 7 February to wait for the **HIGHLAND MONARCH** to finish loading a cargo of frozen meat. A detachment of Royal Marines from the cruiser *AJAX* (photo below) was ready to take custody of them.

At one o'clock on the afternoon of 15 February 1946 "*amid scenes of protest and public lament*", the contingent of 811 men was led to the quayside. The Argentine Army officers who had had charge of the prisoners to the ship's gangplank collected up all the identity documents and dropped them into a single large bag which was handed over to the Royal Marines officer as the ship was about to cast off. In this way the identities of the men could not be verified against the documents, and the British naval attaché on the quayside suspected immediately that "*substitutions must have occurred.*"   Seventy-three more **GRAF SPEE** men came aboard at Montevideo.

According to Newton(**10**) it was discovered during the identity checks on the voyage to Europe that eighty-six U-Boat men were repatriated with the **ADMIRAL GRAF SPEE** prisoners:

It was not clear when and how they had got to Argentina to be repatriated from there.

In his later CEANA Report(**11**) he added a rider to this statement that these eighty-six U-boat men

".....were not necessarily shipped out aboard **HIGHLAND MONARCH** *with the* **GRAF SPEE** *sailors",*

but this does not change the salient point that they were repatriated to Germany and "*it was not clear when and how they got to Argentina to be repatriated from there.*"

EDITOR NOTE – Eighty-six (86) men is the approximate size of two U-Boat crews.

The US authorities in the River Plate region could not discover a Presidential decree or instrument surrendering the U-Boats which brought these men to Argentina, and thus they appeared to be in Argentina illegally. Until such time as evidence becomes available to the contrary, the only inference to be drawn from this is that these eighty-six U-Boat men came ashore in Argentina from their U-Boats clandestinely and with the implicit agreement of the Argentine authorities.

Footnotes:
(1) Not to be confused with the Type VII-C boat **U-235** (Huisgen) used for training duties in the Baltic. This boat was sunk in error by the German torpedo boat **T-17** off the northern tip of Denmark on 14 April 1945. There were no survivors.
(2) Hirschfeld, Wolfgang: *Feindfahrten*, Neff Verlag, Vienna 1983: Hirschfeld/Brooks: *Hirschfeld-The Story of a U-Boat NCO 1940-1946*, Pen & Sword/USNIP 1997, p.199.

(3) Letter from Professor Rohwer to Hirschfeld, 28 March 1996, see Brooks/Hirschfeld *ibid*, pages 199, 228, 231. It is firmly established that Japan made this request in 1943. According to John W Dower (citing *Showashi no Temo*- "The Emperor and Showa History"), publ. Tokyo 1968, Vol 4, p.146-148, Japan was promised a total of two tonnes of uranium oxide to be sent in two submarines. Also see, John W Dower, Japan in War and Peace, New Press, 1993, p.80.

(4) Letter to US author Joseph Mark Scalia from Kunihiko Kigoshi, 7 August 1998, reported in Sidney Trevethan: *The Controversial Cargo of U-234*, (unpublished manuscript), Revision 13, January 1999.

(5): Report on Interrogation of Crew of *U-234*, 27 June 1945 OP-16-Z, last page.

(6) Jochen Brennecke: *Haie im Paradies - der deutsche Ubootkreig in Asiens Gewässern 1943-1945,* Heyne Verlag Munich, 1973, p.26-34.

(7) See Salinas and de Napoli: *Ultramar Sur*, Ed Norma, Buenos Aires, 2002, p.253-254: also Jorge Camarasa, *Puerto Seguro*, Norma, Buenos Aires 2006, p.214. Copies of this document are in possession of the mentioned authors. Special rules apply to the declassification of certain documents in Argentina. In 2003 Jorge Camarasa went to Ascochinga to research this report. Villagers confirmed that a German who went by the name of Otto Rehklau or Otto Freider, a specialist in heavy electrical machinery, had occupied "the big house on the ridge", often used for Nazi reunions, from the early 1950s onwards. He died there of a heart attack in 1984 and his body was removed to an unknown location.

(8) Salinas, *ibid*, p.434 etc.

(9) Once returned to Germany, the Argentine Government approved immediately all applications from **GRAF SPEE** men wishing to return to Argentina as immigrants.

(10) Newton, Professor Ronald: *El cuarto lado del triángulo*, Panamericana, Buenos Aires, 1995, p.336 and 424.

(11) Newton, Professor Ronald: *Actividades clandestinas de la marina alemana en aguas argentinas*, CEANA Report 1998, text and footnote 50.

CHAPTER TEN

The Mysteries of the *U-977* Voyage

"I am just one of the unknown young German survivors of the Second World War. Together with my generation I would say nothing if that were possible; if the secret of U-977, whose last commander I was, did not have to be revealed..."
Heinz Schäffer, *El Secreto del U-977*, HIMSA Editorial, Buenos Aires 2006.

Heinz Schäfer

"Commander, if this chart is correct, you were not within fifty miles of the Equator when the Brazilian cruiser BAHIA was sunk there on 4 July 1945!"
Capitán de fragata Mallea, naval harbourmaster Mar del Plata: *El Secreto del U-977*, p.19.

"Three cheers for our trusty and invulnerable U-977! Hurra! Hurra! Hurra!"
Heinz Schäffer, *ibid*, to his crew at Mar del Plata, 17 August 1945.

After his discharge from Allied captivity in 1948, Heinz Schäffer, former commander of *U-977*, was accepted by the Argentine Republic as an immigrant. He then began writing his memoirs. In order to "*reveal the secret of U-977*" he prepared the manuscript in a particular way so that those who were capable of understanding would understand. There was the fantasy voyage in which *U-977* came down to Argentina at a crawl, and spent sixty-six days on the snorkel submerged, arousing the admiration and sympathy of all and woven into the narrative of the fantasy are the true facts of the voyage, in which burdened with a huge weight of cargo, *U-977* raced to the Cape Verdes and Equator, crossed the Line on 4 July 1945, and was at large in the South Atlantic and Argentine Sea for forty-four days before surrendering at Mar del Plata.

For reasons of political necessity, when the book was published worldwide in 1950(**1**) only the fantasy voyage remained, and has been accepted by the world at large as gospel ever since. Yet even the Argentine Navy and US Navy reports on the interrogation of Schäffer reveal no claim at the time that he had ever done any such thing, and the time frame leaves no possibility for a 66-day run always submerged.

In 1955 the Argentine Navy translated and published the original book privately for internal circulation and reference only, and the book *El Secreto del U-977* appeared on the shelves of the Argentine Navy Library as Volume XXIV, bearing the acknowledgement:
"This translation and impression is authorized by the author for Argentine Navy personnel only".

In 2006 the Argentine Navy decided to publish their 1955 translation through the HIMSA editorial house, and it is now available to the general public in Spanish. This original version, read together with the naval interrogation reports(**2**), provides a far different story to what historians have been pleased to serve up to date.

Schäffer was a Berliner, born 28 April 1921. He was accepted as a naval cadet at the end of 1938(**3**). After obtaining his commission and serving aboard a minesweeper on Channel duties he joined the U-Boat Arm in May 1941. He made six full patrols aboard *U-561* (Bartels, 1941-May 1942) and four under Heinz Fenn as IWO aboard *U-445* (May 1942-October 1943). During 1944 he qualified as a U-Boat commander and spent the year commanding *U-148* attached to 21. U-Bootflottille at Pillau which did nothing but train men for command. At Christmas 1944, Oberleutnant Schäffer was given command of the snorkel-equipped Type VII-C boat *U-977*.

He arrived at Blohm & Voss Hamburg with the boat in March, although the US Navy Report has him at Hamburg on 20 February, and the boat at the Howaldt Yard between 26th and 30 March "*to fit the snorkel*" which according to Schäffer was already fitted when he took command of the boat at Pillau. At the beginning of April 1945 the boat was attached to 31.U-Training Flotilla at Hamburg, "*ready*" but in Schäffer's opinion not operational. He complained of having "*only 70% battery capacity*", "*the main couplings had been in use for more than a year and could start giving trouble at any moment*", he wanted "*armour protection*", "*a new radar*" and some time for "*working up the crew*" since "*not all men aboard were familiar with the boat*". His requisitions were thrown out "*for scarcity of materials*" & he was ordered to Kiel to prepare for sailing.

EDITOR NOTE – This boat was commanded by Kapitänleutnant Leilich from 6 May 1943 until December 1944 when command passed to Oberleutnant zur See Heinz Schäfer.

A few hours after putting in to Kiel he went aboard the HQ ship for a conference with Admiral Dönitz who listened to his complaints and then gave him orders for Operation *Southampton*.

He was to take his old Type VII-C boat around Scotland, down the Irish Sea, around the tip of Cornwall, sail up the Channel to the Isle of Wight, enter the port of Southampton and attack shipping there "*if possible*". Such an operation was obviously a suicide mission for a clapped-out Type VII boat at that stage of the war. The new Type XXIII boats now in commission were purpose-built for this kind of adventure, and here one must suspect that there was more to Operation *Southampton* than meets the eye.

Schäffer now decided to pay one last visit to his mother in Berlin to convince her to leave Berlin before the Russians arrived, and supposedly on the train journey he just happened to fall in with a Waffen-SS officer who spoke to him about the new super-secret weapons the Reich was about to unleash, and invited him to Waffen-HQ in Berlin to see the extraordinary possibilities with his own eyes. Why he has these pantomime scenarios in his book is difficult to fathom. The only conceivable reason for an SS officer to invite a U-Boat commander to Waffen-SS HQ to see some secret weapons would be if they wanted him to install some on his boat and report back on how they worked.

In due course Schäffer arrived, was introduced to the commanding officer and the demonstration began. "*There reigned such confidence in Final Victory as I had never previously experienced, not even at the end of the French campaign,*" he wrote. He was shown photographs of the strangest devices, including the so-called "*death ray machine*", which he was given the chance to see in operation next day, but Schäffer excused himself for lack of time. After visiting his mother and failing to convince her to leave Berlin, he returned to Kiel.

What can this "*death ray machine*" have been? It is known from a USAF report that German ground forces were operating an "*interference phenomenon*" against Allied aircraft. "However incredible it may appear to project from the ground to a height of 30,000 feet sufficient magnetic energy to interfere with the functioning of the ignition system of an airplane, it is believed that the above evidence nevertheless justifies the consideration of counter-measures for such a condition...(**4**)"

In parallel with this report it seems likely that "*interference phenomena*" had been refined for use aboard U-Boats making important voyages or entering enemy harbours for experimental purposes. A man who provides us with an interesting account of such phenomena is former Oberfunkmeister Wolfgang Hirschfeld(**5**), who was senior radio-telegraphist aboard *U-234* outward bound in March 1945 for Japan with strategic war materials.

This Type X-B boat had been converted from a minelayer into a cargo carrier. Eleven military or technical passengers, two of them Japanese, boarded at Kiel. Contrary to the usual practice, the telecommunications station was under the direction of a scientist, Dr Heinz Schlicke, a specialist in radar, infra-red and direction finding, who had been given the honorary rank of Fregettenkapitän (S) for the voyage.

Early on 26 March 1946, *U-234* (Kapitänleutnant Heinrich Fehler) and her minesweeper escort sailed from the Strander Bucht in company with three U-Boats as additional escorts. These boats were the Type VII-C *U-1107* (Parduhn), Type IX-C *U-516* (Petran) and the Type VII-C/41 *U-1274* (Fitting). Once free of the Great Belt, Fehler dismissed the minesweepers and closed up with the U-Boat escorts. Although *U-234* could make seventeen knots, Fehler was obliged to sail at ten knots, the speed of the slowest of the three U-Boat escorts. These latter boats were to accompany *U-234* to Norway and return at once to Kiel. The intriguing question is why one of these escort boats could only make ten knots. Did she have heavy electrical gear aboard we are not supposed to know about? In his book, Hirschfeld sidestepped the question of this slow progress by falsely stating that the three escorts were "*Type XXIII*" boats whose top speed surfaced was ten knots.

The first incident occurred in the following manner. At about 1500 hrs on 27 March 1945, Dr Schlicke told Warrant Officer Hirschfeld to plug in "*the reserve radar*". A few minutes later three enemy aircraft were sighted closing fast. When the range had reduced to 3300 yards, Fehler ordered the flak to fire. Hirschfeld said:

> *"The flak gunners failed to respond and it remained quiet. I sprinted to the bridge and heard Fehler loudly berating the gun crews. Everyone on the upper deck of the boat had heard the order to open fire except the gunners. To our astonishment the enemy aircraft flew on in apparent ignorance of a string of four U-boats below them."*

When I asked Hirschfeld about this incident he gave me to understand that just as he was subordinate directly not to the IIWO but to Dr Schlicke, he thought the flak crew was controlled by Kapitänleutnant Heinrich Hellendorn, the passenger specialist in naval flak, and the flak had orders to obey only Hellendorn in everything, and ignore the commander. This was an unheard of situation on a U-Boat.

The second incident occurred at midnight off Frederikshavn. A German southbound merchant convoy consisting of four steamers and escorted by modern torpedo boats was attacked by bomber aircraft in seas illuminated by starshell. As the four U-Boats, the priority target, looked on, an ammunition ship blew up. Hirschfeld:

> *"Our radar showed a multitude of contacts at all points of the screen. The Kattegat was swarming with enemy aircraft. Fehler's flak crews waited immobile at their weapons. The radar detected an aircraft approaching at low altitude from the*

west. The trace appeared when the contact was about 6000 yards distant and barely skimming the surface of the sea."

Hirschfeld directed the radar beam at the attacker and at 3300 yards;
"The aircraft inexplicably pulled off its headlong course towards us and turned away. At 6000 yards he vanished from the screen....Aircraft were continuing to mill around the sky and after thirty minutes there came another approach from the west. When the radar beam was concentrated fully on the inbound bomber it disengaged at 3300 yards. The game went on all night: three times it was repeated. It could not have been coincidence, but I have never discovered exactly what effect this trick caused on the enemy radar screen. By daybreak it was all over. The four U-Boats cruised unscathed into Oslo Fjord and anchored."

The important points to note from the foregoing incidents are these:
1. The four U-boats never opened fire at any time;
2. Every incident involved Oberfunkmeister Wolfgang Hirschfeld directing the "*radar beam*" at the approaching aircraft.

When Hirschfeld did that, the aircraft always pulled out at 3300 yards and left the scene. From this it may be inferred that 3300 yards was the perimeter of the "*interference phenomenon*" and at this point the aircraft crew suddenly received notice that they were in immediate danger. Because the aircraft then left the scene at once, this immediate danger must have been some kind of threat to the health and well-being of the aircraft crew from the interference phenomenon, thus the term "*death ray*"

Because the four U-Boats never fired at the aircraft, and an officer was appointed especially to impose discipline at the flak guns and ensure that the commander did not get carried away and try to open fire in the heat of battle, it must also have been dangerous to attempt to fire out from within the protection of the "*phenomenon*". Therefore the principal purpose of the interference phenomenon was defensive.

Heinz Schäffer's immediate orders were to take *U-977* to Norway to complete refuelling and exercise for a few days with the new schnorchel.

There would be an intermediate stop at Frederikshavn in Denmark on this voyage to load up. According to the official record, *U-977* sailed on 13 April 1945. At Frederikshavn so huge a quantity of provisions "*and everything else imaginable*" was loaded that the chief engineer protested at the "*excessive weight*" which would make it difficult or impossible to submerge safely. Schäffer also stated(**6**) that he "*only received 80 tonnes of fuel in the days before the defeat. The German reserves were exhausted and the synthetic production plants and railway connections destroyed*," whereas he told the Argentine Navy interrogators that although he had bunkers for 130 tonnes, "*the chief engineer requested that he load only 80 tonnes, 61.5 per cent of capacity, to optimize the stability of the boat.*"(**7**)

This must be explained as providing the intermediate space necessary for sufficient buoyancy to keep the upper seventh part of the hull above water.

The Argentine Ministry of Defence has recently released more details about *U-977* in its archive 35275/07. A photograph of the conning tower shows three aerials of interest. The Argentines remarked with surprise that it was difficult to understand why a boat from a training flotilla which had allegedly escaped from Europe at the conclusion of hostilities to obtain better treatment for the crew, as Schäffer claimed, should be fitted with highly advanced radio-technical equipment, one item of which remains on the top secret list to this day.

Attached to the instrument surrendering the boat is the crew list of thirty-two crewmen aboard *U-977*. This list indicates four men who had passed the Special Course in Electricity and the U-Boat Heavy Electrical Machinery Course. These four men were:
- Funkobergefreiter Harry Hentschel, senior radio-telegraphist:
- Obermachinist Hans Krebs,
- Maschinenobergefreiter Kurt Nittner and
- Machinengefreiter Gerhard Höfler.

The Argentines did not think it worth mentioning all the other courses which the crew might have taken.

It can be seen from the conning tower photograph taken from the stern of *U-977* that the aerials of interest have points of reference marked by a number, but the accompanying reports to which the numbers refer remain classified. The "Fu-M-B" anti-radar device installed on the snorkel head was of a type believed not to be of general issue to Type VII boats. It can be seen fitted in the second photograph of the conning tower. The purpose of the tall aerial attached to the D/F loop is unconfirmed.

The third aerial of importance can be inspected in the Ministry file but not photocopied. This was an aerial of dimensions too large to stow on the bridge and its size and rough shape can be judged by the extent of the area on the upper gun platform blacked out by the censor. This aerial was of semi-circular shape, rotatable and of a variable parabolic configuration.

None of the British and American experts consulted could offer a suggestion as to its purpose. We note, however, that Wolfgang Hirschfeld failed to provide any description of the mysterious equipment whose beams he aimed at incoming aircraft from *U-234*, and since *U-977* achieved the same happy results against aircraft as did *U-234*, it seems fair to assume that this was the aerial for the "*death ray machine*" and was fitted aboard *U-977* as soon as the three escorts to *U-234* brought it back from Norway in late March 1945. It would have been essential for, and the whole objective behind Operation *Southampton*.

As with *U-234*, the voyage to Norway was extremely dangerous because the British exercised a tight watch over the Kattegat. All German U-Boats heading for the front had to pass through it. The sector was very narrow, thickly mined and could be easily blockaded: "*more than half the U-Boats putting out were lost here on their first run northwards principally for the inability to dive in mined areas when under air attack*."

Out of Frederikshavn,

> *"Scarcely had we left our escort than the anti-radar equipment signaled the presence of enemy aircraft. We counted twelve, approaching rapidly. We were in an area of shallows which were mined. We could already hear the sound of the aircraft engines. At first they circled us - it seemed as if they wanted to fix our position with exactitude or were awaiting reinforcements before making their attack. We expected to be hit at any moment by the new rockets from below the wings. If we had remained on the surface we would have been done for and so, ignoring the danger of mines, I gave the order to submerge. All turned out well. Each time we raised the FuMB anti-radar it indicated the presence of aircraft very close. It seemed they knew our course and were following us(**8**)"*

The perplexity of these Allied aircraft in the face of a single U-Boat surfaced is interesting. No less than twelve of them were circling "*as if trying to fix the position of the boat*", suggesting either that it could not be seen on their instrumentation or through binoculars, or they dared not enter, or fire into, the interference phenomenon. If, as Schäffer suggests, they were "*awaiting reinforcements*" how many more aircraft than twelve were required to attack *U-977*?

U-977 arrived safely at Horten, and on 26 April at Christiansand South. On 1 May news was received of Hitler's death and that Admiral Dönitz had assumed supreme command of the Wehrmacht.

> *"Meanwhile the chief engineer had learned to navigate with the snorkel. We were ready to sail. As I had predicted we were feeling the consequences of the wear and tear on the diesel couplings. We made no complaint because we wanted to go to the front. We had a clear and precise mission in which we were not subjected to contradictory orders amidst chaotic circumstances."*

U-977 sailed from Bergen for Southampton harbour on 2 May 1945.

> *"A few days after we sailed we lost the main periscope due to the negligence of the IWO. This was serious because it was indispensable for navigating with the snorkel. When snorkeling we would be blind without it. The sky-periscope was no substitute."(9).*

On 4 May the telegraphists noted Dönitz' Order of the Day to the U-Boat Arm to cease hostilities, at which *U-977* abandoned Operation *Southampton* and turned back for the Norwegian coast. On 10 May 1945 having returned to the coast near Bergen, sixteen crewmen volunteered to be put ashore, leaving 32 men to sail the boat to Argentina.

The Mysterious Voyage of *U-977* from Bergen to Mar del Plata, Argentina

The *"66-day voyage always submerged"* of *U-977* is a fiction. In *El Secreto del U-977* Heinz Schäffer stated:

> *"After I surrendered the boat at Mar del Plata base on 17 August 1945, I went to the wardroom of the coastguard cruiser* **GENERAL BELGRANO** *where I was invited to explain my voyage to the Argentine naval authorities using the nautical charts and astronomical manuals which I had produced to them. The first thing the flotilla commander wanted to know was why I had not scuttled my submarine off the coast. I*

at if we had done so we would have lost all ; of explaining the truth about our voyage.

*..... ..is response I deduced how important it was that we justify our attitude clearly: 'Commander, there are strong suspicions that your boat sank the Brazilian cruiser **BAHIA** some days ago. It is also suspected that you had aboard Adolf Hitler, Eva Braun and Martin Bormann, and that you put them ashore in the south of our continent. First we must clear up these points.'*

"*With great calm I took out my nautical chart, spread it out on the table and explained our itinerary from 9 May. After hearing my discourse, he replied: 'If this chart is exact, Commander, then on the day the **BAHIA** was sunk (i.e. 4 July 1945), you were more than fifty nautical miles from the place where she went down (i.e. the Equator). We shall inspect your documentation.'(10)*"

If *U-977* had actually been still submerged ten days north of the Cape Verde Islands and a thousand miles away from where the *BAHIA* went down, this would have been a good time to say so. From the statement of Capitan Mallea it is clear that *U-977* was more or less 50 miles away from the Equator on 4 July 1945, but not all that far, and it is also clear from Schäffer's book**(11)** that on 10 July 1945, when Wermuth's *U-530* surrendered at Mar del Plata, *U-977* was already between the Equator and Rio de Janeiro.

In the true voyage of *U-977*, the Equator was crossed on 3 July 1945. In the official reports declassified by the Argentine and US naval archives, the Equator was supposedly crossed three weeks later. The Argentine Navy interrogation report states that Schäffer appeared at the interrogation on 20 August 1945 armed with two charts, these being the one he produced at Mar del Plata upon surrendering, and the forged chart he had been asked to draw up by the Argentines and which placed him much farther north of the Equator on 3 July 1945 than his true position. The purpose of this subterfuge was to ward off all questions about his having landed Hitler and other passengers in Argentina, of refuelling from other German U-Boats at sea on the way down or of having sunk the Brazilian cruiser *BAHIA*.

174

The Facts Upon Which All sources Agree

All sources agree that *U-977* left Bergen, Norway, on the morning of 10 May 1945, that the boat arrived at Mar del Plata, Argentina, on 17 August 1945 after a voyage of approximately 7,600 miles. Furthermore that about 85 tonnes of fuel had been loaded at Kiel of which five tonnes remained upon surrendering to the Argentines.

The Official US and Argentine Reports on the *U-977* Voyage

The Argentines do not normally declassify material in the manner to which one is accustomed in the northern hemisphere. In 2002, at the instigation of the Chief of the Argentine Naval Staff, the Argentine naval archive allowed the authors Salinas and De Napoli to copy the Schäffer interrogation for inclusion in their book(**12**). The authors were obliged to report all material honestly in their narrative, but not show it to anybody. I know this from my conversation with them in Buenos Aires. We also know from the US interrogation report declassified later that they upheld the conditions by which they were bound, and so we may be confident that the items in the Argentine report which are absent from the US report are honestly reported and do appear in the Argentine report.

Schäffer told the Argentine naval interrogators on 20 August 1945(**13**) that he had headed for Iceland and then bore south for the Cape Verdes, where after a voyage from Norway lasting 64 days he arrived on 13 July 1945. He was certainly surfaced for a large part of this leg, for he mentioned having to dive on several occasions to avoid being seen by shipping. The course would have been good to allow for the North Atlantic current. Schäffer told them from his forged chart that he spent four hours surfaced each night recharging the batteries and the remaining twenty hours daily submerged.

The Argentines did not like this version because he would have used too much fuel. They calculated:
* Recharging batteries 250 litres/hr x 4 hrs =1000 litres;

* Submerged travel 120 litres/hr x 20 hrs =2400 litres;
* Total daily fuel consumption   =3400 litres;
* Total fuel for 64 days, 3400 litres x 64 =217,600 litres;
* Total fuel shipped at Kiel   = 85 tonnes.

Therefore he would have had to refuel twice to reach the Cape Verdes, and this was not wanted.

According to the US Navy declassified report, *U-977* followed the same course, arriving at the Cape Verdes on the afternoon of 14 July 1945, a sixty-five day run. Apart from the one day's difference, this is the same account Schäffer rendered to the Argentines based on the forged chart. The Americans made no calculations of the fuel consumption nor of "*66 days always submerged*" since obviously nobody had mentioned it because it never happened, and the Americans closed the book on the affair by commenting only that the voyage had been made "*at an extremely slow average speed*".

The "*66-day Voyage Always Submerged*"

In his book Schäffer describes his epic "*66-day submerged voyage*" on eighty tonnes of fuel. He says he sailed always submerged from Norway to the Straits of Gibraltar in sixty-six days(**14**). That distance is 1800 miles as he says. Therefore his average speed over the ground was 1 knot. Although he would have had to battle the eastward-setting North Atlantic current from Scotland down to Cape Finisterre and he had no periscope, he chose to "*hug the coast of Britain*", which would have cost him heavily in fuel to keep him off the lee shore. Surfacing near Gibraltar, Schäffer found he had consumed half his bunkers - forty tones - just to get to Gibraltar, and he had to make the remaining 5,500 nautical miles on the other forty tonnes.

After many discussions and calculations (**15**) Schäffer decided that he must now,

> "*Sail always surfaced for ten hours daily at 60 revolutions on one diesel, and 14 hours daily on one E-motor, which will*

get me from Gibraltar to Mar del Plata by mid-August with five tonnes to spare".

His average speed would be 7 knots daily, moving him southwards at one hundred sixty-six nautical miles per day. It is 3,000 nautical miles from Gibraltar to the Equator, which would take him 17 days, arriving there on 14 July + 17 days = 31 July 1945. This of course does not coincide with the "*official*" reports, which have him crossing the Equator on 23 July nor his true admission that he crossed the Line on 3 July. And as the Argentine Navy knew very well and did not want the world in general to know, *U-977* was at large in the waters of the South Atlantic for no less than 44 days after crossing the Line and no evidence exists to show what Schäffer did during this time.

The Cargo aboard *U-977*

Mention was already made above of the exceptional weight being carried by *U-977*. Schäffer's narrative makes clear that the boat was uncomfortably crammed, and this explains why the sixteen crew members were put ashore near Bergen on 10 May 1945 - not as a gesture of fatherly kindness by Schäffer, but because the voyage had to be made more tolerable because of the lack of space. He alludes four times to this lack of space without hinting what created it. We know now from the Argentine archives that it must have been heavy electrical equipment.

Here we have a Type VII-C U-Boat with only ten torpedoes aboard and provisions for thirty-two men for three months. Since sixteen men went ashore before she sailed for Argentina, there should have been far more space aboard than the remaining crewmen were accustomed to yet the engine room hands "*went into the NCO's quarters*" for the purpose of "*making more room. If we had had the full ship's complement aboard it would have been extremely uncomfortable.*" Schäffer explains that:

"Only two men could move from one room to another at a time, any more movement would have affected the trim making it difficult for the chief engineer to keep the boat at a constant 14

metres" - indicating how tender the boat was - and "the human waste accumulating aboard was excessive"(**16**)
which suggests that both heads were out of use, probably serving as storage lockers. The visits of the crew to the heads being undesirable from the viewpoint of keeping the boat in trim.

Schäffer describes(**17**) how, in the bow compartment, the Type VII-C boats had twelve drop-down cots, two for each three ratings aboard, therefore cots for twenty men. In the NCO's room aft there were eight drop down cots for twelve men. In all there were cots for thirty men, since at any one time ten would be on watch in the engine room, control room and telegraphy section. The commander and three officers had their own cots so taking into account the duty watches aboard *U-977* there was more cot space available (thirty-four) than men on the boat (thirty-two), and nobody even needed to sling a hammock.

Bow room of *U-995*, same as *U-977*, showing 'drop down' cots

"Even though sixteen men were disembarked" however, Schäffer reports that *"the space still remained very much reduced."*(**18**). The IWO, Karl

Reiser, wanted to jettison the torpedoes "*to make more space available in the compartments*"(**19**). There were ten torpedoes aboard. These were stowed four in the forward tubes and four in storage holds below the deck plating forward, one in the stern tube and one in the storage hold below the deck plating aft. They took up no crew space. No doubt there were only ten instead of the usual issue of fourteen in order that no torpedoes would take up space in the interior of the hull. If the ten torpedoes aboard had been jettisoned, the only fresh space created would have been in the torpedo tubes and storage holds below deck. Thus the only way to "*create more space*" for the crew would have been to shift as much as possible of whatever was taking up the space in the pressure hull into the five torpedo tubes and under-deck storage.

The Actual Voyage of U-977

If he followed the course explained in the US and Argentine Navy reports, Schäffer could have reached the Equator on 3 July 1945, fifty-four days out from Bergen, without refuelling by covering 89 nautical miles daily mostly surfaced at an average speed of 3.7 knots. He could have gone from Bergen to Argentina easily without refuelling provided he spent most of the time surfaced. The whole purpose of the voyage was to get this equipment to safety in Argentina. If all aircraft encountered were as perplexed about *U-977* as the twelve over the Skagerak, he should have been quite safe. Whether he was ever surfaced and in sight of the *BAHIA* is a question considered in an earlier chapter. Possibly *U-977* was one of the two boats to unload near Necochea on the night of 27 July 1945.

Unexplained Contacts

On 13 July 1945, nine days after the Brazilian cruiser *BAHIA* blew up on the Equator at 30°W, the Brazilian torpedo boat *BABITONGA*, her commander and crew highly experienced in anti-submarine work, had taken up position at the spot where *BAHIA* had gone down, and immediately detected two or possibly three submerged submarines at a range of 1200 yards. After signalling them for identification and receiving none, the ship's commander called up reinforcements and the hunt for the submarines began. For some mysterious reason it was impossible to obtain a certain fix on their position for five days.

On 17 July a fishing boat off Rio Grande do Sul reported being passed by two submarines heading south which were identified as German, while on 18 July **BABITONGA** obtained a hydrophone contact on a lone boat which she then depth-charged using her *Hedgehog* launchers. During the skirmish an object believed to be a submarine surfaced briefly at 800 yards distance. It was described as "*glowing black*" and had a shape which eluded description. When **BABITONGA** opened fire with her deck guns, the shape dived rapidly as evidenced by the huge bubbles which rose to the surface.

It was some considerable time before another contact was obtained, this time by sonar. A fresh attack was made, and some oil came up from below. A sample was collected for analysis. Upon returning to port Captain Dos Santos Parreira did not consider he could claim a kill but considered it to be "*a viable hypothesis that he surprised enemy U-Boats on their passage south intending to disembark somewhere on the South American littoral.*" The analysis of the sonar recordings in the United States determined that the object was "*beyond any doubt a submarine*" while the oil sampled "*did not come from any Allied submarine in service.*"(**20**)

———————————————————————

Footnotes

(1) Much of the contents in the first edition respecting the **U-977** voyage were condemned as undesirable politically and removed from *Das Geheimnis um U-977*, the original first edition published in Buenos Aires in 1950 before the censored version known as **U-977 - 66 Tage unter Wasser** was published in West Germany that same year. All foreign language translations are based on this latter book. In 2006, the original German volume was translated into Spanish and published in Argentina. See: Heinz Schäffer: *El Secreto del U-977*, Hisma, Buenos Aires, ISBN 987-22996-0-9

(2) US Navy declassified report *Report on the Interrogation of Prisoners from U-977 Surrendered at Mar del Plata 17 August 1945*): *El Secreto del*

U-977, p.191: for the commentary on the Argentine Navy interrogation of Schäffer, 20-23 August 1945 see Salinas and De Nápoli, *Ultramar Sur,* Ed. Norma, Buenos Aires 2002.

(3) According to *El Secreto* (p.27), Schäffer had "no interest in politics and did not belong to the Hitler Youth", while the maritime society he frequented (at age 14 he held a yachtmaster's certificate for all classes of sailing vessel for all German waterways) "had no connection with Nazi ideology". Although he did his compulsory six months' RAD service on the land, he would have needed more affinity to the regime than this for permission to go to the United States "to perfect his English". Besides visiting Cleveland, he told the Argentine Navy under interrogation that he had visited numerous towns and cities in the USA and helped found the pro-Nazi US-German *Bund* at Buffalo. During his career Schäffer was awarded the Iron Cross First Class and the U-Boat Front Clasp in bronze, an important decoration.

(4) NARA Air Intelligence Summary No.53 (US Strategic Air Forces in Europe, 12 November 1944).

(5) Brooks/Hirschfeld, Hirschfeld, Pen & Sword/USNIP, 1997, p.200-202.

(6) *El Secreto,* p.215.

(7) Salinas and De Napoli: *Ultramar Sur,* Ed. Norma, Buenos Aires, 2002, p.235-236.

(8) *El Secreto,* p.186-187.

(9) *ibid,* p.191, 204, 217.

(10) *El Secreto del U-977,* p.19.

(11) ibid, p.222.

(12) Salinas and De Napoli: *Ultramar Sur,* Norma Ediciones, Buenos Aires, 2002.

(13) ibid, p.426.

(14) *El Secreto,* p.210.

(15) ibid, p.215

(16) ibid, p.198, 203, 205.

(17) ibid, p.58-59.

(18) ibid, p.203.

(19) ibid, p.205.

(20) *Ultramar,* p.303-305 quoting *Historia Naval Brasileira,* Vol 5, Servicio de Documentacao Geral da Marina, Rio de Janeiro, 1985.

CHAPTER ELEVEN

The Golfo Nuevo Incidents

So Many U-Boat Sightings

It will be recalled from an earlier chapter that the Argentine Navy began to complain of suspected submerged U-Boats active around Golfo Nuevo from 1941 onwards. No explanation has ever been put forward for this activity, but Professor Newton(1) mentions that *"an habitually reliable anonymous source"* informed the US Embassy in Chile in early 1941 of a German supply base on the Valdez Peninsula between Lobería (near Punta Pirámide) and Punta Delgado (actually on the coast outside Golfo Nuevo).

Newton discounts this but it may explain many puzzling features about the Golfo Nuevo history. The only inshore waters which have sufficient depth to host a secret underwater supply base for U-Boats would be around Punta Pirámide and Punta Pardelas where there is at least depth of 60 feet.

Golfo Nuevo is an almost enclosed body of water within the Valdez Peninsula on the coast of Chubut province. It is a roundish bay no more than thirty-five miles, nor less than twenty-five miles across at any point, and from coastal shallows it shelves deeply to a maximum depth of one hundred fifty-seven metres at its centre. The entrance faces south-east and is nine miles wide. The surface waters of the gulf are relatively calm. The town and important naval base of Puerto Madryn - which lacks any facilities for submarines - is located well inshore on the southern side. For the most part the coast has a dune landscape, the soil being layers of bivalve and crustacean fossils, volcanic ash and a clayish sand with gravel. The single paved road into Valdez Peninsula ends at Punta Pirámide, there is little population except for a few large ranch properties.

(see chart on page 183)

The Golfo Nuevo Incident 1958

During a Press conference at Government House on 23 May 1958, Argentine President Frondizi made the following announcement:

"On Wednesday 21 May 1958 a squadron of our destroyers carrying out a routine exercise north-west of Cracker Point just inside Golfo Nuevo detected by hydophone equipment a submarine proceeding submerged. It is assumed that this submarine is capable of high speed underwater. As is the practice in these cases, being in waters of our national jurisdiction, the destroyers carried out four depth charge patterns. During the operation a periscope was seen. After the attacks, patches of oil were found floating at the surface, which often happens when a submarine suffers damage. Later, our Navy carried out successive searches until the evening of Thursday 22 May, but these had no result. It is therefore assumed that the submarine though damaged has eluded its pursuers, or has been sunk."

The exercise was being carried out by three cruisers, four destroyers, a workshop ship, an oceanographic survey ship and a tug supported by three Catalina aircraft, five bombers, a DC-4 and twelve Corsairs. The submarine was spotted visually from various vantage points on the destroyer **BUENOS AIRES** after a radar contact. All depth charges carried by the surface vessels were expended during the initial patterns.

Late the following week, Navy Secretary contraalmirante Gastón Clerment stated that the Navy was continuing its operation in Golfo Nuevo in accordance with a plan drawn up for such emergencies, and with the same intensity as in the opening days of the hunt.

Military sources quoted by the newspapers stated that the submarine had a speed submerged of between eight and twelve knots, and despite the numerous reports identifying it as one of a type used by Germany in the Second World War, *"the impression amongst naval chiefs is that these submarines are very much more modern"*. The use of the plural *"these submarines*" when only one had been sighted in Golfo Nuevo is significant, for it confirms suspicions that the Argentine Navy knows far more about "*these submarines*" than it makes out.

By 10 June 1958, nearly three weeks after the operation commenced, the special correspondents sent to Puerto Madryn reported that the intruder submarine was suspected to have escaped through the blockade at the entrance to Golfo Nuevo on 7 June. This meant that it was present in Golfo Nuevo for eighteen days without the Argentine Navy having been able to do anything to prevent it.

In October 1959 a submarine was detected in Golfo Nuevo again, but left after five days despite a combined air-sea search(**2**).

The Golfo Nuevo Incident 1960

The night of 18 January 1960 at 45° 03'S x 64° 17'W off the north end of Golfo San Jorge, Chubut province was misty. Aboard the Argentine State Yacht *YAMANA*, returning from survey work on the continental shelf, the chief engineer reported a strange humming sound "*like a turbine*" which he could not identify, since *YAMANA* had no turbines. The commander cut the ship's engines, and shortly afterwards the humming also stopped. On the bridge wing looking over the bows after restarting the engines, the commander saw the fine silhouette of a submarine surface close to his ship's path, and then submerge quickly.

For some reason the Naval Staff placed no credence in this report, but at 1810 hrs on 21 January 1960, after the YPF tanker *LA PLATA* reported an unidentified submarine heading north at ten knots at position 43° 46'S x 63° 58'W outside Golfo Nuevo, the destroyer *SAN LUIS* was despatched from the main naval base at Bahìa Blanca to investigate. The Naval Staff was interested in the fact that if this was the same submarine of both sightings, it had progressed only twenty-five sea miles in a three day period and was edging closer to Golfo Nuevo.

In the early hours of 23 January 1960, a P2V anti-submarine-warfare aircraft left Puerto Belgrano to fly a search pattern over the region of the first two sightings. This machine was equipped with AN/APS-20 radar with a range of 150 sea miles. A contact was established at 20 miles, and upon approaching the submarine it dived rapidly. Sonar buoys were dropped and sound recordings made. The silhouette was described as grey with a tall, narrow sail, and moving fast on the surface. No sign of life was seen on deck.

Golfo Nuevo is clearly seen on this chart. We also note how near this is to San Antonio Oeste, site of the German spy HQ in this area during the war as well as Caleta de los Loros where it is rumored there currently are two U-Boat wrecks.

As can be assumed, if the submarine was intending to enter Golfo Nuevo clandestinely, the sound of the "*humming turbine*" would betray its presence, and so entry would have to be delayed until it could be masked by other vessels entering the gulf.

At 0820 hrs on 28 January 1960 just inside Golfo Nuevo, Task Force 54 consisting of the old destroyer **CERVANTES** and patrol boats **KING** and

MURATURE carrying naval cadets on their annual training cruise sighted a periscope trailing a wake and heading for the interior of the gulf. The boats were not sonar-equipped, but the sighting was confirmed by hydrophones. After no response had been received to the demand that the boat surface and identify itself a depth charge attack was made.

Upon receiving the report, the Naval Staff sent the destroyers *BUENOS AIRES* and *SANTA CRUZ*, and the anti-submarine frigates *HÉRCULES* and *SARANDI* to the location, and put on alert its two P2V Neptune anti-submarine aircraft which carried better electronic detection equipment than the surface vessels. The Navy Secretary decided not to announce the incident to the general public until the situation became clearer, but had the Chief of the Naval General Staff contact the US naval attaché to ask if the United States would be prepared to offer any kind of advanced anti-submarine weaponry.

CERVANTES meanwhile was patrolling the nine-mile wide entrance to Golfo Nuevo while the two patrol boats worked as a pair hunting the submarine. With the arrival of the two destroyers and two frigates, the Task Force was now seven ships and renumbered 86, being arranged in three search pairs with *CERVANTES* watching the gulf entrance. The minelayers *GRANVILLE* and *PY* left Bahía Blanca with a cargo of mines. The coastal lights at the gulf entrance were extinguished and normal maritime navigation diverted away. When *HÉRCULES* and *SARANDI* made a contact at Punta Conscriptos along the southern shore, they attacked with depth charges but were surprised when the submarine slipped away at twelve knots and headed for the gulf entrance where the thermal layers offered very poor audibility for sonar and hydrophone operators. Because all their tactics for this kind of emergency were based on a submerged submarine having no greater speed than eight knots, the Argentines were left without a plan.

The national daily *La Nación* was the first to report the incident to the public in its edition of 2 February 1960:

"The Navy has sent a number of units in search of a submerged object detected last Saturday in the waters of Argentine jurisdiction",

and on 3 February Navy Secretary Clement announced that other ships were being sent. He considered it probable that there were two submarines "*because these boats generally operate in pairs*". This was the fourth submarine incursion in Golfo Nuevo in less than a year, and by now no doubt the Argentine Navy had a fair idea of the capabilities and *modus operandi* of the submarines involved, as the incident late that night proved.

Near Punta Cracker just inside the gulf entrance the destroyer *SAN LUIS* obtained a submarine contact at 3000 yards, moving at 15 knots through the 50-metre shallows. When the sea was illuminated by the Leigh light of a P2V circling overhead, a slim grey periscope was seen. Two rounds were fired from the deck gun, forcing the submarine to submerge. As the depth charge attack was being prepared aboard the pair destroyer *BUENOS AIRES*, the submarine arrived directly beneath her keel. When the rudder was put hard over, the submarine followed suit. This demonstrated that the submarine could make a very tight circle. At this point it released an *Alka Seltzer*, a capsule which develops tumescence in the sea to baffle shipboard detection devices, and ran off at high speed submerged.

EDITOR NOTE – The item referred to as an '*Alka Seltzer*' was in reality, a counter measure device known as '*Pillenwerfer*'. This was a chemical '*slug*' fired from a special tube on the boat that would fizz and bubble, causing the sonar devices to think they were locking onto the propellers and machinery noises of a submarine while the submarine made its silent escape.

On 4 February after hours of continuous depth charging, *SAN LUIS* and *SANTA CRUZ* had expended their stocks and returned to Puerto Madryn to reload, leaving the patrol boats *KING* and *MURATURE* to make sporadic attacks against a target of whose whereabouts they were never sure. A ploy was attempted. The two patrol boats sailed close together, each using only one propeller. When approximately overhead of the submarine, *MURATURE* cut her engine while *KING* made a few simulated sweeps on both before leaving the area. The purpose of this manoeuvre was to deceive the submarine commander into believing he was alone. The silent *MURATURE* was certain that the submarine was below her keel, and she moved ahead suddenly, firing one depth charge from the stern tube and six from the lateral tubes.

This ruse looked successful, for after the explosions died down iridescent patches of oil were found on the surface, but as **MURATURE** approached, the submarine headed for the gulf entrance at high speed to obtain the protection of the poor audibility there. The respective temperatures of the water layers and the fast current there resembled the conditions at Gibraltar(**3**).

On 5 February, the commander of Task Force 86 signaled Commander Naval Operations that his depth charges were not able to damage the intruder "*due to limits on depth*". Argentine manufactured depth charges were ineffective below 150 feet, and if the intruder knew this, it could escape all depth charge attacks by going deeper. Because of the submarine's high speed underwater, the warship sonars were of limited usefulness. They had short range, did not function when the carrier ship moved faster than 18 knots and did not provide the depth of a contact.

This meant that depth charging was a matter of trial and error. Better quality equipment had to be introduced immediately or the outlook "*was not promising*". In particular, homing torpedoes were needed. These were equipped with an inbuilt sonar guidance system and were virtually infallible, but the nations approached were not keen on supplying Argentina with weaponry still on their secret lists. Instead one hundred depth charges and the technicians to install MAD equipment aboard the P2V aircraft were despatched. The MAD system is based on an analysis of the change in the vertical magnetic component of the waters produced by the presence of a metal submergible.

The Naval Staff was concerned that the intruder submarine was making them look fools. Over the last five days there had been contacts which led to attacks, but the submarine had never been pinpointed and tracked in the normal manner. At night hundreds of flares lit the sky while ships' searchlights swept the waters and the depth charges crashed and thundered. By 10 February the anti-submarine corvette **LA REPUBLICA** had arrived with replacements including many experienced sonar operators, followed next day by the destroyer **ENTRE RIOS** and the frigate **SANTISIMA TRINIDAD**, but the decision was taken not to mine the gulf entrance, since the overriding desire was to force the submarine to flee, and not sink it.   On 12 February the tanker **PUNTA MÉDANOS** anchored off Punta Pirámide to enable swifter refuelling.

On 13 February La Nación quoted military sources as saying that the submarine had "*the profile of a Type XXI German U-Boat*", and the Spanish periodical *Las Provincias* published a cable from its correspondent William Horsey in which he reported that the submarine in Golfo Nuevo had surfaced briefly on seven occasions and had been positively identified as a Type XXI German U-Boat.   In unconfirmed reports, oil samples leaked by the boat had been analyzed, and were alleged to be an oil of the kind produced to a formula used by the Third Reich.

Type XXI

President Frondizi had thirteen warships and forty aircraft available and on 13 February he took custody of modern depth-charges, flares, sonar buoys and other advanced weaponry and equipment sent by the United States together with anti-submarine warfare veterans led by Captain Ray Pitts, USN.   Pitts reported directly to almirante Rega, Commander Argentine Naval Operations.   The depth charges were of terrific destructive effect and could destroy a submarine down to 200 metres, which was deeper than any point in Golfo Nuevo. The P2V aircraft would each carry two homing torpedoes below the wings and have MAD search equipment fitted.   All this should have been sufficient to sink one submarine in a round gulf no wider than 35 sea miles.

On 14 February, reported in *La Prensa* two days later, the Argentine Foreign Ministry had sent a Note to all nations known to operate submarines asking that "*if the submarine of unknown flag in waters of our national jurisdiction at Golfo Nuevo, Chubut province, is a submarine of your State*", would the naval attaché be so kind as to "*ask your*

Government to issue instructions to the submarine in question to identify itself to the naval authority of the zone" since the Argentine Government now considered itself "*legitimately authorized to take those steps necessary to uphold the law with respect to the territorial sovereignty of the Republic.*"

The Soviet naval attaché, Kourin, and Vice-President Mikoyan both denied that the submarine was Russian. The formal denial of the Soviet Government was reinforced over the next few days when the USSR made no diplomatic attempts to allow the submarine to go free. Mikoyan also made a cynical comment that so far as he could see the only beings in peril in the Golfo Nuevo were the fish. Argentine newspapers disclosed from unofficial sources that the commander of the submarine had also replied in negative vein to the demand to surrender.

The newspaper *La Razón*, under a heading *Destruction of Enemy Submarine in Golfo Nuevo Imminent* reported on 14 February:

"*Navy Secretary Gastón Clement announced last night in response to a question regarding the inordinate delay in destroying the enemy submarine in the South, that he thought it was "fundamentally a matter of hours". He reiterated that there were two submarines present and one of them was presumed to have propeller damage, judging by the noises picked up by the hydrophones. These were submergibles which possessed very advanced equipment. For example, when submarines of this type suspect they are being tracked by radar, they use a special ray to destroy the precision of the instrumentation...*"

La Razón also ran an article under the banner *Body Appears at Puerto Madryn*:

"*An unconfirmed report states that the body of a frogman-diver has been found near Punta Ninfas just inside Golfo Nuevo. By the state of decomposition it is thought the man has been dead four days. Until now he has not been identified. The frogman suit is of standard design and two oxygen tanks were found. No manufacturer's labels or marks were found on the clothing or equipment. The body has injuries leading to a belief that the man may have been a crew member of the damaged submarine killed due to the effects of blast while attempting to make repairs."*

Also on 14 February 1960 two strange submarines arrived and manoeuvred near the Argentine flotilla outside territorial waters. These vessels were described as "*gigantic*" and the type "*could not be determined with exactitude.*" Inside Golfo Nuevo, depth charging with the new, extremely powerful explosives began. One depth charge was dropped every ten minutes day and night. Naval forces thought that the intruder had "*the mysterious ability to elude electronic detection*", and on 15 February the Argentine Defence Minister, Justo Vilar, announced that in his opinion "*the submarine must have escaped*". The same day *La Nación* reported a communiqué from Washington:

"...*The US Navy has sent a team of thirteen anti-submarine experts to help the Argentine Navy in its hunt for the submarines in Golfo Nuevo. Their assistance will be purely advisory. The Navy also confirmed that additional anti-submarine material has been despatched south. A cargo of depth charges, sonar buoys, sonar and electronic detection equipment was sent to Argentina last week.*"

In its editorial of 16 February 1960, *La Nación* stated:

"*The general anxiety to know the true situation regarding the events in Golfo Nuevo is growing rapidly in the face of reports that the submarine bottled up by Argentine warships has slipped though the net and left. However, naval circles maintain that there may yet be a favourable outcome to the matter, especially after the Navy Secretary confirmed that the patrols are being intensified.*"

The newspaper also reported sources less optimistic than the Navy Secretary:

"*As advised in previous reports, the possibility is not being discounted that the submarine has fled. It had recently become much more manoeuvrable, and was faster than at any time during the first seventeen days in Golfo Nuevo. If it could make 20 knots submerged, as appears likely, it would not be difficult for it to mock its pursuers. To support this conclusion one thinks of our frigates, unable to manage 18 knots, and of our destroyers whose radars go fuzzy when the ship goes faster than 15 to 17 knots..."*

On 17 February **KING** and **MURATURE** in Golfo Nuevo re-established contact with the submarine, and the biggest naval-air concentration since the Second World War gathered in the small gulf for a fresh onslaught, yet *La Prensa* was not optimistic about a successful conclusion being achieved:

"There have been no new developments in the search for the submarines in Golfo Nuevo. The lack of fresh contact with the intruders, and the prolonged nature of the operation, has led people to speculate that the submarines have fled. This hypothesis, and the other to the effect that they have been sunk, is not supported by concrete facts or even claims..."

In the early hours of 21 February when a Type XXI submarine surfaced, homing torpedoes were fired but *"incomprehensibly missed"*. A fresh salvo was fired and missed. More sonar torpedoes were fired from the air, but these also failed to find the target. On 22 February when the submarine surfaced briefly to discharge oil it was shelled by warships but no hits were observed. By now the Argentine Navy had had enough and on 23 February reported:

"The waters of Golfo Nuevo were carefully combed on 21st and 22 February without any further contact being made with the intruder, which is believed to have escaped. It is presumed however that it may attempt to return. Nevertheless the search has been stepped down."

On 22 March 1960 the *New York Times* published the following article under the caption *Submarine Held Real - Leader of US Unit Backs Argentine Report*:

Washington, 21 March (UP):

" Captain Ray M. Pitts, who headed a US unit in Argentina during last month's submarine scare, believes there was a foreign submarine in Golfo Nuevo. He said in an interview that there was much evidence he was not free to speak about. He

added that he had talked with persons who said they had seen the intruder. He said he was confident those persons were telling the truth. Captain Pitts is Assistant Director the Navy's undersea warfare division. Eight of the thirteen-man US expedition sent to Argentina to hunt for the submarine were killed in the plane collision on 25 January over Rio de Janeiro."

On 24 February 1960 the Argentine Navy Secretary announced:

"The operation in Golfo Nuevo has ended without the capture or destruction of the intruder submarines. However, the Navy has fulfilled its duty, which is in essence to protect our sovereignty at sea and along the sea and river coasts, on the surface, below it and in the air above. Its duty was done in effect, since it detected the intruder, attacked it offering no quarter, forced it to vacate our waters and prevented it from carrying out its mission, which was to violate our national sovereignty..."

This platitude glosses over the fact that the Argentina Navy and its surface ships were never sure where the intruder was at any material time unless it was surfaced, when they fired shells and torpedoes at it and always missed. "*Forced it to vacate our waters*" is an interesting statement in view of Gastón Clement's presumption of 23 February that the submarine might "*attempt to return*". This suggests an awareness on his part of the purpose for which the submarine had come to Golfo Nuevo. Perhaps an agreement had been reached between the Navy Secretary and the submarine operators that it would withdraw temporarily to enable him to make his claim of having forced it out, and then return for one last period of attention before closing the facility permanently(**4**).

The Type XXI boats which visited Golfo Nuevo over the period of the preceding several years did not go there to proclaim their strange advanced technology to the world, nor for some other mundane task such as refuelling, which could be done almost anywhere along the Patagonian coast without too much notice being taken. In Golfo Nuevo near Punta Pirámide, as the Chilean spy had detected in 1941, there was probably a clandestine underwater U-Boat base where a single U-Boat could be attended in absolute security. Regarding the risks for a U-boat in entering an almost enclosed body of water hosting a naval base, the refit must have been essential and linked to the secret technology.

The Navy Secretary had stated openly that the submarine appeared to be

equipped with some kind of ray which neutralized or caused electronic equipment such as sonar, radar and the MAD analyzer to give false readings. This would also explain why their torpedoes did not home in on the target. Yet most interesting was the failure of the depth charges "*of terrific effect*" to damage or sink the boat. The submarine crew would never have remained in Golfo Nuevo had there been a real risk that the boat could have been sunk. Therefore it is fair to conclude that the boat *was* invulnerable to attack once the danger became too great.

ABOVE – Standard Type XXI U-Boat

The accidental revelation of the existence of this technology brings to light the extraordinary advances in U-Boat weaponry by Germany at the end of the Second World War. The scientists and materials, and the technical specialists to handle them, were transported to Argentina with the tacit agreement of the Argentine Government, and after a decade or so there began to appear mysterious U-Boats of the final wartime breed endowed with strange capabilities which made them invulnerable.

These capabilities had already been tried out during operations in 1945. As recounted in Chapter Six, while the coast of New York was at a state of high alert; dirigibles scoured the waves for U-Boat periscopes *U-530* came close inshore, if not into the harbour itself, and Wermuth allowed each crewman time to observe everyday life in the streets of New York through the periscope apparently without fear of being discovered.

Heinz Schäffer's *U-977*, a Type VII boat considered unfit for the front by her commander, was ordered by Admiral Dönitz to sail to Southampton harbour and sink shipping there, a mission which not only made no sense in the first week of May 1945 but was moreover suicidal unless the boat had some form of "*interference influence*" which gave her invulnerability. In the Skagerak, *U-977* was caught on the surface by twelve or more RAF fighter-bombers which circled her but never attacked, and allowed Schäffer to submerge and continue his voyage unscathed.

During the run northwards through the Kattegat on 26 March 1945, Oberfunkmeister Wolfgang Hirschfeld reported similar incidents affecting *U-234* which he considered bizarre and for which no explanation offered itself.

In his visit to Waffen-SS HQ in April 1945, Heinz Schäffer was offered the opportunity to see a practical demonstration of the new "*death ray apparatus*". Schäffer avoided knowing what this was by explaining he had to be somewhere else at the time. The term "*death ray apparatus*" recurs in a strange little book(**5**) which was brought to my attention a few years ago, and I have been assured that this is the area to where research should be directed for understanding.

EDITOR NOTE – I was a Special Weapons technician in the US Air Force in 1960 when this story was unfolding. Even though the Air Force was not involved in the hunt for these mysterious submarines, we were kept abreast of the pursuit and I remember we wondered how these intruders could defeat the world's best and most modern anti-submarine technology and specialists. True, we did enjoy a chuckle or two in the beginning that our Navy was unable to catch or destroy these submarines but soon we were amazed that, no matter what our Navy, the most advanced in the world did, the mysterious submarines evaded them with ease.

Footnotes:

(1) Newton, Professor Ronald C: *Actividades clandestinas de la armada alemana en aguas argentinas*, CEANA Report February 1998, text around footnote marker 24.

(2) *Blanco y Negro*, Madrid, No 2494, 20 February 1960.

(3) Hirschfeld/Brooks: *Hirschfeld, op cit*, p.78-82 for the experience of submarine *U-109* near Gibraltar in 1941.

(4) The sources for this account are Camaras, Jorge, *Puerto Seguro*, the website, and Schwarz, Captain Jorge F. (ret'd), *Operación Golfo Nuevo*, Instituto de Publicaciones Navales, Buenos Aires, 2002. An officer of the Argentine Navy communications branch, at the time of the 1960 incident Captain Schwarz was attached to the Secretaría General Naval which allowed him the opportunity to gather the basic material necessary to reconstruct events and interview naval and air force crews. His fictional account based on the true events finishes at 14 February 1960 before the introduction of the advanced weaponry from the United States, for reasons of national security and secrecy. Although his fictionalized account uses a hypothetical Soviet submarine as the intruder, Captain Schwarz admits that the origins of the submarine remain a mystery.

(5) Polo, Ángel: *Otra civilización nos domina - los Intraterrestres*, Ediciones Ramos Interamericana, 1977, p.71-74.

CHAPTER TWELVE
Caleta de los Loros: The
Mysterious Postwar Sightings

"There is a persistent idea, amply set out in the sensationalist genre of literature, according to which the Nazis were inspired and even directed by occult forces from 1920 to 1945. This mythology owes its origins to a postwar fascination with Nazism. This fascination has perhaps been caused by irrationality and the macabre policies of Nazism, and the brief continental domination of the Third Reich."
Professor Goodricke-Clarke: *The Occult Roots of Nazism*, Appendix D.

Few people have ever seen ball lightning, those mysterious balls of fire which float through the air and can pass through solid matter. Even scientists know very little of them, but many in general they conclude that ball lightning is a spherical whirlwind of heated plasma with great electrical conductibility, previously charged with energy from electrical storms, which produces an intense magnetic field.

The electrical potential of the magnetic field was calculated scientifically based on an event in England in the 19th century. During bell-ringing practice in the parish church at Stanford Courtney, Devon, on the evening of 7 October 1811, a ball lightning entered the nave and halted the bells in mid-swing. At the moment when the ball lightning disintegrated, the bells were released from the force holding them. Dr Blair calculated from this that there are magnetic fields which are five hundred times more potent than that of the Earth, which oscillates at between 0.5 and 0.7 gauss. The spherical ray in Devon appeared inside the church at a distance of ten metres from the bells. Its magnetic force can be worked out from the amount of force needed to move the bells, being 150,000 gauss at one metre from the centre of the ball lightning.

Dr. Blair concluded that it would not be possible to reproduce in any laboratory on Earth magnetic fields of such extraordinary potential.

The reader will see that if such a phenomenon could be created radiating outwards from a U-Boat, the magnetic field would deflect or refract all electronic rays aimed towards it, would make the boat invulnerable to all explosive forces, and also possibly affect the conditions of visibility inside the spherical ray. The reader will also see that if the Type XXI boats in Golfo Nuevo could operate within the protection of such a phenomenon, it would explain their invulnerability. But "*it would not be possible to reproduce in any laboratory on Earth a magnetic field of such potential*" say the scientists, and so the motivation and technology would have had to come from sources beyond the Earth's geography.

An example of the magnitude of the task is provided in a scientific paper by American researchers Seward, Chen and Ware entitled *Ball Lightning Explained as a Stable Plasma Toroid*. These gentlemen are of the opinion expressed in the title of their paper but cannot prove it until such time as "*a phenomenon is captured*" and definitely analyzed. The problem is that all their plasma toroids, of a uniform 10-cms in diameter, last a maximum of a fifth of a second and so cannot be "*captured*", and that is as far as the United States has come in over sixty years of experimentation.

If ball lightning is a stable plasma toroid, and is the phenomenon used by the naval Hitlerists postwar to protect their U-Boat force, then the German plasma toroids are spheres of anything up to six miles in diameter in all directions and absolutely stable until such time as the operators desire to dissolve the toroid by electrical signal.

This enormous difference in the stages of achievement between the modern United States and end-of the-war defeated Germany seems to confirm that the Germans must have had help from a non-terrestrial ally which provided the technology under its own supervision for its own purposes.

Obviously there is little archive information on anything connected to this branch of science, but of interest is the fact that in the 1930s, the giant electrical concern AEG set up a laboratory on the roof of the Charité hospital in Berlin to study the phenomenon of ball lightning.

There was a single project in Hitler's Germany which qualified under *Sonderstufe SS/1940* as a "*special priority case*". Professor E. Schumann, head of the Research Division at the Army Weapons Bureau (*Heereswaffenamt*), awarded an AEG project the highest known priority rating ever awarded in the Third Reich, *kriegsentscheidend* - decisive for the war. The work was to continue "*until at least the end of the war*", a phrase indicating that whichever way the war went, the work would continue until Final Victory, whenever that happened to be. The document of approval for the rating is the record of the Heereswaffenamt session of 21 July 1942. The Reichsmarschall's Plenipotentiary for Nuclear Science, Professor Esau, emphasized the great urgency of proceeding with the development in the war interest. Half the project, involving high-tension transformer work, was headed by AEG Senior Engineer Richard Crämer. The project was given the cover-name *Charité-Anlage* (Charité Installation), which was of course an allusion to the work on ball-lightning carried out by AEG on the Charité hospital roof during the 1930s(**2**).

Scuttled U-boats in Caleta de los Loros

Between the early 1950s and 1990 numerous Argentine witnesses, particularly private aviators, claim to have seen one or two sunken submarines no farther out than a mile from the low water mark at Caleta de los Loros on the northern shore of Golfo San Matías. This gulf forms the seaboard of Argentina's Rio Negro province, and on its southern shore it is adjacent to Golfo Nuevo and Golfo San José. The north shore of the gulf extends between the town of San Antonio Oeste, the HQ of German military intelligence in Argentina in both world wars, and El Condor, a distance of over 100 miles. The section of the shore which is of interest in the first half of this narrative runs just south of the 41st parallel South, and lies between the Mejillones headland marking the western entrance to the Caleta de los Loros cove, and the lighthouse on Punta Bermeja, a distance of about 40 miles. The coast is a mixture of cliffs up to 100 feet in height, of rocky platforms and sandy beaches having a typical dune vegetation. Windless days are a rarity.

The first occasion on which the Argentine Navy appears to have shown unusual interest in this strip of coastline occurred on the morning of 18

July 1945 when the torpedo boat *MENDOZA* arrived in Golfo San Matías to investigate a reported U-Boat. The Argentine warship approached to within two miles of the coast to reconnoitre Caleta de los Loros and adjacent beaches. After the attack on a submerged submarine off San Antonio Oeste late that afternoon, retold in an earlier chapter, at 1907 hrs *MENDOZA* steered 107° to leave the area and patrol the northern stretch of coast close inshore again.

After reaching the Belén light (41° 09'S x 63° 46'W) at 2105 hours, *MENDOZA* reversed course and proceeded on hydrophone watch from there back to San Matías light (40° 49'S x 64° 43'W), which she reached at midnight. Why the commander of *MENDOZA* decided to concentrate on this length of coastline in the expectation of finding a U-Boat there rather than anywhere else is not mentioned in the report. The torpedo boat, in company with at least three naval aircraft, spent the next two days navigating up and down this strip, but eventually gave up the search following receipt of the order on 21 July 1945 from the Chief of the Naval General Staff to call off all coastal patrols. This intensity of this search indicates a degree of suspicion, if not knowledge, held by the Argentine Navy about this bleak shoreline in the months just after the European War terminated.

EDITOR NOTE – It is stated by Don Angel Alcazar de Velasco in our first of the Hitler Escape Series (***Hitler in Argentina***) that after the U-Boat put him and Martin Bormann ashore at Puerto Coig, the captain planned to take the boat to a spot halfway between Puerto Coig and Buenos Aires and scuttle the boat in a little cove there. Look at a map of the Argentine coast and you will see that Caleta de los Loros (Parrot Cove) at the northwest corner of Golfo San Mathias is right where Don Angel predicted. ***Hitler in Argentina*** is still available from Sharkhunters. Details at the end of this book.

The Postwar Sightings

Aviator Manfredo Braunmüller made two significant reports. His first was news of his sighting a sunken U-Boat in the zone in the 1950s. Next came Mario Chironi flying a Government aircraft in 1956.

Ernesto Duca, co-piloting a Cessna aircraft for the provincial Salud Pública in 1965 stated:

"We were going to San Antonio Oeste and I saw the wrecks off the Caleta about 1800 metres out, a sort of strange cone shape, oriented at 45° to the coast, the tips were more pointed than the rest. At the end on either side they had propellers shining like the sun. On the beach side was a large drum or the remains of a boiler of some two metres in diameter. It looked as though the hull had parted."

Hotelier Antonio Ribeira made three sighting reports between 1958 and 1966. Vidal Perayra of Viedma, a former employee of Lahusen, saw a submerged U-Boat from a beach in March 1980:

"With the wind from the north you could see the bow perfectly 200 metres out from the low water mark."

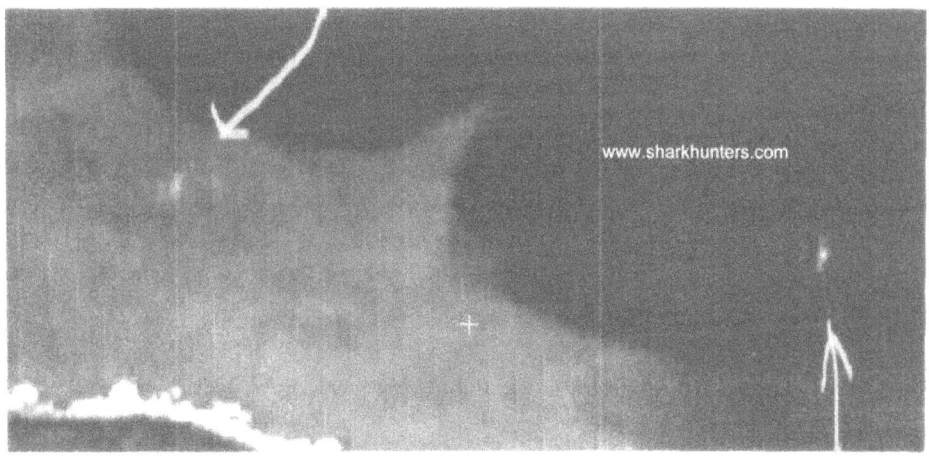

The breakers on the beach are seen to the lower left; two *'targets'* further out are seen in this aerial photo.

On a day of extreme low water in 1990, veterinary surgeons Marcelo Ochoa and Eduardo Frias hired an aircraft and tried to photograph a submerged sighting. Frías' photo is the only known exposure in existence outside the classified naval archives. It shows two elongated shapes estimated at 60 metres in length lying parallel to the coast. The photo was taken from inside the pilot's cabin during a private flight using an inadequate lens and the quality is not good. Charts of the Service of Naval Hydrography do not indicate a sunken wreck at this position.

In 1978 Carlos Massey, a salvage expert, was engaged in refloating a sunken fishing vessel at Puerto Madryn in Golfo Nuevo. He was called to the naval base at Bahía Blanca to give his opinion on the possibility of salvaging two U-Boats sunk in waters near Caleta de los Loros, and given access to secret documentation, a file of about 100 pages with photographs, nautical charts, maps and sketches. Massey recalled seeing statements signed by a very senior naval chief, giving the conditions and exact time of sighting. This was in 1960, totally by chance. A Neptune aircraft from the Almirante Zar base at Trelew had seen the sunken hulls during a flight close to the northern coast of Golfo San Matías while patrolling those waters in a search for possible intruder submarines. The aircraft was equipped with magnetic sensors (MAD), and the pilots had noted down the coordinates.

Massey went to say that in August 1978 the sighting had been made in ideal conditions of low water and solar zenith, enabling the hulls to be photographed. The Argentine Navy had then sent a team of divers for the purpose of completing the inspection.

> *"In the photographs one can clearly distinguish the silhouettes of the boats which lie at some 16 metres with the hulls close together, facing towards the coast, and the sterns fifty metres apart. Apart from the silhouettes one sees the dark coloration indicating the position of the conning towers."*

Massey said that he could not remember (or more likely the Argentine Navy cautioned him not to relate) the exact position of the two boats, stated precisely in degrees, minutes and seconds, but it was on the northern coast of Golfo San Matías and in waters close to Caleta de los Loros at between 800 and 1000 metres from the low tide mark. Allegedly the reflotation of the submarines was finally abandoned at the request of the West German Embassy in Buenos Aires on the grounds that the boats might be booby-trapped. The Argentine Navy denied Massey's allegations.

During the Falklands War in May 1982, Diego Ginaca was master of the YPF fleet tanker *CAMPO DURáN*, the only civilian vessel in service as a fleet auxiliary at that time. About the middle of the month his ship had met up with the frigate *SANTISIMA TRINIDAD* (photo below) on the north coast of Golfo San Matías between Bahía Rosas and Punta Bermeja, some sixty kilometres east of Caleta de los Loros, when a helicopter gave the warning,

"You have company astern".

The helicopter crew had seen the silhouettes of two submarines which they suspected might be British. The refuelling was broken off abruptly but an hour later it was confirmed that the submarines sighted were not enemy. Ginaca, as might be suspected, does not remember the exact coordinates.

On 17 August 1971(**3**), pilot Manfredo Braunmüller took off from Viedma for the Valdez Peninsula. It was a day without wind, the sea in Golfo San Matías was exceptionally calm and had no swell, the sky was fully overcast. While flying 35 sea miles west of the usual Punta Delgadi-Jabalí Island maritime track, the pilot observed three Type XXI submarines together, one trailing oil, and heading for the northern coast. Braunmüller used two rolls of film to photograph the submarines from very low level, and took the stills from one roll to show the Commander-in-Chief,

Argentine Navy, almirante Gnavi. This officer, who had participated in the Golfo Nuevo incident in 1960, expressed recognition of the three submarines but declined to launch an aero-naval search, apparently on the grounds that they presented no threat to Argentina(**4**).

The interesting point about this report is that no print from either roll of film exposed was ever published, which leads one to suspect that all the material was declared top secret immediately and confiscated. The position of the three boats when seen, about thirty-five sea miles west of the Punta Delgado-Jabalí track, indicates their destination as being east of Caleta de los Loros on the north shore of Golfo San Matías. Two factors were favourable as regards weather conditions which may have dictated 17 August 1971 as a good day to make the run. The sky was totally overcast, enabling the voyage to escape observation by spy satellites, thus protecting the entrance to the secret location of the new repair base. If the third boat was in a sinking condition, the millpond conditions will have helped her complete the voyage.

The Audacious Theory

The two sunken U-Boat hulls lie parallel to the coast. They are oriented at 45° to the coast. They lie in sixteen metres, their bows together facing the coast but the sterns fifty metres apart. They lie between 800 and 1800 metres from the low tide mark at or near Caleta de los Loros. Once they exhibited "*a strange cone shape*" and their propellers "*gleamed like the sun*". This phrase reminds one of the submarine which surfaced near the Brazilian torpedo boat **BABITONGA** (Chapter 10) glowing and possessed of a shape which defied description.

The Germany Embassy in Buenos Aires has virtually admitted that these scuttled U-boats are of German origin and are so inherently dangerous that they should not be visited, while the Argentine Navy knows more than anybody about them and pretends it knows nothing. Both Governments remain the guardians of a tremendous secret.

Despite all the mysterious shifts of their position near Caleta de los Loros, and the inability of searchers to find the scuttled hulls or the slightest piece of convincing evidence of their existence, all the sightings of these two sunken U-Boats over the last forty years at Caleta must be held genuine.

The clue is that although the boats are very occasionally visible supposedly "*at ideal conditions of low water and solar zenith*", all the trawling in the world cannot snag them. In my opinion they cannot be found for the following reason. Ball lightning is a plasmoid which can pass through solid matter, and therefore it originates from another gravity field. Anything contained within the plasmoid will share its properties. The boats in Caleta de los Loros must have been sunk within a permanent, stable plasmoid. Though occasionally visible, in general they remain invisible, but even when visible they are intangible, since they are not present in the gravity field of the Earth geographically.

In the 1958-1960 incidents, the Type XXI boats in Golfo Nuevo were totally invulnerable whenever inside the gravity field of the plasmoid, but ᴜd not have fired out of the plasmoid into the gravity field of the Earth even if their intentions had been hostile. This explains the mysterious incident aboard *U-234* in the Kattegat on 26 March 1945 when the flak gunners disobeyed the commander's order to open fire at enemy aircraft. The flak gunners had been instructed beforehand to obey one of the twelve officer-passengers and ignore the commander in the event of his giving the command to fire when the officer-passenger had charge of them. This was what I was led to understand by Wolfgang Hirschfeld in my conversations with him.

Why were these hulls scuttled so close to the coast, and not in the deeps of the South Atlantic only a relatively few miles offshore to the east? We find that Caleta de los Loros is a calm lagoon of triangular shape and immense size. At high tide it fills to a depth of six metres but drains to reveal a sandy bottom at low water. Recalling the inexpressibly dangerous nature of the mercurial substance which spilled aboard *U-530*, undoubtedly the ideal location for unloading it from two Type XXI boats was considered to be the remote calm lagoon of Caleta de los Loros at high tide by night. This substance is dangerous to the world environment. As soon as it was safely ashore, the contaminated boats were towed one sea mile out from the low tide mark and scuttled within the plasmoid protection in a position where the integrity of the protection could be constantly monitored from the shore for ever.

The Searches of the Late 1990s

The first major search at Caleta de los Loros took place on 23rd and 24 November 1996. The Institute of Marine Biology *Almirante Storni* expedition was led by Uruguayan Tony Brochado. Support for his team came from the Prefecture, the municipality of San Antonio Oeste and various interested parties (the aviators Chironi, Pereyra, Rivera). The Argentine Navy declined to assist. After the unsuccessful search, Brochado said that a magnetometer was required and he thought the submarines "*must be further out because the pilots had seen them at an extraordinarily low tide.*"

At the end of November 1997 over a period of twenty days the minelayer **GURRUCHAGA** explored the Caleta de los Loros zone with a team of tactical divers and a robot machine equipped with a video camera. Grumman S2F Tracker aircraft from the anti-submarine squadron and Institute of Marine Biology and Fisheries scientists were also present. In its edition of 21 January 1998, the *Ámbito Financiero* newspaper confirmed that the expedition had been ordered by President Menem. The Tracker aircraft were fitted with MAD (Magnetic Anomalies Detector) equipment, and after compiling a map to chart the highest intensities of metal, divers armed with electronic aids were drawn by sleds over the sea bottom. It was the unofficial verdict that the zone is near the Sierra Grande and "*a lot of metallic material in nugget form had found its way to the sea bed*".

At the end of 1998, an expedition led by Frederik Soreide and Marek Jasinsky, and including scientists from the Norwegian Institute of Submarine Archaeology, the Faculty of Maritime Technology of Oslo and the Museum of Maritime Hydrology of Trondheim reconnoitred the sea bed at Caleta de los Loros using a high definition sonar. They found the same magnetic anomalies detected by previous expeditions but no scuttled U-Boats.

Thus the scuttled U-Boats near Caleta de los Loros remain elusive "*for lack of a precise position and because of changes on the sea bed on a daily basis*" (writer Patrick Burnside) while writer Abel Basti thought that "*after a half century, the U-Boats would have become totally entombed in the sand.*" His opinion therefore discounts the aerial photo of the two apparent U-Boat hulls seen in 1991, and on which the recent searches were founded.

EDITOR NOTE – Seen on the right of this photo, ABEL BASTI is Sharkhunters Member #7305-2008 and is one of the best researchers in South America on this subject.

HARRY COOPER (1-LIFE-1983) on the left
        NAHUEL COCA (7304-2008) in the center

The Scuttled U-boat at the South End of Golfo San Matías

Ronny Friman, a Norwegian diver, photographer and adventurer, had been involved in the 1998 expedition at Caleta de los Loros. In 2001 he contacted scientists at the Norwegian University of Technology (NTNU) with intriguing new information.

During the Second World War, the Kriegsmarine set up a base for U-Boats in Norway which became important at the end of the war particularly for signals traffic with units in the Atlantic. Following the cessation of hostilities, a number of U-Boats headed for Argentina carrying important technological documentation, weaponry, strategic materials and passengers. One of these boats was damaged on the way down. While attempting to obtain instruction on where to unload from naval intelligence at San Antonio Oeste, the periscope was spotted by the Argentine torpedo boat ***MENDOZA*** on 18 July 1945 and the boat sustained serious depth charge damage.

She headed for the southern end of Golfo San Matías. Close to the coast the engines broke down, leaving the boat at the mercy of the strong current. It began to drift eastwards towards the open sea. Not having charts of the gulf, believing the boat to be over shallows the commander decided to abandon and scuttle her for later salvage of the cargo. The boat went down in waters too deep for later salvage. This information was reported to the Kriegsmarine signals station in Oslo which continued to operate long after the war ended.

Although its files were eventually destroyed, a number were copied and kept by three Norwegian collaborators, and the survivor of the three was now offering the material for sale. According to Friman, the files were considered genuine. Of the greatest interest was the U-Boat scuttled off the mouth of Golfo San José at the south end of Golfo San Matías. It was said to have been carrying twelve tonnes of gold ingots, important documentation and materials. Friman proposed to NTNU a cooperation with the US-run Albenga Foundation and he renewed his contacts with the

Norwegian Institute of Oceanic Investigation (IOE ProMare). He hoped that the search would have the most advanced technical equipment.

Friman co-opted an English entrepreneur and navigator, Terry Neilson, the owner and operator of the 15-metre 28-ton Bermudan sloop *ICE MAIDEN ADVENTURER*. The boat is a single mast, two-sail steel-hulled ocean voyager equipped with Raytheon radar, Skanti SSB and VHF, GPS and other electronic aids to navigation and seafloor searches. The idea here was to generate a multi-part BBC TV documentary about the search which would help finance the project.

The Albenga Foundation assumed responsibility in Buenos Aires for all the logistics, planning and importing, took on the scientific direction of the work with its own personnel and the IOE ProMare technicians from Norway.

ICE MAIDEN ADVENTURER put into Mar del Plata and remained there until all the electronic search equipment had been installed aboard. Meanwhile Terry Neilson and TV producer Sarah Aynesworth arranged interviews with historians and documentary makers in Buenos Aires, San Clemente del Tuyú and Mar del Plata to compile information and locate surviving witnesses to the incidents involving alleged U-Boats in Argentina in the postwar era.

On 29 January 2002 having completed fitting out, *ICE MAIDEN ADVENTURER* sailed for Golfo San Matías, and next day took aboard Javier García Cano, scientific director of Albenga, and Morten Kvamme, Norwegian specialist of IOE ProMare. Also aboard was an Argentine Navy observer to control the operation and gain experience in the use of sonar. The actual coordinates of the wreck's position are kept a closely guarded secret, but the general area is not far from land off the mouth of Golfo San José.

Now You See It, Now You Don't

Despite the drawbacks of navigating a yacht with restricted space for the operation of all the electronic search equipment aboard, and the changeable weather conditions which often forced the boat to shelter in Golfo San José, a grid area was searched and sonar images taken. One of these drew the excited attention of all aboard. The image left little room for doubt. Below the keel of *ICE MAIDEN ADVENTURER* lay the wreck of a German U-Boat of the Second World War.

The position of this sunken submarine is known for certain on the basis of GPS and other navigational aids including radar. According to Terry Neilson the U-Boat was found exactly on those coordinates where it was expected to be found from the signal transcript.

It was decided to make a number of passes over the coordinates to confirm. The wreck could not be found again. Finally the expedition was abandoned for lack of time. The 1200-ton body of a U-Boat nearly sixty years underwater cannot be on the 1945 coordinates one day and gone the next. That is a scientific impossibility, the wreck must be there, and the technical operation had been witnessed by the independent Argentine Navy observer.

A fresh expedition was authorized, financed in part by the BBC in London. New sonar equipment came down from Norway together with a Seaeye Falcon RoV (remotely operated search vehicle) and a state-of-the-art Argentine Navy magnetometer. On the basis of the accord of scientific cooperation between the Albenga Foundation and the Argentine Navy, it was agreed that the naval vessel ARA *CUIDAD de PUNTA ALTA* would be used as the mother ship. Expenses were fronted by Pro-Mare USA. The Argentine Navy was keen to use the operation for experience in the use of high technology instrumentation, and its specialized team would work the RoV and sonar equipment.

My Personal Involvement in the Project

In April 2002, Terry Neilson contacted me at Paysandu in Uruguay. He proposed that I should translate into English from German and Spanish all documentation retrieved from the sunken U-Boat and collaborate in the writing of a book on the search. We spent a whole day discussing the overall project. Terry was absolutely certain they had the U-Boat. I asked if there was anything worrying him and he said he thought he was being constantly shadowed, not by Argentines but by Germans.

Our next meeting was in London in July 2002 when Terry showed me the sonar image of the U-Boat. It is lying on its side. He allowed me to take measurements of the image, which is wonderfully sharp. From the various hull ratios I concluded that this was a Type IX-C/40 U-boat.

Our third and last meeting was in Buenos Aires in August 2002 when I went to the Puerto Madero marina to be shown over *ICE MAIDEN ADVENTURER* and meet the crew. I was impressed by their enthusiasm and I left convinced of their honest belief that they had the U-Boat; it was just a matter of time. That evening Terry introduced me to the Argentine naval captain in charge of the salvage team. This man was absolutely confident that they had the boat, it was a scientific certainty, he said.

The second expedition searched the zone for five days in February 2003. They began at the coordinates and radiated outwards. Repeated passes were made over the coordinates using the magnetometer and sonar. The RoV explored the seabed. Despite the strong 5-knot current, underwater visibility was excellent. No U-Boat was ever found. Philosophically the Argentine Navy suggested they must have mistaken a rock for a U-Boat.

Conclusion

This was a multi-million dollar exercise in which everybody involved believed wholeheartedly. The scientific evidence at the 1945 coordinates confirmed the wreck of a submarine at that position in 2002, and a few hours later it had vanished.

Once we have ruled out all the possibilities to explain a mystery, whatever remains, however improbable, must be the truth. In favourable conditions at the location, the sunken U-Boat was detected by electronic equipment aboard *ICE MAIDEN ADVENTURER* as she passed overhead. When a subsequent pass was made to confirm the detection, the boat was not there. Where have we read of this kind of thing before? In the 1960 search for a Type XXI intruder in Golfo Nuevo, the submarine was detected briefly from time to time by electronic equipment before vanishing again for long periods. The only reasonable conclusion to be drawn about the sunken U-Boat at the south end of Golfo San Matías is that she lies within an immaterial protection such as was used by the 1960 Type XXI U-boat. She may be detected infrequently by electronics but never found because the protection puts her geographically beyond the world. For the Germans to go to all this trouble to hide her, forget the gold, this is probably a very, very dangerous wreck.

In the quote at the head of this chapter, Professor Goodricke-Clarke stated it as his opinion that the mythology of the Nazis being inspired or even directed by "*occult forces*" from 1920 to 1945 originated from "*irrationality, the macabre policies of Nazism and the brief continental domination of the Third Reich.*"

In July 1942, the Army Weapons Office granted the ball lightning project the highest of all priorities. How did Hitler's scientists just happen to stumble on the idea in the first place, obtain funding, know that their developments were on the right track, successfully complete all the testing and come up with the finished product two years three months later? *This* is irrational, yet the evidence points that way.

It must be that exterior forces operated Hitler. Their ultimate aim was not his victory but for his scientists to create the means for their future colonizing purposes. We cannot see beyond that concept, but I propose that it is far more logical than the muddled causation put forward by Professor Goodricke-Clarke. Moreover it does not require me to be obsessed by "*the macabre policies of Nazism*".

Footnotes:
(1) Blair, Dr A. J., of the Centre for Nuclear Investigations, Jülich, in the magazine *Nature*. Quoted in Polo, Ángel: *Otra civilización nos domina*, Ed. Ramos Americana 1977.
(2) NARA/RG 330, Foreign Scientist Case Files Box 28, "K.Debus".
(3) *Crónica*, Trelew, 27 November 1996.
(4) Camarasa, Jorge: Puerto Seguro, Ed. Norma, 2006, p180-197: 257-259.

This is the end of the story well researched and written by S.E.I.G. Agent **MICHAEL IVINHEIM**.

What follows are excerpts from the KTB Magazine of Sharkhunters. This is history you will not find anywhere else.

A - "Spook" Stuff and Secret Charts
Excerpted from our **KTB** Magazine

Introducing Feldwebel Schultz; new S.E.I.G. Agent

This is an Intel report from our newest S.E.I.G. Agent Feldwebel Schultz, former 4th Panzer Division, 36th Panzer Regiment.

PART 1

I think it is possible that Doctor Green was in USA from beginning 1948 but he was a big war criminal. We received in 1980 from ▮▮▮▮▮ Agency that Dr. Green has died in Hawaii in 1979 and all files are closed in the archive of the former American CIC and that these files are missing after 1961. So it is possible that Dr. Green was in the USA but only a small handful of CIC (later CIA) Special Agents have had consolidated knowledge about the real name of Dr. Green.

EDITOR NOTE – It was revealed by GREGORY DOUGLAS (4253-2008) that Dr. Grün (German word for Green) was in fact, Heinrich "*Gestapo*" Müller who came to work for the US after the end of the war and that he retired to Hawaii with the rank of Colonel.

Why are we concerned with Dr. Green? For the same reason we're interested in Señor Gomez. Keep reading.

You know Mr. Bochen – he was in Western Germany and he gave an interrogation in ▮▮▮▮▮ Agency and he told that he has not knowledge and that he has fear of one's life and he told to be worried about his family so he can tell nothing more. But he told that a big shadow is alive but he told not where is shadow. So we think shadow was in USA alive in this time. So it is possible that Dr. Green was in USA because he was very important. He has knowledge about Russia Secret Service in this time in 1948, 1949 and later and later and he has knowledge about the Russian double codes. This code from beginning 1945 to 1951 was a double code and after 1951 a ternary code beginning with numerarys and second with alphabetic letter so like 3-7-5-5-9 was C-I-K-K-L and in clear code after third key G-R-E-E-N.

The code was used once only once on one day and the next radio or letter has another code. Then one day later the code was possible 7-8-2-2-0 as R-X-V-V-C and clear it was G-R-E-E-N. This is only an example.

BOCHEN in 1943

EDITOR NOTE – PAUL BOCHEN (5051-1996) was a German U-Bootfahrer in the Kriegsmarine and he rode a "***Black Boat***". After the war he emigrated to the USA and lived in the woods in Pennsylvania. There was a lake behind his property and he was always concerned about security. **BOCHEN** gave us a code that we reported years ago.

PART 2
Mr. Gomez you know, we think not that Mr. Gomez (Hans Kammler) was NOT in USA. After 9 May 1945, Kammler is missing in the forest southwest of Prague, Bohemia approximately 30 kilometers distance were American troops, west of his last position…..but in 1947-1948 the American CIA was in search of General Kammler in Austria but did not locate this war criminal. We think that in the office of Dr. Debus (more on him later) was another Kammler, not General SS Kammler. It is possible that was Luftwaffe Officer Engineer Heinz Kammler who was in Luftwaffe Research Center like Colonel Dr. Knemeyer (more on him later).

PART 3
Engineer Heinz Kammler worked in 1944 for Special Luftwaffe Research Office too. This was "*Untersuchungsgruppe 13*" called office "*U-13*". Chief of this German Reich Top Secret Office was Professor Dr. Georg Kamper and this Top Secret Office "*U-13*" gave information to Dipl. Engineer Rolf Engel; and Engel was Rocket Missiles principal engineer

and Chief Consultant in RHSA in Amt VI – Secret Service SS – Chief was General SS Schellenberg and in At VI-D4 in 1944 was Hauptsturmführer '*Kurt Gross*' and Gross was head of '*Sargo'* in South America.

EDITOR NOTE – Remember that SARGO was the codename for Becker, one of the top German "*Spooks*" in South America. This was his police booking photo when the Argentina secret police captured him in Buenos Aires just before the German surrender in early May 1945.

Walter Schellenberg

So after 1945 many researchers of Office "*U-13*" came to South America. The Office "*U-13*" was the highest Top Secret Research Office for newest weapons in the Reich in 1944 to 1945.

After the war agents of the CIC or CIA asked Luftwaffe Generalmajor **ADOLF GALLAND (2854-+-1993)** and General Josef Kammhubber and Generalleutnant Dipl. Engineer Frodl and Dipl. Engineer Carl Francke (principal engineer of Heinkel HE 162) Chief in "*Erprobungsstelle in Rechlin*" and Dipl. Engineer Wolfram Eisenlohr, principal engineer in the Luftwaffe but none have information about Top Secret Luftwaffe Office "*U-13*" but all this knowledge rested with SS General Kammler and he is missing after 9 May 1945 and SS General Schelenberg but in the interrogation of Schellenberg you cannot find "*U-13*". Only a handful of people in the Reich has information about Luftwaffe Top Secret Office "*U-13*" for winning the war with newest weapons – jets and rockets, but it was too late. Göring never gave information about "*U-13*".

EDITOR NOTE – We are still asking about Hans Kammler. The third scenario was that he died fighting at the head of his troops. Nobody believed that – not even the person who invented that story. What troops? What fighting? While it is true that Hans Kammler was a General of the SS, he was a Doctor of Engineering, not a combat soldier. He had no combat troops under him; only scientists, engineers etc. So what did happen to

Hans Kammler? Who was in the office of Dr. Debus? Who was Dr. Debus? What ties all this together? As we said before, keep reading!

The CIA should have Spooks like Sharkhunters does.....

Who <u>IS</u> Feldwebel Schultz?

We normally do not identify our S.E.I.G. Agents but in this case, we are told that we can reveal the following:

Feldwebel Schultz was formerly in the Reich in the 4th Panzer Division in the 36th Panzer Regiment. In April 1945 he has a very good (rare) Sturmgeschütz – Panzer IV with long 7.5cm gun.

In 1945 he has command of this Sturmgeschütz Panzer in April 1945 in the German Reich Sturmgeschütz Brigade Nr. 202 and he told that his Sturmgeschütz crew in April 1945 was in last fights and destroyed nine Russian T-34 tanks in one day. This was in grid like Liepaja in Latvia.

He said he thought his Sturmgeschütze crew has destroyed the last T-34 Russian tank in the war near Libau short time before 14 hour (2 pm) on 8 May 1945. On the evening he destroyed his Sturmgeschütz himself because the war was over.

He was wounded and came in the evening on a small German Reich torpedo boat with other wounded German soldiers and in the night 8 to 9 May 1945 went to the West and he was in western Germany on evening 9 May 1945 but his tank crew went to Russian prison and all his friends are missing after 9 May capitulation. This is the true story of old Feldwebel Schultz.

B – VERTRAULICH – CONFIDENTIAL Charts and Information from **PIZZARRO**

The charts on the next few pages reveal a massive amount of formerly unknown Top Secret information. We have already reported that **PIZZARRO** had a meeting with one of the pilots of KG 200 and this meeting took place on 30 October 1969 at the huge memorial to *GRAF SPEE* in Uruguay and we also reported a couple months ago that this pilot had just died, so **PIZZARRO** can reveal this. **PIZZARRO** also told us the name of the son of Dr. Kammler and where he is living, but that will remain untold.

Here are the notes that came with these charts from **PIZZARRO** exactly as they came to us in this packet.

PART 1
Regarding the giant JU 390-V1; Interrogation 1044/1945 German Luftwaffe Unteroffizier (Sergeant) former in photographic unit in France (Mont de Marsan; FAGr. 5 Airfield) told under USA interrogation (files USA 9th Air Force Report A.P.W.I.U. Report 44/45) that one JU 390 flown 12 miles off New York January 1944. Name of the German sergeant was Wolfgang Baumgart.

PART 2
1945 JU 390-VA; test pilot logbook Oberleutnant Joachim Eisermann 9 February 1945;
>   1.   JU 390-V2 fifty minute test flight start and circuits around airfield Rechlin and Bad Rechlin airfield;
>   2.   Flight 9 Jan. 1945 with JU 390-V2 from airfield Rechlin to next test airfield Laerz (Lärz) only 20 minutes test.

PART 3
February 1945 JU 390-V2 was in Lärz (Laerz Airfield) 9th Feb. 1945 – 12th February 1945 and 13th February back. Next time after 13th February to 1 April 1945 nothing. But after war in USA German General Fritz Morzik (Transportflieger) told JU 390 in March 1945 was on airfield Bardufoss,

Norway and on 28 March 1945 about polar route to Japan, to Tokyo and back to Norway 30 March 1945 to Bardufoss.

In April 1945 JU 390 back to in Germany (Prague??) and according to General Bauer was on the airfield Rechlin from 23rd to 29th April 1945.

PART 4
On 30 April 1945 to airfield Prague later to Schweidnitz (southern of Breslau) 1st May 1945…..60 kilometers southwest of Breslau. (see the map next page)

EDITOR NOTE – This is the JU 390 that was assigned to Obergrupenführer Dr. Hans Kammler…….and his headquarters were in the Skoda Works in Prague just 60 kilometers away. It was in fact, the only JU 390 airworthy at this time. Does anyone REALLY believe that Kammler walked into the woods, either alone or with his SS guard, with the intention of quickly being dead, either by his own hand or by that of his adjutant?

The war was over; he was in a position of power with the Allies, either to the West or to the East and so many of the top German scientists, Intel specialists and officers were going to one side or the other why would he seek death rather than a better life as the others did. It makes no sense that he would kill himself – and we believe that he came to the USA in Paperclip.

PART 5
Part 5 is actually the chart on the next page with all the details on it. Pay close attention to the chart and all that is written on it and you will note about in the center of the chart is the word "**BELL**" with a circle drawn around it.

During our conversation, **PIZZARRO** said that this is where *die Glocke*, otherwise known as the "*Nazi Bell*" was loaded aboard this JU 390-V2. Where did it go? Keep reading………….

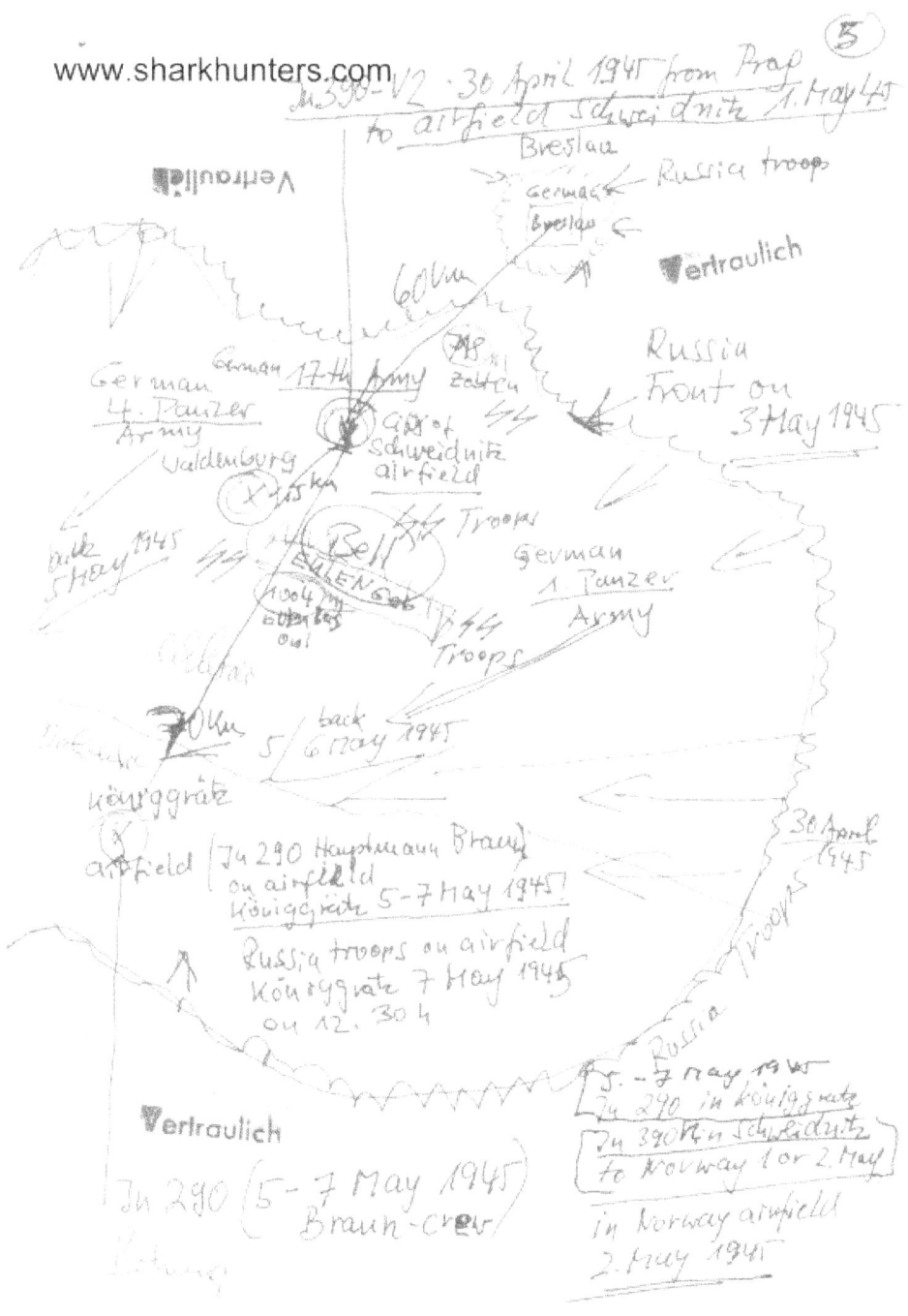

www.sharkhunters.com

⑤

Ju 390-V2 · 30 April 1945 from Prag
to airfield Schweidnitz 1. May 45

Breslau

German ← Russia troops
Breslau ←

Vertraulich

Russia
Front on
3 May 1945

German 17th Army zahti
German
4. Panzer
Army   GRI of
            Schweidnitz
Valdenburg   airfield

X 15 km

Bell
EILEN GO6
1004 kg   Troops
Eilentes
Owl
            Troops

German
1. Panzer
Army

back
5 May 1945

70 km   back
            5/6 may 1945

Königgrätz
(X)
airfield (Ju 290 Hauptmann Braun
          on airfield
          Königgrätz 5-7 May 1945)
          Russia troops on airfield
          Königgrätz 7 May 1945
          on 12.30 h

30 April
1945

Russia Troops

Vertraulich

Ju 290 (5-7 May 1945)
        Braun-crew)

5.-7 may 1945
Ju 290 in königgrätz
Ju 390 in Schweidnitz
to Norway 1 or 2 May

in Norway airfield
2. may 1945

PART 6

30 October 1969 **PIZZARRO** was in Mercedes, Uruguay for a meeting with RS, former pilot of 1. KG 200 (First Group) and as we reported, RS died earlier this year. RS came from the small German town named Nuevo Berlin (New Berlin) north of Mercedes in this time 1969.

Before they said goodbye, RS gave all information we have seen here. **PIZZARRO** remembers – at last RS smiled and said:

1. JU 390-V2 in north Norway 2nd of May 1945. It carried a crew of seven and also six passengers – AND very important cargo. So in JU 390-V2 only 13 persons.
2. JU 390-V2 has range of 12,500 kilometers! So it went non-stop to Uruguay!! He received radio console signal on 311.5khz in Paysandy Province. JU 390-V2 came from northeast.
3. Landing not on normal airfield but on long, very good hard street northeast of Esperanza.

EDITOR NOTE – Look to the chart on the previous page and to the left you will find the penciled note '*JU 390-V2*' and an "X" on a road running left to right on the chart. At the left end of this road you will find a circle with five diagonal lines running through it. This was the small woods in which the radio transmitter was placed to give the plane a homing signal and he landed on that road as seen on the chart.

And what **WAS** that very important cargo? The pilot, RS, told **PIZZARRO** that it was "*die Glocke*"!

———————————

The rest of the story of RS written "*Top Secret*" in 30 October 1969 in Mercedes, Uruguay. This is a handwritten short protokoll and RS told **PIZZARRO** and we continue from above:

4. On airfield Königsgrätz (Bohemia) was at last JU 290 (crew of Hauptmann Braun). This JU 290 was in KG 200 too. On 5 May 1945 Braun received order to Königsgrätz Airfield 60km southwest of Schwednitz. In this time the JU 390 was in Norway.

Typical JU 290 as referenced on previous page

5. JU 390-V2 to South America evening 5 May 1945; start okay so JU 290 not to Norway for help! JU 390 non-stop to Uruguay. In this time Villa Cisneros was closed.

6. He told, I received information that JU 390-V2 was on airfield Villa Cisneros in Spain Sahara but this is false. Possible this was plan for JU 290 but not for JU 390-V2.

7. In Uruguay a group of nine good Germans gave radio signals on 311.5 KHZ to find lost place.

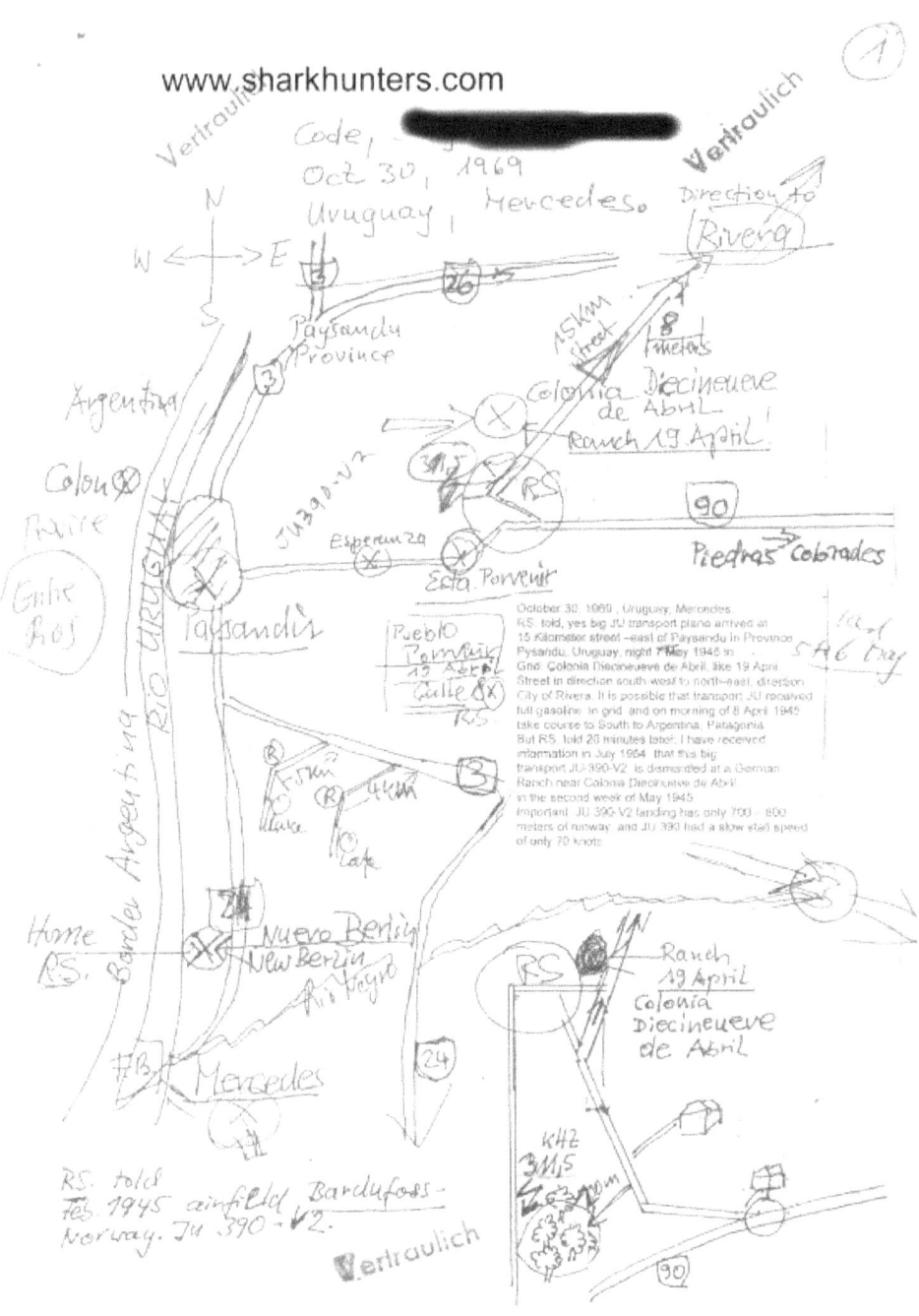

TOP SECRET

8. 1947 (two years after) important cargo goes to Argentina (Patagonia) to island (very secret island) in a big lake! But 1950/51 special top secret command destroyed top secret base.

EDITOR NOTE – We are told that this "*important cargo*" was "*die Glocke*" and we are quite certain that the top secret island was Heumel Island, the big lake was Nahuel Huapi at the town of San Carlos di Bariloche. This is the area where Adolf Hitler lived in the estate "*Inalco*"; this is where Juan Perón built his mountain troop training school just across the water from Heumel Island; this is where a large armed German security force existed both on land as well as lake patrol for some years after the war; where SS **ERICH PRIEBKE (7598-2011)** and many others lived.

Dr. **JOSEPH FARRELL (7353-2008)** suggested that a certain building in the nuclear research compound of Dr. Ronald Richter was the one that housed "*die Glocke*". He said it would be the large building with all the square holes in the walls. We first visited this mysterious island in 2008 and here we see

Sharkhunters President **HARRY COOPER (1-LIFE-1983)** in this very building. We are still unclear why this building had all these square holes in the walls and what was the purpose of the very

large and oddly shaped doorway.

Here are recollections of S.E.I.G. Agent **PIZZARRO** regarding his many communications with RS who died just a few months ago:

"He told first in 1947 – I received a small information about cargo in JU 390-V2. This very important cargo came from city of Waldenburg to airfield Schweidnitz with approximately 100 SS guards.   Waldenburg is only 15km southwest of airfield Schweidnitz and I received information all cargo came from a top secret SS base Stetin in the Euler (Owl) Mountains and this base (research center) was destroyed by SS troops on 30 April 1945 in direct order of General SS Kammler."

We mentioned in **KTB #258** under "**Editor Note**" that many veterans of the SS (and other branches of the Wehrmacht) lived in Bariloche and the surrounding area. Our research tells us that there was always a big party at one of the very upscale hotels in the area, usually Llao-Llao just outside Bariloche or another resort just over the border in Chile.

Above – one such party in Bariloche many years ago.

Below – Llao Llao a

www.sharkhunters.com   Photo by Nahuel Coca

Nice place to have a party, eh? Both times there has been a Sharkhunters *"Patrol"* to this area, we have enjoyed dining in this beautiful place…….and we could almost hear the ghosts of those who were here before us.

Here are some additional notes made by Sharkhunters President **HARRY COOPER (1-LIFE-1983)** when he spoke with **PIZZARRO** presented in random order. **HARRY** was writing very quickly as **PIZZARRO** spoke.

Bauer said that he could *"go anywhere in the world"* with the gigantic six engine JU 390-V2. He said this on Rechlin in late April 1945.

"die Glocke"…..he said that the Bell was found on the island Heumel then moved to Area 51 where it was reverse engineered and a larger one was built by American scientists at Area 51.

He told Sharkhunters the new name of the son of General SS Dr. Kammler and the town in which he lived – but that information is locked away in a safe place and we will not reveal it.

C - "Now you see them – now you don't!"
The Vanishing Scuttled U-Boats in Golfo San Matias

By GEOFFREY BROOKS (7531-2010)

In April 2002 in Uruguay, I was contacted by Mr. Terry Neilson, a stranger. He told me he had a project. He had seen my book "*Hirschfeld; The Story of a U-Boat NCO*" and wanted me to translate from German and Spanish all documentation which would be retrieved from a sunken U-Boat just discovered in Golfo San Matias, Argentina. I did not think there would be one but out of curiosity I spent a day listening to his project. In London three months later he showed me a wonderfully shaped sonar image of the boat. It lies on its starboard side, and from measurements taken on the image I concluded that it was a Type XI-C/40.

Our third and last meeting was in Buenos Aires in August 2002 when I was shown over Terry Neilson's 15 meter 28 ton Bermudan sloop *ICE MAIDEN ADVENTURER*. She is a single masted, two sail, steel hulled ocean voyager equipped with Raytheon radar, Skanti SSB and VHF, GPS and other electronic aids to navigation and seafloor searches. A multi-part BBC-TV documentary about the search had been generated. Terry Neilson and TV producer Sarah Aynesworth arranged interviews with historians and documentary makers in Argentina. The US Albenga Foundation had assumed responsibility in Buenos Aires for all logistics, planning and importing, the scientific direction of the work with its own personnel and for the Institute of Oceanic Investigation ProMare technicians from Norway. The Argentine Navy was also involved and would supply the SeaEye Falcon ROV (Remotely Operated Underwater Search Vehicle).

I was impressed by the enthusiasm of everybody I met and left convinced of their honest belief that they had a U-Boat; it was just a matter of time. That evening Terry introduced me to the Argentine Navy Captain Villas, in charge of the salvage team. I learned that the Argentine Navy had made available the latest magnetometer. It had been agreed by the Albegna Foundation that the naval vessel *ARA CUDAD DE PUNTA ALTA* would be used as the mother ship. The Argentine Navy was keen to use the operation to obtain experience in the use of high technology instrumentation. Its specialized team would operate the ROV and sonar equipment. Villas told me he was absolutely confident they had the boat; it was a scientific certainty.

I was a person of no importance to the project until the documentation was salvaged; if then. Furthermore, the coordinates were a closely guarded secret and so persistence of unessential personnel aboard ship was not desirable. Thus I was left ashore when, in February 2003, the second expedition sailed off to search the zone for five days. They began at the coordinates and radiated outwards. Repeated passes were made using magnetometer and sonar. The ROV was dropped on the coordinates and explored the sea bed. Despite the five knot current, underwater visibility was excellent. No sunken U-Boat could be found. This was an extensive exercise in which everybody believed so wholeheartedly that several million dollars had been invested in it, but there was nothing there. Why did they believe there might be?

At the end of the Second World War and for long afterwards, the U-Boat Arm had continued to operate a signals office in Oslo to keep in touch with U-Boats heading for Argentina and elsewhere with important technological documentation, weaponry, strategic materials and passengers. Although its original files had been destroyed, a number were copied and kept by three Norwegian collaborators. In 2001 the survivor of the three offered the material for sale to scientists at the Norwegian University of Technology in Trondheim (NTNU).

Once the signals were held genuine, what interested everybody was one sent by a U-Boat about to be scuttled at the southern end of Golfo San Martin with twelve tons of gold ingots aboard. A check was made with the Argentine Navy. They thought they might have depth charged this boat the day before the date of the signal.

Putting together the signal and the Argentine Navy report, we come up with this scenario:
On 18 July 1945, a German U-Boat had approached the port of San Antonio Oeste in Golfo San Matias. This port housed the German Etappandienst Headquarters.

EDITOR NOTE – The reader will remember that the store and offices of the Lahausen Wool Company in this town was the Headquarters for the German agents coming and going by way of U-Boats and sailing boats in the war.

In the roadstead, the boat's periscope was sighted from aboard the Argentina torpedo boat ***MENDOZA*** which pursued and dropped a pattern of depth charges based on hydrophone plotting. Then the U-Boat, seriously damaged during the attack, headed for Golfo San Jorge but lost engine power and began drifting towards the open Atlantic. The commander decided to scuttle the boat for later salvage of the cargo. It sank in eighty metres about seven miles north of the entrance to Golfo San Jorge. A signal reporting the event and the precise coordinates of the sinking was transmitted and received in Oslo.

On 9 January 2002, Terry Neilson's consortium had decided to make a preliminary check of the coordinated given in the signal. *ICE MAIDEN ADVENTURER* took aboard the Albenga scientific director and a Norwegian specialist from IOE ProMare and an Argentine Navy observer to monitor the operation and help monitor the sonar. Terry Neilson placed the boat precisely on the coordinates by the use of the GPs and took sonar images. One of these images excited everybody who saw it. Without any doubt, below the keel of *ICE MAIDEN ADVENTURER* lay the wreck of a German U-Boat of the Second World War.

Half an hour later when they decided to check their observations and data they could not locate the sunken U-Boat. They searched over and around the coordinates until nightfall. Nevertheless, because they irrefutable proof (the sonar images) they reported back in jubilation.

Based on the results of Terry Neilson's expedition, the multi-million dollar second expedition had been set up. When upon his return in February 2003, Terry Neilson informed me that the second expedition had failed to find the U-Boat, I was astounded. How could a large 1,200 tonne U-Boat resting on a sandy bottom at 80 meters for almost sixty years have suddenly vanished off its resting place within half an hour of discovery? Believe me, there were some long faces. The project was abandoned. The gold aboard the U-Boat was to have paid the bill for it and now they were left with footing the bill themselves.

I recalled when collaborating with former Oberfunkmeister **WOLFGANG HIRSCHFELD (34-+-1984)** on our joint book *HIRSCHFELD* published in 1997 (pages 201-202) we had discussed the northbound transit on the Kattegat by *U-234* in late March 1945 during which time the boat appeared to have mysterious immunity from attack. From what Hirschfeld had told me I developed the theory that *U-234* must have obtained this immunity by sailing for a while in another energy field.

Now I suspect this theory accounted for the disappearance of the sunken "*gold*" boat. I shall explain what I mean in the Conclusion to Part 2.

I knew of course about the legendary scuttled U-Boats at Caleta de Los Loros which nobody had been able to find and I had discounted them previously as pure invention. Following knowledge gained with the "*gold*" boat project at the southern end of Golfo San Matias, I thought to take another look at the U-Boats said to lie at the northern end of the same gulf.

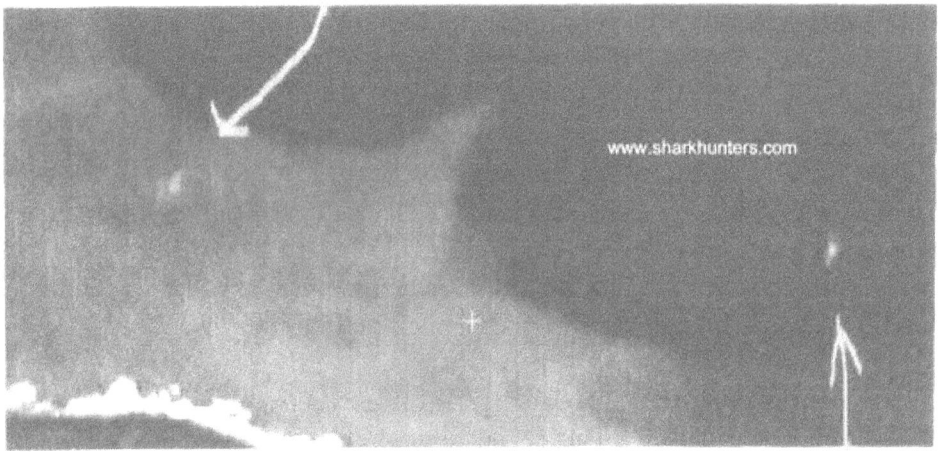

Aerial photos of what appears to be two sunken U-Boats

PART 2

The northern shore of Golfo San Matias extends eastwards from the town of San Antonio Oeste (Headquarters for the German Etappendienst in both World Wars). Just south of the 41st parallel South about forty miles long is the Mejillones headland marking the western entrance to the Caleta de los Loros Bay. The coast, of very sparse population, is a mixture of cliffs up to 100 feet high, rocky platforms and sandy beaches with typical dune vegetation.

Since the early 1950's numerous Argentine witnesses claim to have seen one or two scuttled U-Boats no farther out than a mile from the low water mark at Caleta de los Loros. It is a calm lagoon of triangular shape and at high tide it fills to a depth of eighteen feet but drains to reveal a sandy bottom at low water.

Here are three typical reports:
1. Ernesto Duca in 1965 piloting a **Salud Publica** aircraft saw two wrecks *".....about 1,800 metres off the Caleta oriented at 45° to the coast, propellers shining like the sun, boats seemed to be breaking up, saw a large drum, maybe the remains of boiler."*
2. Hotelier Antonio Ribeira made four reports between 1958 and 1980, all sightings being from the beach. In the March 1980 report he stated *"With the wind from the north, you could see the bow perfectly 200 meters out from the low water mark."*
3. Veterinary surgeons Marcelo Ochoa and Ediardo Frias; *"On a day of extreme low water in 1990 (photographed from a hired aircraft) two elongated shapes about 60 metres in length lying parallel to the coast."*

A report to which much credence must attach is that of Carlos Massey, a marine salvage expert called to the Argentine Navy base at Bahia Blanca in August 1978 to give his opinion on the possibility of *"salvaging two scuttled U-Boats in waters near Caleta de los Loros."* He was given access to secret documentation, a file of about 200 pages with photographs, nautical charts, maps and sketches.

He recalled seeing statements signed in 1960 by a very senior naval chief giving the conditions and exact time of sighting. During a flight along this stretch of coast in 1960 in search of possible U-Boats in the Golfo Nuevo incident, a Neptune aircraft from the Almirante Zar Base at Trelew equipped with magnetic sensors (MAD) had photographed the wrecks and noted the coordinates.

The sightings had been made in *"ideal conditions of low water and solar zenith"* enabling the hulls to be photographed. *"In the photos one can distinguish clearly the silhouettes of the boats which lie at some 16 metres depth with the hulls close together, facing towards the coast with the sterns fifty metres apart. One can see dark coloration indicating the position of the conning towers."*

Massey said that he could not remember (or more likely the Argentine Navy told him to forget) the coordinates, although it was *"in waters close to the Caleta de los Loros at between 800 and 1000 metres from the low tide mark."*

There have been three major accredited searches for the scuttled U-Boats off Caleta de los Loros:

1. On 23/24 November 1996 the Institute of Marine Biology Almiranti Storni Expedition supported by the Naval Prefecture and the municipality of San Antonio Oeste failed to find the submarines.

2. At the end of November 1997 the minelayer ***ARA GURRUCHAGA*** explored the Caleta de los Loros using a team of tactical divers and a robot machine equipped with a video camera. Grumman S2F Tracker aircraft from the anti-submarine squadron were also present together with Institute of Marine Biology and Fisheries scientists. The expedition had been ordered by President Menem (*Ambito Financiero* 21 Jan. 1998). Nothing was found.

3. At the end of 1998 Norwegian scientists, marine archaeologists and hydrologists reconnoitered the sea bed with a high definition sonar. Nothing was found.

This according to Chilean writer Patrick Burnside:

"The U-Boats scuttled near Caleta de los Loros remain elusive for lack of positive coordinates and because of changes on the sea bed on a daily basis."

Oh, I think they would have been spotted by now if they were there. Moreover, this theory does not explain the 2002 vanishing U-Boat at the southern end of Golfo San Matias where the precise coordinates are known and the sea bottom is firm.

CONCLUSION

Although the two U-Boats off Caleta de los Loros are occasionally visible *"at ideal conditions of low water and solar zenith"*, all the trawling in the world cannot snag them. That is a crucial factor. Too many reports have been made by responsible witnesses for wrecks of some kind or another not to be there. So the solution must lie in what are known as SS-Earth Sciences, perhaps Vril.

To explain what seems to have been copied: 'There are in the world a number of haunted island which are inconsistent. On rare the occasions when they are present in this world they always appear at the same coordinates. For example, San Borodon Island, occasionally present 40 kilometers west of La Gomera in the Canary Islands has appeared for perhaps a total of fifteen days each century since first noted by Ptolemy in Roman times.

These appearances, when the island can be visited, occur generally during intense electro-magnetic storms.

When inconsistent islands vanish, they *dematerialize* into another energy field. This must have been what Dönitz meant when he was reported to have said that the Kriegsmarine had found;
"einen absolut uneinsehbaren Versteck wo der Führer vor allen seinen Feinden sicher sein wird."
(An impregnable and hidden fortress for the Führer)

Nowhere on Earth is totally impregnable, although another energy field is. The three scuttled U-Boats in Golfo San Matias will have been *dematerialized* by an artificial process which was not perfect, as evidenced by their being seen very occasionally from an aircraft, yacht or on the beach when the circumstances were right. Why the Third Reich in Exile went to all this trouble to dematerialize them so close inshore instead of enlisting the help of the ever-willing Argentine Navy to tow them out to the South Atlantic deeps to their last resting place must remain a mystery.

FOOTNOTE
The role of the Argentine Navy in the 1960 Golfo Nuevo incident might lead one to think that senior Argentine naval commanders knew far more about the Third Reich in Exile U-Boats than they ever cared to admit.

On 17 August 1971, Manfred Braunmüller, a professional pilot of Argentine nationality who two years earlier had reported seeing the sunken U-Boats at Caleta de los Loros, took off from Viedma Aerodrome at the northeast corner of Golfo San Matias on a flight to Puerto Piramides on the north shore of Golfo Nuevo. It was a day without wind, totally overcast and the sea was calm. On the way he was surprised to see three Type XXI U-Boats proceeding through Golfo San Matias on a heading which would take them towards the deserted north coast between 63° and 64° west. One of the boats was trailing oil. Braunmüller always carried a camera and used two rolls of film to photograph the small flotilla. He did not have enough fuel to remain in the air to watch them, but on landing he took one roll of the film to Admiral Gnavi, Commander in Chief of the Argentine Navy.

Gnavi had been involved in the 1960 Golfo Nuevo incidents. After seeing the photographs, he formed the impression that there was no purpose to be served by searching for the three submarines, which represented no threat to Argentina. No photograph from either roll of film has ever been published ad the total overcast prevented the movement being observed by spy satellites.

EDITOR NOTE – We are aware that this is a lot to handle and the reader must proceed as he//she feels comfortable. We can attest to the 1960 U-Boat incursion into Golfo Nuevo as I was in the US Air Force at the time and we got almost hourly updates for the couple weeks this submarine hunt went on, even using borrowed very high tech US Navy ASW equipment and US Navy men operating this equipment. The submarines were trapped in a small gulf, were frequently seen but never forced to surrender and never damaged. They eventually got away. This is not conjecture, this is hard fact. Thanks to **GEOFFREY** for this story

D - What Boat Was Really Sent South of South America?

Input from S.E.I.G. Agent **FELDWEBEL SCHULTZ**

German U-Boat Staff (BdU) that Russian troops are near Berlin and British troops near Hamburg and French bases closed – only German Norway bases are free. So Skipper Schneewind said we are sailing to south of South America.

EDITOR NOTE – SOUTH of South America? Can anyone think of any place south of South America that is anything but Antarctica? This is getting interesting.

On board of *U-183*, so said the survivor, are twelve torpedoes, 400 kilograms (about 880 pounds) of Quinine, 500 kilograms (about 1,100 pounds) of Opium and 700 kilograms (about 1,540 pounds) of iodine for the German Reich and some tons of rare metals and rare Earth oxides (for German Reich newest weapons) and many supplies (food) in *U-183* for five months.

Eighteen years ago **Feldwebel Schultz** with a historian had a meeting with members of the officers' families on *U-183* and received same information. This information is never printed before.

EDITOR NOTE – We will print more information; when we receive it from our S.E.I.G. Agents.

―――――――――――――――――

It was reported in another book that several U-Boats deliberately let themselves be discovered so they could fake their own destruction. We wonder where these authors came up with all this drivel but they claim that *U-518* and *U-1235* faked their sinking so they could proceed elsewhere and ultimately pick up special guests and cargo for onward voyage to Argentina. These boats were sunk – they did not play dead as these writers claim.   Here we have additional information on *U-880* courtesy of S.E.I.G. Agent **FELDWEBEL SCHULTZ** who tells us -

In 1947 **FELDWEBEL SCHULTZ** received this photo of *U-880* from the widow of the Skipper, Schötzau. **FELDWEBEL SCHULTZ** said he has received this photo of the Indienststellung (commissioning ceremony) in Bremen. Both photos are of the commissioning on this page and the next.

He was told by the wife of Kapitänleutnant Schötzau that he has a child, a little daughter. This meeting was in the region southwest of Köln in the town of ▮▮▮▮▮▮.

The widow of Skipper Schötzau said to **FELDWEBEL SCHULTZ** that *U-880* is missing. She told that after the war in May 1945, Großadmiral Karl Dönitz told her that six big snorkel U-Boats from Norway were in the Atlantic and he said that three of these U-Boats were missing – no more radio messages after 12 April 1945.

Later she received information that *U-518*, *U-880* and *U-1235* were missing and that *U-546* with survivors were sunk by US Navy destroyers.
EDITOR NOTE – Two Sharkhunters Members rode *U-546*. They were the Skipper **PAUL JUST (206-+-1986)** and crewman **WERNER KRÜGER (325-+-1987)**.

JUST   KRÜGER

He was also told that *U-805* and *U-858* came to the USA to surrender and all crews in USA prison.

EDITOR NOTE – THILO BODE (304-1987) photo left was Skipper of *U-858*.

E   ....and What About *U-530*?

More from S.E.I.G. Agent **PIZZARRO**

A Member asked some interesting questions. My apologies, I do not remember who asked but here are the questions:

1. Why would some of the crew and Captain Wermuth have copies of a Spanish/German dictionary if this was just a standard war patrol with them returning to Germany?
2. Why did a lot of the crew have smokes, chocolate and pesos made in Argentina unless they stopped someplace and spent some time somewhere in Argentina before arriving at Mar del Plata? They left Kristiansand in Norway in March?
3. What happened to the large raft that they carry? It was not found when they did a search of the boat.

Once again we turn to **PIZZARRO** who tells us:

One of the former 1943 officers of *U-530* told Wermuth in 1945 more about the third patrol of *U-530* in 1944. After her third patrol *U-530* was in Lorient, France – German U-Boat base on 22 February 1944. The next, the 4th patrol beginning 22 May 1944 from Lorient; Skipper of *U-530* was Kurt Lange. In the time from April 1944 to first weeks in May 1944 was Skipper Lange and his crew in home leave and some holiday in Paris.

So the officer on *U-530* said in this time in 1945 in time of home leave was another U-Boat crew for two weeks on *U-530* for a short patrol to Spain port. He thinks with cargo and back to Lorient. He told this was in the last week of April and the first week of 1944 and it was Spanish harbor on the Gallegan coast (North of Spain).

EDITOR NOTE – This is interesting because **DON ANGEL ALCAZAR de VELASCO (158-+-1985)** stated that he was picked up by a U-Boat off the Gallegan coast in early June 1944 that took him to Hamburg. Furthermore, he also said that when he left Europe with Martin Bormann aboard a boat that took him

to Argentina, they boarded a boat off the Gallegan coast. You will read all this in our newly released book:
"Hitler in Argentina"

Very interesting – Wermuth told me that this information is in later USA interrogation too. Wermuth told me that he has a meeting, he thinks it was in summer 1941 in Hamburg with some (three) officers of the battleship *ADMIRAL GRAF SPEE*. These *SPEE* officers escaped from Argentina in 1940 and were later all U-Boat Skippers (U-Kommandanten).

EDITOR NOTE – We believe that two of these officers were Fregettenkapitän **JÜRGEN WATTENBERG (154-1985)** who was Navigation Officer aboard *SPEE* and later commanded *U-162*; the other was Kapitän zur See **KURT DIGGINS (3518-1994)** who was an Adjutant on *GRAF SPEE* and later Skipper of *U-458*.

WATTENBERG   DIGGINS

So he received information about Argentina, Bay Rio de la Plata, Montevideo and Buenos Aires but he has not friends or relatives in

Argentina. Wermuth told me that no persons or treasure were on *U-530* on last patrol or had been landed in Argentina or elsewhere for surrender and never treasures aboard *U-530* – only torpedoes, weapons and Flak.

Wermuth told me that he did not know of any other submarines and his crew has never seen another German U-Boat after German Reich surrender.

Only one of the radioman has received in beginning July 1945 short waves radio signals like short waves of the German U-Boats (Grenzwellen-Kontakt) before *U-530* was in Argentina, but he told me that it is possible that another U-Boat was on course to south in South Atlantic. Later he received information in USA prison about *U-977*. But in this time, beginning July 1945 *U-977* was not in South Atlantic and Wermuth told me that it is possible that another German U-Boat was on course to South America.

EDITOR NOTE – Since **WERMUTH** picked up radio traffic from another Boat in the South Atlantic but *U-977* was not yet in the South Atlantic – what U-Boat was it?

He told me that in March and April 1945 approx. 15 big German U-Boats were in Atlantic against USA and he has heard the radio short signals of the U-Boat base in Berlin; these were signals of the BdU to many U-Boats. Wermuth said to me that the last radio order from Berlin for *U-530* came on 26 April 1945. Only received attack order but he did not answer. Course of *U-530* this time was attack in Grid for New York.

All boats have fuel refill and provisions for six months. *U-530* in this time March 1945 so Wermuth told me *U-530* has carried 16 torpedoes with six T-5 (Zaukönig) in torpedo room and three T-3 torpedoes and eight LUT torpedoes and torpedo pistols for all torpedoes. Wermuth told me he was never Skipper on *U-853*; this is in all books false. He told me that in the American interrogation of the *U-530* is error – crew member of *U-530* told in USA prison that *U-530* has only 14 torpedoes but correct number is 16 torpedoes.

After U-Boat Command Training in 1944 Wermuth was I.W.O. on *U-530*. In this time *U-530* was in shipyard and *U-530* received cut out deck before conning tower for high speed diving. *U-530* at first had the old 1942 design so *U-530* beginning 1945 in shipyard for new cutout deck, he has received command.

> **EDITOR NOTE** – The original design of the Type IX boat had a wide foredeck which caused it to "*hang*" on the surface. It was this trait that kept *U-110* on the surface after Lemp ordered abandon ship and allowed the Brits to capture the boat. Later model Type IX boats came out of the yard with the cutout deck and others brought back and retrofitted so they could dive faster.

U-530 received the newest stealth snorkel – the head and top of trunk was rubber covered and *U-530* has a strong radio system with Tunis Antenna with Radio Mücke System and Fliege Radio System and one Naxos amplifier with cathode ray tube visual indicator and two Rundipole, one on the bridge and one on the stealth rubber snorkel head. Wermuth said the radioman of *U-530* received a short signal book with newest short codes from February 1945. This was not the normal Enigma code – this was a short signal code book with book keys. On *U-530* was a strong 200 watt radio transmitter and one 40 watt emergency transmitter and an emergency transmitter for life rafts (hand operated), two main receivers and one all wave receiver with Welle 600 and one Radione receiver.

Question 2 – We think this is error. Wermuth told me that after arriving in Mar del Plata, high ranking Argentine Navy Officers gave him Argentine cash, Pesos, to buy drinks and food in the Argentine Navy Base or Argentine Officers Restaurants so the crew received same gifts like chocolate and smokes.

Question 3 – *U-530* has not cargo **IN** boat – never. We have no more information. Otto Wermuth told me his first intention was to go to Chile to city of Punta Arenas in the canal to Chile but his Engineer told him that *U-530* did not have enough fuel so he decided his first Argentine city was Miramar to surrender but later decided to go to the Argentine submarine base at Mar del Plata. Otto Wermuth told me that he first sighted Mogotes Light and Lighthouse at 0300 of 10 July 1945 from a distance of 19 or 18 miles. His position at that time gave him a true bearing of 239° or 240° on the light. He then submerged *U-530* and he waited for the first daylight of dawn to look over the port of Mar del Plata.

At that time he approached nearer the port and cruised some three miles offshore awaiting for light to enter. At 0630 he is seen and lit his navigation lights and entered the port. In answer to Argentine Navy signals he flashed with his lamp the letters:

A-L-E-M-A-N S-U-B-M-A-R-I-N-O

Wermuth stated that fifty-four men was the normal complement of a submarine of the Type of *U-530* but on *U-530* was only two officers, the Engineer, one radioman and nine crewmembers "*Spook*" Spain because some of the crew members were in Spain in 1942 and 1943 on another ship, not a U-Boat and very interesting, a former officers of *U-530* told Wermuth more about the third patrol in 1944. *U-530* began her third patrol October 1943 from La Pallice. About 1,000 miles northeast of the Caribbean a Type XIV U-Boat supplied her with about 40 metric tons of fuel and two weeks provisions.

After two unsuccessful attacks had wasted five torpedoes, a hit was scored on a 10,000 ton tanker north of Colon in December 1943.

EDITOR NOTE – That would be the 10,195 ton American turbine tanker *CHAPULTEPEC* on 26 December 1943 at 10° 30' N x 78° 58' W. Damaged, not sunk.

A few days later *U-530* attacked another tanker and was rammed by the tanker and lost her bow buoyancy tank and sustained damage to main ballast tank. Later the U-Boat was passing between the French island Martinique and Dominica the U-Boat started back to Lorient, was in port 22 February 1944.

Harry this is new! Top Secret cargo transport in last week April 1945 to first weeks May 1945. *U-530* entered a Spanish harbor Gallegan coast and back to Lorient!

The long fourth patrol of *U-530* began from Lorient 22 May after fitting out first snorkel on *U-530*. Two weeks later *U-530* passed the Azores and two weeks later in a grid between Freetown and Trinidad *U-530* rendezvoused with Japanese submarine *I-52*. The guest on *U-530* was Kapitänleutnant Schäfer with newest German Enigma keys and maps and two radiomen were with rubber dinghy from *U-530* transferred to *I-52*. After diving *U-530*, many detonations were heard and all think that Japanese boat *I-52* sunk.

EDITOR NOTE: *I-52* was sunk in very deep water; she did have tons of gold and silver aboard but she is at about 19,000 feet.

F – The "*Spook*" Boat......*U-530*

Third Reich in Exile

We know a great deal about this boat......and there is much we do not know.   After **OTTO WERMUTH (1344-+-1990)** took command, her missions became clouded. We have already read a great deal about *U-530*, about **WERMUTH** (P.O.W. photo right) and about his missions.

Some believe that it was his boat that brought Martin Bormann and **DON ANGEL ALCAZAR de VELASCO (158-1985)** out of Europe and landed them at Puerto Coig on the Patagonian coast. Even though **DON ANGEL** stated in his 114 page long letter to us in 1985 that he brought Bormann to Patagonia one year after the end of the war while *U-530* surrendered end of July 1945 – it may be that **DON ANGEL** was using deliberate mis-information, not a rare thing for "*Spooks*". He did bring Bormann out of Europe, that cannot be denied – but maybe it was in summer 1945 rather than 1946 as he admitted. There is no one to confirm or deny the dates.

"The Government of the Third Reich Came Ashore at Bahia Blanco in Summer 1945"

That statement was told to **HARRY COOPER (1-LIFE-1983)** by our very dear friend **INGRID SCHARFENBERG (3308-1993)** some years ago. This was not a stupid woman and she was not given to crazy stories. Further, she never let go of the "*old ways*" and she had a great many friends who had been very high in the Party......and who still kept close contact with these men. We met some of them in her Hotel zum Türken.

When **COOPER** pressed her for an explanation, she merely smiled her coquettish smile and asked;

"Who do you think I mean?"

COOPER said that he assumed she meant Bormann, as that is who **DON ANGEL** said was aboard. Again she smiled at him and said;

"Bormann was not the head of the Government of the Third Reich. That was only Adolf Hitler."

She refused to say more but we read more here from **PIZZARRO**;

EDITOR NOTE – S.E.I.G. Agent **PIZZARRO** interviewed Captain **OTTO WERMUTH (1344-1990)** in his home some years ago and here is what **PIZZARRO** tells us.

I asked Wermuth about Horton, Norway and he told me:

PART 10. *U-530* departed Kiel at 1800 hours on 19 February 1945 and was in Horton, Norway on 23 February 1945. In the deep water bay at

Horton, *U-530* (photo here) has snorkel training and deep diving training. *U-530* departed from Horton on 3 March 1945 together with *U-714*. Commandant of *U-714* was H. J. Schwebke. It is possible that Wermuth knew Schwebke in 1944 as both Skippers, Wermuth and Schwebke, were in French U-Boat base. Wermuth has told me that he has seen *U-714* and later he received information that Schwebke sank with his boat *U-714* days later on 14 March 1945. I have seen many photos of *U-714* in Horton; Schwebke in Horton on 22 February 1945.

EDITOR NOTE – Schwebke & the entire 50 man crew of *U-714* was lost on that date when sunk by the Royal Navy destroyer *HMS WIVERN* and the South African Navy frigate *NATAL* ten miles NE of Berwick.

From Horton, *U-530* sailed on 3 March 1945 approximately 150 miles to Kristiansand and from Kristiansand on the same day, 3 March 1945 to her last patrol against the United States.

From Kristiansand, Wermuth took up a course to the north 25-30 miles away from the Norwegian coast and approximately 100 miles north of Bergen he gave order for a west course. At this point, 100 miles north of Bergen, he used his rubber covered snorkel.

EDITOR NOTE – The boat had been retro-fitted with a new rubber coated snorkel in which the head and shaft were coated with rubber, but not just raw rubber applied. The inner coat of rubber had scientifically designed holes cut into the rubber to defuse and deflect radar signals. The outer layer was smooth to allow it to go through the water with less drag and resistance. This was called "*Alberich*" after the main character in a German folktale called the Niebellungenslied. "*Alberich*" had a magic hat and when he wore it, he was invisible.

Ten days after departure from Horton-Kristiansand a radio message was sent to *U-530* for weather reports but Wermuth told me that *U-530* had no radio contact and he has never sent any radio signal. So *U-548*, Kommandant Erich Krempl received this order for weather reports. On the *U-714* photos in Horton I have seen one big U-Boat and I think it was *U-548* because Krempl sailed from Horton against the USA on 5 March 1945 and was sunk weeks later with all hands

So *U-548* gave weather reports and Wermuth told me he has never sent one radio signal back to the U-Boat base.

PART 11. I asked him in what Grid he has order for weather signals and he told me that *U-530* has radio order to send reports from approximately 61° North to 20° West. Wermuth told me that after 27° West his *U-530* surfaced each night for 3 or 5 hours and on 26 April *U-530* received radio signal for attack Grid New York.

In this time the newest and biggest worldwide radio transmitter with the name *GOLIATH* was destroyed. American troops came to small town

Calbe on the Milde River and some days before 11 April 1945 German soldiers destroyed *GOLIATH* – this one megawatt transmitter systems for U-Boat underwater radio signals, the most powerful tune transmitter in the world for tuneable frequency – Längstwellen on 3 to 30 Khz with wave length of 10 to 100 Kilometers. *GOLIATH* has three big antennas with a height of 204 meters.

But after *GOLIATH* was destroyed the German Reich Navy has in April 1945 newest mobile transmitter in sea with codename *FELIX* so it is possible that *U-530* last radio order came from the *FELIX* transmitter on 26 April 1945 as radio signal to the snorkel head.

Wermuth told me that after 26 April many short waves from the German Reich U-Boat bases were picked and he thinks that fifteen or twenty big German U-Boats were in the Atlantic in April 1945.

PART 12. I asked him about his meeting in 1941 in Hamburg with three Leutnants of the former battleship *ADMIRAL GRAF SPEE*, sank 1939 in the Rio de la Plata. Many officers of the *GRAF SPEE* escaped 1939 and 1940 from Argentina to the German Reich. He said to me that he did not know the names, but later all three were U-Boot Kommandanten and in French base he has received information that two sank in 1943 with their U-Boats and were killed. So we look together in the files and it is possible that two of these escaped *GRAF SPEE* officers were:
- Friederich Mumm, *U-594* sunk 4 June 1943
- Hermann Kottmann, *U-203* sunk 25 April 1943   or
- Heinz Kummer, *U-467* sunk 25 May 1943

Many more *GRAF SPEE* officers were later U-Boot Commanders:
- **KURT DIGGINS (3518-1994)** *U-468*
- Hans-Joachim Kuhn, *U-1233*
- **JÜRGEN WATTENBERG (154-1985)** *U-162*
- Rolf Schaünburg, *U-536*
- Johann Reckhoff, *U-384*
- Jobst Hahndorf, *U-864* in training, killed 1945
  - Hans-Joachim Schmidt-Weichert, *U-9*

PIZZARRO sent email to this Author - This is my last mail about *U-530*. In *U-530* report three of all thirty pages are closed for 80 years. I have sent you all important extracts from the 30 page report so I cannot send more and can never send the rest of the story – the three pages; I do not have these pages. They will not be available until 2060…..or never.

My last question (to Wermuth) was – I think that *U-530* was not in Grid New York. Wermuth said on 4 May 1945 he has shot three LUT torpedoes at a convoy with more than ten ships. Two torpedoes did not hit and the third was hung up in the tube.

On 6 May 1945 the next convoy was sighted. Wermuth shot two new LUT torpedoes but no hits, no detonations. Three hours later the next LUT torpedo was fired at a big ship, possibly a tanker, but missed. One hour later the next single T-5 torpedo hit but did not detonate. On 7 May 1945 the next two T-5 torpedoes missed ships in the convoy and after Germany surrendered on 9 May 1945, four or five torpedoes fired at the next convoy all missed.

So Wermuth told that on the American coast he has fired fourteen torpedoes and all were duds. I said to Wermuth this is a crazy story – and I think *U-530* was never in Grid New York.

Wermuth smiled and said no more………….

G – 3rd U-Boat at Sea in mid-1945

….. from S.E.I.G. Agent **PIZZARRO** about another boat, a third U-Boat in addition to *U-530* and *U-977*, confirming what we already knew.

Harry – last year you have emailed to me the telephone number of a former *U-977* crewman. He told me the same story like the radioman of *U-530* and later the Skipper of *U-530* **OTTO WERMUTH (1344-1990)**. This former member of *U-977* told me in July 1945 *U-977* was in the door to the South Atlantic and our radioman of *U-977* received short wave signals like short waves of the German U-Boats (Grenzwellen) he told me that Schäfer (Skipper of *U-977*) said he thinks another German U-Boat was on course to south in South Atlantic and he said one name of a German U-Boat commander. He said that he has a meeting with another U-Boat Skipper and this U-Boat commander said to him after the war his course is to South America.

This was in the week approximately 20 to 28 July 1945.

The former radioman of *U-977* told he picked up seven radio traffics from another U-Boat and all seven were on the last German U-Boat wave code from April 1945 – and the radioman of *U-977* said this is the handwriting of German U-Boat code.

So we think in July 1945 a third U-Boat was in South Atlantic in Grid between Brazil island Fernando Noronha and Rio di Janeiro but the radioman said 800 or 900 miles east of the South American coast, near to the African coast and he told me than in April 1945 approximately 50 German U-Boats departed from their Norwegian bases to patrol against England and the USA.

EDITOR NOTE – This was *Operation* **MERCATOR**, meant to pull Allied ASW assets out of middle Atlantic and clear a freeway so to speak, all the way down into the South Atlantic.

EDITOR NOTE - Some years ago our S.E.I.G. Agent **PIZZARRO** sat down with **OTTO WERMUTH (1344-1990)** to talk about that last patrol of *U-530* and here is some of what he learned. Before we begin this interview, we mention that in all correspondence we had with **WERMUTH**, he did not refer to this final patrol as a Feindfahrt (war patrol) but rather as a "*Reisen*" which means "*Journey*".......like a trip or a vacation.

1. **WERMUTH** told me that he was Kommandant of *U-530* selected by Admiral von Friedeburg, Chief of BdU Op. 2 in beginning of 1945 and he was sent from French base to Hamburg to take command of *U-530*. I asked him about is Iron Cross First Class and he told me that he was holder of the Iron Cross First and Second Class and he has the U-Boat Service Badge (U-Abzeichen) and the rare U-Front Medal (Frontspange).

Above: Iron Cross 2nd;   Iron Cross 1st;   U-Boat Badge
Below – the U-Boat Frontspange

He had received all crosses for his service on other boats. He was on *U-37* as a Watch Officer in 1941. In July 1942 he was II.W.O. (2nd Watch Officer) on *U-103* until June 1943 then in that month he became I.W.O. (1st Watch Officer) on *U-103* until February 1944. He rode *U-103* during three Feindfahrten (war patrols) and in this time sank three enemy ships.

EDITOR NOTE – That would be:
   31 Oct. 1942 the 6,405 ton British motorship *TASMANIA*;
   6 Dec. 1942 the 5,025 ton British steamer *HENRY STANLEY*;
   13 Dec. 1942 the 13,945 ton British steamer *HORORATA* *
     (HORORATA was only damaged and made it to a repair port.)

   3. He told me that in February 1945 he was with *U-530* in Kiel and his boat in Kiel received fresh provisions for one week and good long special U-Boat provisions for approximately 18 weeks and order for Norway base, so he sailed from Kiel 19 February 1945 to Horton, Norway and was in Horton 23 February 1945. He sailed from Horton on 3 March 1945 with course to the USA.

3. In Norway his *U-530* received approximately 230 tons of (diesel) oil and more than 5 tons of lubrication oil (Schweröl), and *U-530* received fresh provisions like bread, fresh meat and many vegetables for 14 days so he has on *U-530* provisions for 19 weeks; approximately five months.

4. **WERMUTH** told me that *U-530* was never in the last German Group *SEEWOLF* in the Atlantic. His boat was alone in the Atlantic with course to USA. He told me all orders came directly from Berlin. Last radio for *U-530* on 26 April 1945 but he did not reply and he had orders not to reply. He has paper orders in *U-530* for attacking enemy ships only and in last radio to *U-530* was on 26 April 1945. Attack orders for Grid New York.

5. He told me his course from Horton, Norway was wide to the north of England rounded in the Atlantic, many nights with snorkel. His snorkel was rubber covered. He told me that after German Reich surrender he was

in Grid New York and in middle of May 1945 his *U-530* was on course to South America. *U-530* was approximately 800 or 900 miles northeast of Puerto Rico and *U-530* was on snorkel march (running submerged using the snorkel to breath and run the diesels) and on many days during the daylight *U-530* was underwater. Later he passed in the night between the islands of Rocks of Saints Peter and Paul, and the island of San Fernando Naronha approximately in the middle of these  two islands. **WERMUTH** has told me that he thinks he has seen in darkness a light of a lighthouse and on 17 June 1945 at 1000 hours in the morning *U-530* crossed the Equator. In this very time one very high aircraft came from northeast to southwest.

The Mysterious Final Voyage of *U-530*

By S.E.I.G. Agent **MICHAEL IVINHEIM**
Argentina Correspondent

PART ONE

U-530 was the first of two German submarines to surrender to Argentina postwar. Fifty-seven years later, the interrogation file of Commander Oberleutnant zur See **OTTO WERMUTH (1344-1990)** was partially declassified in June 2002 when Admiral Stella, Chief of the Argentine Naval Staff, released Spanish language photocopies under license to Juan Salinas and Carlos de Napoli for their book Ultramar Sur.

The US National Archives then declassified an intelligence report and enclosures submitted by the U.S. Naval Attaché at Buenos Aires on 24 July 1945. Because this was a translation into English of the Argentina report, the U.S. Naval Attaché was responsible for any deviation between the two accounts.

In 2009 when I read through the eleven pages of the translation on a website, I noticed a deviation from the Argentine report which could not have been a simple error. There was also a statement from which it was clear that **OTTO WERMUTH** who sailed *U-530* from Germany was replaced later by another commander using his name. A great effort has been made and continues to be made, to cover over this fact and also for some reason to hide the identity of most of the crew members and in **PART ONE** of my article, I am concentrating solely on this aspect of the mystery.

Will the Real Otto Wermuth stand up please?

"At Mar del Plata this 10th day of July 1945 before those present and the commandant, submarine division, Argentine Navy, capitàn de fragatta Julio C. Mallea, the commander of the German submarine U-530, Oberleutnant Otto Wermuth, hereby surrenders unconditionally his vessel, his command and his crew, the list of whose members is appended hereto…"

List of Crew Members of *U-530*

Officers: Otto Wermuth, Karl-Felix Schuller, Karl-Heinz Lenz, Peter Leffler, Gregor Schlüter.

NCOs: Jürgen Fischer, Hens Setli*, Johannes Wilkens, Paul Hahn, Georg Rieder, Kurt Wirth*, Heinz Rehm*, Rudolf Schlicht*, Rolf Petrasch, Ernst Zickler, Georg Mittelstadt*, Robert Gerlinger*, Viktor Wojsick*, Günther Doll*, Rudolf Bock*, Werner Rosenhagen*, Arno Krause, Karl Kroupa*.

Ratings:
Herbert Patsnick*, Sigismund Kolacinsky*, Friederich Mürkedick*, Arthur Jordan*, Eduard Kaulbach*, Rudolf Muhlbau*, Franz Hutter*, Harry Kolakovsky*, Franz Rohlenbücher*, Johannes Oelschlager*, Willy Schmitz*, Heinz Hoffmann*, Heinz Paebzold*, Gerhard Nellen*, Ernst Liewand, Reinhard Karsten*, Hans-Wolfgang Hoffmann*, Arthur Engelken*, Hans Sartel*, Erhardt Piesnack, Joachim Kratzig, Erhardt Muth*, Friedrich Ourez*, Werner Zerfaz*, Erhardt Schwan*, Hugo Traut*, Engelbert Rogg*, Franz Jendretzki*, Georg Wiedemann, Günther Fischer*, and Georg Goebl.

Why the asterisk (*) behind the names?

The number of crewmen aboard *U-530* was five officers, eighteen NCOs and thirty-one ratings being a total of fifty-four in all. The thirty-seven (37) men whose names are marked with an asterisk (*) were unknown at the U-Boat Museum in Cuxhaven when I made the check. Why these thirty-seven men should have wanted to throw their soldbuchs and other identity documents into the sea and adopt a false name is unknown, but it is obviously a part of the great **U-530** mystery.

The instrument of surrender also contained this strange final clause
"Oberleutnant Wermuth declares that the submarine U-530 from which all the crew has now disembarked is in a safe condition, that the only explosive aboard is a torpedo warhead without percussion cap, and that there is no element or device aboard intended to sink the boat or damage it partially or totally."

The face of the real **OTTO WERMUTH** is on an Argentine Police identity card. This man was born at Aalen, Württemberg on 28 July 1920 and therefore was twenty-five years of age at the time of these events. He had very dark hair and was 5 feet 8 inches tall. On his uniform can be seen the *Frontabzeichen* and above it the *Iron Cross, First Class*. It is important to note that he does not have the *Ubootfrontspange* above his left breast pocket and is not listed as ever having been awarded it.

If we look at the photographs (on next page) taken on 10 July 1945 when **U-530** arrived at Mal del Plata, the commander of **U-530** alleged to be "*Otto Wermuth*" who brought the boat into Mal del Plata and signed the instrument of surrender is the Nordic looking officer with the black roll-neck sweater wearing the *Ubootfrontspange*.

11 July 1945
Captain Julio Cêsar Mallea, commandant of the Argentine submarine base at Mar del Plata, watched the Nordic "*Otto Wermuth*" bringing **U-530** alongside the U-Boat quay on 10 July and accepted from this tall, blond officer the instrument of surrender of boat, contents and crew. As far as Mallea was concerned, this man was Otto Wermuth.

Arrangements were made by Captain Mallea to lodge the Nordic "*Otto Wermuth*" and his four officers aboard the Coast Guard ship **BELGRANO** and joined them there for lunch the following day, 11 July 1945. The Press were also in attendance and were allowed to take photos and ask questions during desert. (reported by Salinas and deNapoli in Ultramar in 2006.)

When "*Otto Wermuth*" was asked where he had won his **Iron Cross (First Class)** he told reporters from the newspapers *La Razón* and *Noticias Gráficas* that it had been awarded to him as an officer of the surface fleet. (The swarthy Otto Wermuth had only served in a surface ship for two months; aboard the destroyer **Z-23** while working up in the Baltic.)

12 July 1945

"I was an anti-aircraft officer with a local coastal battery at Mar del Plata and went to the submarine base to see the U-Boat and speak to the naval authorities. I was allowed aboard the U-Boat on 12 July. Some of the crew was still aboard. They gave a general impression of exhaustion and starvation. They wore their hair and beards long and unkempt. I spoke to the commander, Otto Wermuth, who spoke good English and French. He was lodged on the Coast Guard ship **BELGRANO**; his crew lived in tents on a football pitch while recovering from scurvy. Stubble for a blond beard covered his chin and he was hoping to grow a fine elongated blond moustache."

This from Colonel Rómulo Horatio Bustos in the article Yo fui testigo in the newspaper La Nación 23 March 2008.

We can see from the identity card issued to the real Otto Wermuth that on this 12 July he was 300 miles away from Mar del Plata being investigated, photographed and fingerprinted at Police Headquarters in Buenos Aires.

He did not have the beginnings either of a blond beard nor a fine, elongated blond moustache and nobody would possibly think he was Nordic.

Otto Wermuth???   Otto Wermuth???

EDITOR NOTE – We post the two photos here for your comparison. You may make your own decision. Note the officer in the right photo wears the Ubootfrontspange.

13 July 1945
The Argentine Naval interrogation of Oberleutnant zur See Otto Wermuth, his four officers and four NCO's began at Mar del Plata submarine base on 13 July. US Navy observers were present but only as onlookers.

The swarthy Otto Wermuth now presented himself as the *U-530* Commander. Because the boat had arrived on 10 July with no log, charts or other documentation under the actual command of an imposter who had signed the instrument of surrender and the real Otto Wermuth's only means of identification was an identity card issued by the Argentina Federal Police the day before, the members of the interrogation board were understandably not happy about him.

This part is from the US Navy Report on Interrogation of Prisoners from *U-530* Surrendered at Mar del Plata on 10 July 1945 under the item 'US Naval Attaché Buenos Aires observation of the Argentine Navy interrogation of prisoners from *U-530* surrendered at Mar del Plata; Interrogation of Oberleutnant Otto Wermuth.'

"He has no identification of any kind to support his statement that he was actually in command of the submarine. Upon being questioned as to whether or not he could substantiate this, after much reflection, he recalled that one of his seamen married a girl in Kiel by proxy and radio during the voyage and that he, as commanding officer of the submarine, had signed the marriage document."

This document when obtained from Joachim Kratzig sufficed to convince the tribunal. The Nordic '*Otto Wermuth*' faded away, never to be identified or heard from again.....yet somebody must be able to identify him. There were only about fifty holders of the silver Ubootfrontspange.

EDITOR NOTE - A Uboatfrontspange – the first is in Bronze and since the Ubootfrontspange was introduced so late in the war, only a handful were awarded in Silver and there were none in Gold. Who can send us a list of Silber Ubootfrontspangeträgers?
PIZZARRO – we bet you can add much to this.

What was the 0purpose of this switching of commanders? Why did the US Naval Attaché at Buenos Aires falsify a passage in his translation of the Argentine interrogation report?

PART TWO – The Horror Voyage

The *U-530* story is shrouded in deception. *U-530* and *U-853* worked in concert for a brief period in April 1945 close to the US East Coast. The KTBs (war log books) remain top secret in Argentine and Allied archives respectively nearly seventy years after the events related hereunder.

U-530   *U-853*

Operation Regentröpfchen (Raindrop)

On 18 June 1944 at Strasbourg, Martin Bormann set in motion a series of measures to transfer to safe havens abroad the secret armament technologies and wealth of Germany with the aim of developing the potential of the Third Reich in Exile. The operation was code-named *Regentröpfen* and its primary target point was Argentina.

One of the U-Boats used in this operation was *U-530* commanded by Oberleutnant Otto Wermuth.

The Participation of *U-853*

In July 1944 when the 10th U-Bootflottille was being disbanded at Lorient, Flotilla Commander Günther Kuhnke assigned temporary command of the Type IX-C/40 boat *U-853* to Oberleutnant Otto Wermuth. On 24 August,

Kuhnke assumed command of *U-853* himself and led the exodus from Lorient to Flensburg at the end of September. He kept Wermuth as his I.W.O. At Flensburg when Kuhnke took over the 33rd Flottille, he gave command of *U-853* to Oberleutnant Helmuth Fromsdorf. *U-853* left Flensburg in early February and sailed from Stavanger, Norway on 23 February for the US coast (1).

It is believed that *U-853* had aboard millions of dollars' worth of jewels and foreign currency in sealed steel containers.

This belief is supported by the testimony of Hans Bergerdans at the Nürnberg trials that he personally;
> ".....had been paid to stow an enormous amount in US travelers' cheques inside empty shell casings aboard *U-853*."

This boat also had aboard the active component of the Death Ray device mentioned below.

EDITOR NOTE – That there were large amounts of valuables aboard *U-853* has been reported in the past, thus verifying this report by **IVINHEIM**. Scuba divers dive on *U-853* sometimes but we understand it is a dangerous dive with "*black water*", no visibility and swift currents. In fact, LARRY DAUPHEMIA (423-1988) and his dive buddy dived this boat some years ago. They apparently were not properly prepared for this dive, and LARRY watched his friend die that day.

The Participation of *U-530*

At the beginning of 1945, Kuhnke appointed Otto Wermuth as the commander of *U-530*. According to what Otto Wermuth told the Argentines, after leaving the yards *U-530* sailed for Norway at nightfall on 19 February 1945 and then from Oslo for US waters on 5 March 1945 (2). This is disputed. Admiral Eberhard Godt, former head of the Kiel base, stated that Wermuth had left Kiel for Norway on 3 March and not 19 February. His allegation was counter-signed by a former cruiser commander who had watched *U-530* sail and by Kurt Lange, former commander of *U-530*. (3)

EDITOR NOTE – EBERHARD GODT (344-1987) was a Member of Sharkhunters until his passing.

Wermuth told the Argentines that he was acting under direct orders from *"his commanding officer in Berlin, and was not attached to any U-Bootflottille"*.

This was also incorrect. The chain of command was Dönitz at Bernau/Berlin to Flotilla Commander Kuhnke and from Kuhnke to the commanders of *U-853* and *U-530*. These two boats were to meet up during the first week of April off the coast of New York.

The fuel capacity of *U-530* was 245 tonnes but the Chief Engineer shipped twenty tonnes short *"so as to aid stability"*. What tended to make the boat unstable was not stated but it is interesting to note that *U-977*, the only other boat to surrender to Argentina, loaded eighty tonnes of fuel at departure, fifty tonnes short – also *"so as to aid stability"* and discharged about forty tonnes of heavy electrical machinery and strange aerials on the quayside at Mar del Plata (4).

Whereas a Type IX-C/40 boat commonly sailed with twenty-two torpedoes, for this mission *"to attack shipping"* Wermuth took only fourteen (eighteen T-3 LUT and six T-5 FAT) thus creating much free space otherwise taken up by torpedoes. These weight gains from having aboard less fuel and torpedoes enabled heavy electrical machinery weighing over thirty tonnes to be transported.

EDITOR NOTE – The LUT torpedo (lagen-unabhängiger torpedo) had a pre-set gyro angle and zig-zag course.

The FAT torpedo (flächenabsucheder) had a pre-set course.

Wermuth said that his only defensive armament was two twin-20mm and one 37mm flak on platforms abaft the bridge. This statement also appears to have been incorrect. By 1945 it was rare for a U-Boat to be fitted with a deck gun. At his interrogation on 13 July Wermuth told the Argentines that he sailed from Germany leaving it ashore. This was at variance with the statement of harbourmaster Captain Mallea who told the Argentine

Press on 11 July that (the substitute) Otto Wermuth had ordered the crew to *"jettison the 105mm anti-aircraft gun into the sea."* *U-530* crew members describe the episode of ditching the 5-tonne deck gun as one of the memorable events of the voyage. Colonel Bustos, an Argentine AA battery officer who saw over *U-530* at Mar del Plata on 12 July 1945 wrote;

> "The naval authorities told me how surprised they were that the deck gun had been unshipped and ditched at sea (5)."

It is therefore clear, despite what Wermuth claimed, that there had been a deck gun on the foredeck at some time during the voyage.

The Death Ray

Heinz Schäfer, commander of *U-977*, stated in the unexpurgated original version of his book (6) that he was shown photographs of the Death Ray device at Waffen SS HQ in April 1945 presumably before being given one to transport to Argentina. Oberfunkmeister Wolfgang Hirschfeld described the Death Ray used aboard *U-234* in his book (7).

EDITOR NOTE – WOLFGANG HIRSCHFELD (34-1984) was a Member until his passing on 24 April 2005.)

The active element was linked to the shipboard radar and an aerial aligned with the radar aerial emitted the beam. Allied aircraft would not approach to within 3 kilometers of *U-234* when the ray was operating and would immediately disengage and flee after detecting it. In the original version of his book, Hirschfeld stated incorrectly that *U-234* had been escorted by three Type XXIII boats during the transit of the Kattegat. In the updated version (8) it was pointed out that the escort was formed by *U-1107, U-516* and *U-1274*. Whichever of these three could make only ten knots carried the heavy electrical equipment for the Death Ray. Thus, the Death Ray in operation needed one boat to carry the heavy equipment and a second boat to operate the beam. As will be seen from the two examples mentioned further, when the beam was being operated, and it was always operated on the surface, there might have been a difficulty in seeing this second boat.

The *U-853* Mysteries

Some time in mid-April 1945, *U-530* and *U-853* met up near the US East Coat. At midday on 23 April 1945, the 256 tonne corvette *USS EAGLE 56* was taking part in an anti-submarine exercise about three miles from shore in Casco Bay, New England near the city of Portland. The corvette was towing a target which looked like a submarine for US Navy fighters to practice bomb with bags of flour. At 1213 hours an explosion blew off the poop of the corvette, which sank very rapidly.

The naval aircraft saw the incident but not the U-Boat, and within about fifteen minutes two US warships arrived to pick up the thirteen survivors. A depth charge attack was then made by the *USS SELFRIDGE* on a submerged contact detected by sonar but which escaped. Two of the survivors stated that while they were in the water, they saw the conning tower of a U-Boat 400 yards distant and that one of the men, John Breeze, reported seeing painted on the conning tower a red horse on a yellow shield. This was the emblem of *U-853*.

Twelve days later, just after midnight on 6 May 1945 close to Rhode Island a hunter-killer force detected a submerged submarine and destroyed it. Navy divers from *USS PINGUIN* went into the wreck the same day, recovered the log of *U-853* and now the US Navy knew that *U-853* had been responsible for sinking the corvette *USS EAGLE 56*.

EDITOR NOTE – The last ship sunk in American waters was the old collier *BLACK POINT* and it was *U-853* who sank her but the mystery remains – why would a U-Boat sink such a worthless target as a coal ship and worse yet, why would she hang around in water too shallow for safe submarine operations? Why didn't she head for the open sea where she had maneuvering room instead of hanging around in shallow waters near the biggest anti-submarine base of the US Navy?

Why, therefore, later in the year did the US Navy state that the cause of the sinking of **EAGLE 56** had been a "*boiler explosion*" and not a torpedo hit? Perhaps a very similar sinking "*later in the year*" in mysterious circumstances, carried out on the best day of the year to make a point to the United States, made the point.

BAHIA

At 0900 hours on the morning of 4 July 1945 at the Equator off Natal, Brazil just like the **EAGLE 56**, the Brazilian cruiser **BAHIA** had been towing a target for anti-aircraft practice when an explosion occurred which blew off the pop and the cruiser sank very rapidly.

The US/Brazilian Board of Enquiry discounted the eye-witness evidence of ten survivors. All these ratings wanted to testify that they saw a submarine "*suddenly appear fully surfaced two miles off the starboard quarter where nothing had been a second before.*" That type of testimony is obviously inadmissible in evidence and so the Board of Enquiry preferred the evidence of the only officer survivor, Lt. Torres who at all material times had been in the engine room and saw nothing. A verdict was conjured up that by accident a shipboard Oerlikon had been fired into the depth charges stacked on the poop, which then blew up. Since depth charges are so manufactured that this cannot happen, the Brazilian admirals remain skeptical of the verdict to this day.

The US Navy knows the truth about these two similar sinkings and for its own reasons keeps them a closely guarded secret. Only after the publication of Albert Baime's magazine article in MAXIM, May 2002 p 140-148 with the remarkable title "*In Shallow – a psycho sub commander, a plot to level New York, a beach awash in the blood of American sailors*" did the US Navy suddenly realize that **USS EAGLE 56** had been sunk by a U-Boat and awarded the crew a Purple Heart nearly fifty years later.

EDITOR NOTE – Why the US Navy doggedly hung on to the boiler explosion explanation for decades after the war is up for speculation, but it was attorney **PAUL LAWTON (4628-1996)** who refused to let this false story lie and after an incredible amount of work, **PAUL** convinced the US Navy that it was indeed, *U-853* that sank *EAGLE 56.* The Navy corrected the historical records and more importantly – the men were finally awarded the medals they had earned as well as benefits they should have had many decades earlier.

In April 1945 *U-853* and *U-530* had met up to try out the Death Ray. The unfortunate **USS EAGLE 56** became their victim. Afterwards the valuables from Frömsdorf's boat (*U-853*) to Wermuth's boat (*U-530*) while the flak on the stern platform and the deck gun with flak ammunition on the foredeck protected the operation. This meeting also explains how *U-530* arrived off Mar del Plata with her provision lockers almost full although she had only loaded enough for seventeen weeks at Kiel. The rest we must imagine. Frömsdorf, who had the active element of the Death Ray aboard for experimental purposes and used it to sink **USS EAGLE 56** by "*blowing up her boiler*" transferred it to *U-530* to be taken to the Third Reich in Exile in Argentina with all the millions of dollars' worth of cash and valuables…..and they parted.

Footnotes for this part of the IVINHEIM report:

1. Salinas & De Napoli, *Ultramar Sur* 2002p 237-239;
2. Declassified US Navy report, *Report on interrogation of prisoners surrendered at Mar del Plata on 10 July 1945, item US Naval Attaché Buenos Aires, Observation of Argentine Navy Interrogation of Oblt Otto Wermuth*;
3. Associated Press (AP) release, Kiel, 20 July 1945;
4. Heinz Schäfer, *El Secreto del U-977* Hisma, Buenos Aires 2006 P191. This book is a translation of the original German language edition published in Argentina in 1949 under the title *Geheimnis um U-977* then quickly withdrawn from circulation;
5. Col. (Ret) Romulo Horacio Bustos, *Yo ful testigo, La Nacion*, March 2008;
6. Heinz Schäfer;
7. Hirschfeld/Brooks, *Hirschfeld, the story of a U-Boat NCO*, Pen & Sword/USNIP 1997 at p201-202. Reported as occurring during the passage of the Kattegat by *U-234*, 27/28 March 1945
8. Hirschfeld/Brooks, *Hirschfeld*, Frontline Books reprint 2011 at Appendix p. 228

PART THREE – The Radio Dead Zone; *U-530*

After parting from *U-853*, **WERMUTH** apparently had orders to operate off New York. *U-530* carrier two short-wave receivers; one all frequency and one radione receiver. **WERMUTH** thought that one of the short wave receivers might be damaged but the others were in good order. While in his area of operations he was to follow procedure and not transmit except for the daily weather reports. His last contact with Berlin was on 26 April, but at the end of April he entered a mysterious *"radio dead zone"* where not even the coastal radio stations could be heard and the boat remained in total radio silence *"until 8th or 10th May"*.

U-530: Ten Days in the Total Dead Zone

At some time before 4 May 1945, *U-530* was in US territorial waters where **WERMUTH** *"allowed all crew members to view New York through the periscope. They saw very clearly skyscrapers, trains and cars as well as dirigibles of the coastal defence overhead (1)."* Never during all this sightseeing was there a fear that the periscope might be detected by those dirigibles overhead whose only purpose in being there was to scour the coastal waters for U-Boat periscopes. Confidence that the boat could not be seen when the beam was operating?

The LUT torpedo was almost infallible. It ran loops either side of a mean course and also had an acoustic guidance system. The FAT did not have the latter but was generally very effective. On 4 May, **WERMUTH** said that *U-530* attacked a convoy of up to twenty ships in fog. One LUT stuck in the tube; the others had no effect. On 6 May *U-530* fired two LUTs which had no effect against a large convoy. Then a LUT missed a tanker and a FAT missed a straggler. On 7 May two FATs had no effect against another large convoy. No convoys reported being attacked by a U-Boat during this period.

At this point, **WERMUTH** jettisoned the five remaining torpedoes as *"being in a condition to explode"*. He refrained from stating what condition they were in. A reasonable theory for the *U-530* radio total dead zone and the torpedo failures is that the Death Ray had an electro-magnetic basis and a leak shut down the electrical systems of the radio and torpedoes aboard *U-530*.

Emergency Action Aboard *U-530*

Once **WERMUTH** suspected a leak he had to act fast. If the leak combined with the torpedo warheads to being them to a condition where they were likely to explode, deck gun, torpedoes, flak, all munitions, the Death Ray device from *U-853*.....anything which might be tainted with a residual trace had to be thrown overboard at once. The entire outer structure of the boat would have to have been scrubbed repeatedly with the virulent corrosive cleaner carried aboard, no doubt for that purpose.

After all, **WERMUTH** would not wish his boat to be sunk by some kind of mysterious "*boiler explosion*". The fact that the tower and decks were split and cracked, apparently due to corrosion and the deck casing had been the seat of a major fire, were reported widely when *U-530* arrived at Mal del Plata but the causes are never mentioned in the interrogation papers. No true crew list for the final voyage of *U-530* exists. Possibly there was an exchange of crewmen with *U-853* to accompany the Death Ray and so the fictitious *U-530* crew names would conceal the identities.

Heading South for Argentina

After radio contact with the outside world was restored on the 8th or 10th May, *U-530* headed to the waters 1,000 sea miles ENE of Puerto Rico. Here lies the Sargasso Sea and the Doldrums with little winds or swell, ideal for work re-scrubbing the boat with corrosive cleaner, burning contaminated materials and taking stock for the run to Argentina. **WERMUTH** then set course to the south, crossing the Equator on 16 June 1945 and maintaining a slow speed until 20° south; the men having no food because the leak had poisoned the provisions.

WERMUTH told the Argentine naval interrogators that he saw the Punta Mogades light at Mar del Plata at 0300 hours on 9 July 1945 from 18 miles offshore and went down the coast to Miramar arriving there at 0600 hours on 9 July.

> "At nightfall on 9 July I surfaced and made my way eastwards back along the coast keeping three miles offshore until reaching Mar del Plata submarine base where I drifted until the early hours (2)."

The US Naval Attaché did not like this jaunt to Miramar and so falsified his translation to read:

> "Wermuth told the Argentines of first sighting the Mogades light at 0300 hours on 10 July, thought about going to Miramar to surrender and then he submerged and waited for dawn to view the port of Mar del Plata (3)."

Why Did Wermuth go to Miramar?

At the end of 1943, Generalmajor Friedrich Wolf, Naval Attaché at the German Embassy, commissioned Wilheld Seidlitz to search for a suitable Etappandienst location on the Atlantic coast of Buenos Aires Province where German submarines could disembark agents and materials necessary for the intelligence organization in Argentina.   Seidlitz contacted Gustav Eickenberg, a German-Bolivian tin magnate who had a ranch at Mar del Sur which offered great possibilities for disembarkation of submarines. The best spot for the arrival of a U-Boat was equidistant between the lighthouse at Miramar and Necochea where a path led up to Eickenberg's ranch (4).

The End of the *U-530* Voyage

The probability is that **WERMUTH** got off the boat at Miramar. Here the containers of cash, jewels and traveler's cheques (5) were unloaded and he took with him the *U-530* logbook, charts and books for the conference with German naval intelligence officers of the Etappendienst. At Miramar the tall, blond imposter took his name and replaced him for the last leg of the voyage. The latter told the Argentines that he had personally ordered the diesels to be sabotaged off Mar del Plata, no reason being given. The Argentines recorded that no documents of any kind had been on board of *U-530* when the boat was surrendered, and they were reported to have been jettisoned at sea.

Documents from the two boats that "*were jettisoned at sea.*"

EDITOR NOTE – on the previous page and here below are just some of the documents from ***U-530*** (and ***U-977***). The skippers said they had jettisoned ALL documents at sea but as we see here, there were plenty remaining on board. These photos were taken by this author **HARRY COOPER (1-LIFE-1983)** at the submarine base Mar del Plata in 2008.

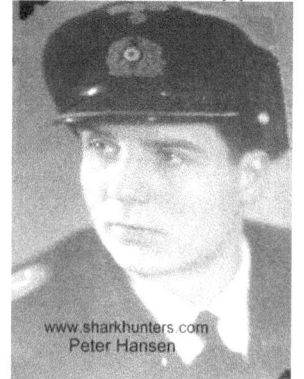

www.sharkhunters.com
Peter Hansen

U-Boat officer and Abwehr agent **PETER HANSEN (251-1987)** was brought to Buenos Aires by the Argentina Navy in 1947 to translate all the documents.....*that were not aboard these boats.*

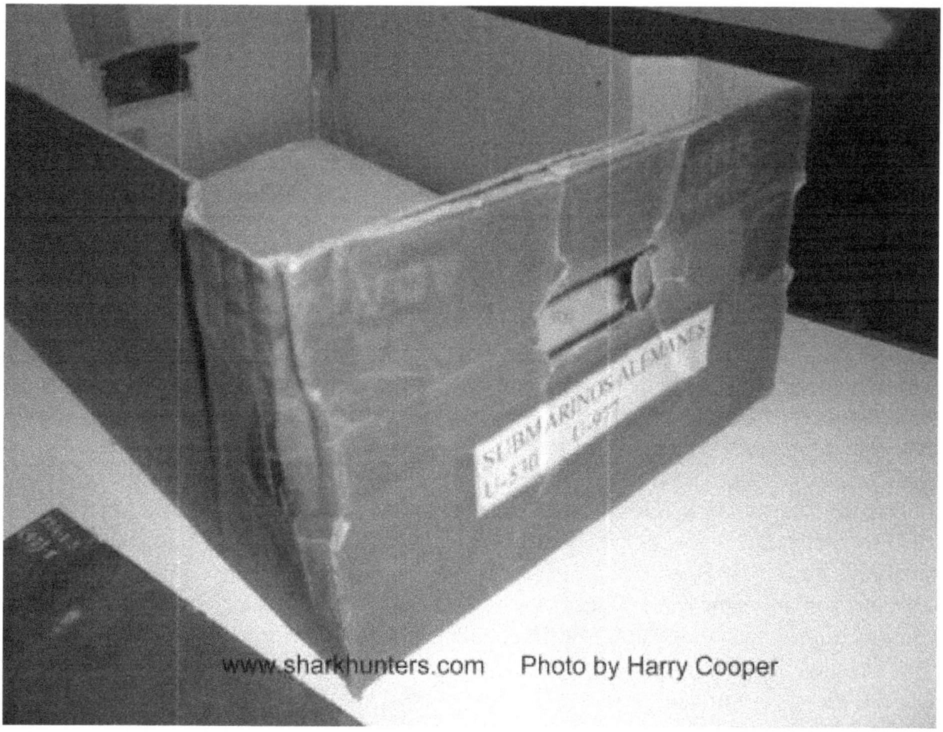
SUBMARINOS ALEMANES
U-530 U-977
www.sharkhunters.com Photo by Harry Cooper

However, it had been established (6) that they went ashore before ***U-530*** put into Mar del Plata and eventually reached the hands of the Argentine Navy, though heavily censored.

"*U-530* appeared to have survived some dreadful calamity. The great rusty hull, its paintwork shredded and peeling contrasted vividly with the smart, steely grey, small Argentine submarines at the base. The decking was very corroded and had been the seat of a major fire. The conning tower had cracked and was falling apart.....the interior was covered with mould."

Colonel Bustos was appalled by the *"vile, nauseating stench in the interior despite the boat having been aired for three days,"* by the *"haggard and exhausted appearance of the crew"* and to cap it all, for the first time in the history of the German U-Boat Arm, a submarine had arrived in port with its provision lockers almost full but the crew suffering from scurvy. The worst affected were *"put on a diet of boiled potatoes and lemons (8)."*

Footnotes:

(1) Salinas and diNapoli, *Ultramar Sur*, p 401: Helmut Kraft, *Submarinos alemanes en laArgentina*, Buenos Aires, 1998

(2) Salinas and diNapoli, opt cit p.424

(3) See the declassified US Navy Report, *Report on Interrogation of Prisoners Surrendered at Mar del Plata on 10 July 1945*, item *US Naval Attaché Buenos Aires, Observation of Argentine Navy Interrogation of Prisoners from U-530 Interrogation of Oberleutnant Otto Wermuth*

(4) *Ecos Diarios*, Necochea 22.2.1944 quoted in Jorge Camarasa, *Puerto Seguro*, Buenos Aires 2006, p63. The Miramar zone was very important for German naval planning and with the tacit cooperation of the Argentines was the centre for a major disembarkation from two U-Boats on the night of 27 July 1945 to another German ranch near Necochea known as Moromar

(5) These clandestine deliveries to Argentina by U-Boat were fairly commonplace during 1945. See the article by Deuxiéme Bureau agent Alain Pujol, *Le Figaro*, 1 September 1970 regarding millions of dollars worth of foreign currency, platinum, gold and diamonds unloaded from a U-Boat on 7 February 1945 at San Clemente del Tuyú with the collaboration of named Argentines at the highest level. This particular transfer was confirmed in a memorandum from the counter-intelligence organization Direcciôn de Coordinaciôn Federal to the Argentine Navy Minister (facsimile of this document in Ladislas Farago Aftermath, Avon Books, New York 1974).

(6) Sharkhunters International

(7) Salinas and diNapoli, *op cit*. p.293

(8) Bustos, *Yo ful testigo, op cit*

U-977.....the Other "Spook" Boat

EDITOR NOTE – S.E.I.G. Agent **PIZZARRO** is our most prolific Agent and **PIZZARRO** finds things even regular "Spook" agencies can't find – and shares them only with Sharkhunters. Here is a great amount of Intel, presented in random order.

We all know that two boats were in the South Atlantic after the German surrender – well, three that we know about. The two that surrendered at the Argentine Naval Base at Mar del Plata well after the German surrender: *U-530* surrendered in late July 1945 and between our S.E.I.G. Agents **PIZZARRO** and **MICHAEL IVINHEIM**, we are learning a lot about this boat.

U-977 surrendered more than a week after *U-530* and aside from the book "*U-Boat 977*" written by Heinz Schäfer the Skipper, there is precious little easily available on this boat and as we have read from **MICHAEL IVINHEIM**, much of Schäfer's book is fantasy; especially the story of their 66 days running fully submerged to save fuel.

Now we have even more information just received from **PIZZARRO**.

PIZZARRO tells us:
More about *U-977* and Schäfer to Argentina – you can print in your KTB.....newest information, many years SECRET.

I have received more information about *U-977* from Spain agency friends. In these files I have found much new information.

PART 1.
On *U-977* were six crewmembers of *U-262* (names withheld) from *U-262* and on board in Kiel first on 15 April 1945 and on 16 April 1945, *U-977* departed from Kiel to Frederikshaven, then Denmark and next port Horton, Norway. All six men of *U-262* on *U-977* and surrendered in Argentina 17 August 1945.

The six crewmembers of *U-262* had many war patrols with *U-262* in 1943 with Skipper Kapitänleutnant Heinz Franke (photo here) Knights Cross Holder; and in 1944 with Oberleutnant zur See Helmut Wieduwitt three war patrols and after November on *U-262* was Skipper Kapitänleutnant Heinz Laudahn; no more war patrols as *U-262* was a school boat.

In April 1945 these six crewmembers of *U-262* came to *U-977*, Kapitänleutnant Schäfer. All former six *U-262* crew members with Iron Cross First Class and Second Class, and with U-Boat Service Badge and Ubootfrontspange too.

PART 2.

In the Spain files **PIZZARRO** read report of one of former *U-977* radiomen; he was after the war in Spain in 1950 and he said in his report to Spain Agency much about *U-977*. He told me he has received short wave signals like signals from German U-Boats in the night 22 to 23 July 1945. In this time *U-977* passed the Brazilian island St. Paul. *U-977* passed this St. Paul Island only in distance of twenty miles off starboard and he told me in the night 24 to 25 July he received the last radio short waves like the '*handwriting*' of German U-Boats and Skipper Schäfer said that this possibly the boat of Meyer (*U-1055*) to South America.

> **EDITOR NOTE** – The official records state that *U-1055* was sunk on 30 April 1945 in a depth charge attack by US Navy planes of VPB.63 southwest of Ushant. If one looks at the file on *U-1107* we find that *U-1107* was sunk on 30 April 1945 in a depth charge attack by US Navy planes of VPB.63 southwest of Ushant. There's obviously an error in the reports and if we look at the facts, we realize that both boats were not sunk by the same planes at the same place at precisely the same moment. They did sink *U-1107* but *U-1055* is one of those whose final fate is unknown.....well, it is no longer unknown.

PART 3.

The radioman told that in this time near St. Paul Rocks, *U-977* has only 38 tons of oil (diesel fuel) and later in Argentina on 17 August 1945 only 5 tons of oil has *U-977*, not more. On *U-977* were ten torpedoes – four new

T-5 Zaukönig Torpedoes and six LUT Torpedoes and all newest torpedo pistols for the detonation.

PART 4.

The radioman told in Spain he has received on 2 May 1945 in Norway on *U-977* radio signal that Hitler is dead, fallen in Berlin. This was in afternoon 2 May 1945 in the Norway port Kristiansand and all crewmembers of *U-977* came on deck. On the conning tower the big Swastika Flag was set at half-mast and all crew members outstretched the arms in the last salute with flag salute. In this time on the conning towers of many U-Boats was a white painted slogan "*Lieber tot als Slave*".

Translation……….."*Better dead than slave*".

The last Flag Ceremony for Hitler's death he has seen on all boats and ships in Kristiansand.

PART 5.

Evening 2 May 1945 at 2200 hours in the evening *U-977* begins her last war patrol with order to coast of England using snorkel and submerged along the Norway coast, course north and later course west to England attack Grid.

In this time the L.I. (Engineering Officer) name ▇▇▇▇▇ gave report to Schäfer he has only 89 metric tons (diesel) oil and 3½ tons of Schwer-Schmieröl (heavy lubricating oil) on *U-977* and food for three months. At this the photo of Hitler was not more in the Officers' Room, only the photo of Dönitz.

All crewmembers think the war is not over and beginning new from Norway bases. In this time many hundreds U-Boats were in Norway and at sea, and there were many airplanes and approximately 1.6 million German soldiers were in Norway too.

Skipper Schäfer told the Engineering Officer ▇▇▇▇▇ that he was in Berlin and he has seen near Berlin the newest weapons and he thinks in the next weeks many of the newest weapons will be in Norway for the last fight and the war is not to end.

U-566 and more "Spook" Stuff .....off to Argentina

We learned from **DON ANGEL ALCAZAR de VELASCO (158-1985)** and later confirmed in many ways, that German cargo ships were in the harbor at Vigo, Spain to replenish U-Boats and also that U-Boats and other vessels departed from the little fishing village of Villa Garcia up the coast from Vigo.

Here is another email from **PIZZARRO** and it answers more questions. **PIZZARRO** sent photos, never seen before, of the crew of *U-566* being rescued by a Spanish fishing boat and there is a story with this. You will see the photos when we highlight *U-566*. Here is the news from **PIZZARRO**:

"This is in the KTB (logbook) of Dönitz, only a short note.

24 October 1943, the Spanish Naval Attaché reports by teletype that *U-566* was sunk by aircraft in about CG 2839. The entire crew was rescued by a Spanish fishing trawler (named *FINA*

from La Coruna) and brought to Vigo because this is a question of the shipwrecked men as *U-566* was in transit to the Mediterranean.

U-566 returning from earlier Feindfahrt. Note the crushed aft portion of the bridge.

In the later KTB of *U-566* we can read exact grid. Skipper Hornkohl wrote in last *U-566* KTB;
'Aircraft attack in Grid CG 2834, Catalina aircraft at 0127 hour in the morning of 24 October 1943.'

U-566 last radio with BdU was:
'Hard bomb hits, Grid CG 2834, no more diving and no more drive.'

U-566 crew in rubber boats coming toward fishing boat *FINA*

How does the sinking of *U-566* play into this history? Keep reading.

Rescued crew of *U-566* aboard *FINA*

PIZZARRO continues:

"MORE INFORMATION – This was 30 sm (statute miles) before the Spanish coast and Skipper Hornkohl sank his *U-566*. In the last KTB entry we read.....in Vigo Skipper Hornkohl has meeting with a Spanish Navy Commander and with the German Consul, and one officer of the German Naval Attaché in Madrid. This officer was Fregettenkapitän Lorek. After the war, Lorek went with his family to Argentina."

Fregettenkapitän Lorek

PIZZARRO continues to tell us about this officer.

This was a very important German Reich Naval Officer in Spain 1939 to 1945. He was a very important coordination officer in Spain for all German U-Boats provisioning in Spain for U-Boat supplies in Spain ports like El Ferrol or Cadiz, in the Muros Bay and in Vigo etc. Supplies with oil (diesel fuel), torpedoes, food and more from German ships in Spanish harbors. In some U-Boat KTBs you can read his name Lorek, but not in KTB of Dönitz.

Fregettenkapitän Lorek and his family were in Spain and after the war, all in Argentina. He was the most important officer in Spain for German U-Boats but I can find not many biography in German and nothing in books.

More on the 3rd U-Boat in the South Atlantic

PIZZARRO asked the radioman of *U-977* and he told me he picked up radio traffic "*Grenswellen*" from another U-Boat in beginning of July 1945 in Grid by Brazil island Fernando Noronha to South Atlantic but he has not the code key and he made this report to his U-Boat Commander Schäfer, and Schäfer said this is possibly another German U-Boat headed for South America and Schäffer said one name is possible; Meyer, but he did not say the U-Boat Number!!!

Possibly the name was Oberleutnant zur See Rudolf Meyer. He was 25 years old and Skipper of *U-1055*, Type VII-C. Meyer and *U-1055* was in April on his second patrol in North Atlantic and he is missing – no more radio after 23 April 1945.

His first patrol December 1944 to March 1945 was 53 days long. His second patrol beginning with the departure 5 April 1945 from U-Boat base Bergen, Norway to the grids near England coast and North Atlantic and so it is possible he has on his second patrol beginning April 1945 food for three months or more and his snorkel boat *U-1055* was filled with oil (diesel fuel). After the war the first information in 1947 was *U-1055* was sunk on 30 April 1945 in the Bay of Biscay west of Brest, France in approximate position 48° 00' N x 06° 30' W sunk by depth charges from US Catalina aircraft, but this was not right!

This aircraft attack was to *U-1107* (Parduhn) and this was a rubber stealth boat and it was this boat sunk, not *U-1055*. After last radio report, *U-1055* was not west of Brest so *U-1055* is missing today with a crew of 49 very young hands – all missing today.

U-880.......Another "Spook" Boat Headed South?

PIZZARRO goes on to tell us that *U-880* was the newest Type IX-C/40 and was in the shipyard in Kiel for twelve days over end of December 1944 into January 1945 for new equipment for a special war operation. What containers came on and into *U-880* ahead of the conning tower?

PIZZARRO – we do not have this answer; what will you tell us?

PIZZARRO poses the scenario that it did not make sense that special passengers would go aboard the old boat *U-518* that was commissioned in April 1942 and not the newest boat *U-880* which was commissioned May 1944. On board *U-880* was a doctor (Doctor Rosenbach) and also a Sanistäts (corpsman) Maat Kurt Lasch but on *U-518* ....no doctor and no Sanistäts Maat.

U-518 in Lorient in 1942

U-518 had a crew of 56, all were lost when the boat was sunk, but *U-880* had a smaller crew of 49 men including the doctor and corpsman. *U-880* had a strong officer contingent including Kapitänleutnant Gerhard Schötzau (the Skipper) plus three officers with the rank of Oberleutnant zur See – Uhde, Nieland and Flindhammer. In addition there was the doctor, the corpsman, two men at the position of Obersteuermann (helmsman/navigator), two Obermashinisten (chief machinists), one Oberfunkmeister (Chief Petty Officer, Radio) and several with the rank of Funkmaat (Petty Officer, Radio). So this was a very high ranking crew on *U-880* (photo below) but not on *U-518*.

With this question you can see that the story of *U-518* and last passengers in false and mid-tempo bullshit. **PIZZARRO** has reported more but said it must remain confidential. Okay, it is locked away in the vault.

CONCLUSIONS:

We have read solid proof that Germany was well entrenched in Argentina from the very early 20th Century and their involvement grew at an ever increasing rate as evidenced by the involvement of the German Navy and their attempts to take the Falkland Islands.

As the light cruiser **DRESDEN** made her escape through the Straits of Magellan, the wily Oberleutnant zur See Wilhelm Canaris took detailed notes of the hidden harbors along the way.

In 1938 the old line ship **SCHLESWIG-HOLSTEIN** went back through the Straits to update the data and we note that during World War Two, South America was rife with German agents and the headquarters was located in the heart of Buenos Aires.

When Canaris made his escape from Chile on horseback over the Andes and came upon the little village of San Carlos di Bariloche, he saw the value for a future time.

Kapitänleutnant Heinrich Garbers showed Martin Bormann, Großadmiral Karl Dönitz and others that is was a simple effort to smuggle people and anything else into the quiet coves along the Patagonian coast of Argentina where there either were no people in the area or the few people they would encounter would be staunch, patriotic Germans. At that point, Dönitz was heard to say:
   "We have found an impregnable Shangri-La for the Führer."

Did he mean San Carlos di Bariloche? We can never be certain, but it is most likely this is precisely what he meant since that is where Adolf Hitler lived from 1945 until 1955. At that time, the town grew in popularity as a resort area that it became necessary for Adolf and Eva to find other, more unpopulated areas and so they moved to Cordoba Province.

OTTO WERMUTH – Submarine Commander; Sharkhunters Member #1344

Over the years he was in Membership, Captain **WERMUTH** and I wrote back and forth. In one letter I asked if they carried any cargo and I asked if they met with a Japanese submarine to transfer personnel and goods.

Here is one of the more important of his letters as pertain to this subject. This is the translation of his 13 July 1990 letter:

Dear Mr. Cooper,
First I would like to thank you heart-fully for sending me your KTB Issue and for honoring me as an Honor Member.
   In response to your question, I can clearly and truthfully assure you that:
   U-530 carried no deadweight when she left Kiel on 19 February, 45 on her last journey. She arrived on 10 July 45 in Argentinean Mar del Plata with no silver or uranium on boats.
   U-530 also did not have a meeting with the Japanese I-52.
   With this statement, I hope to have been able to help you. And remain with best regards.

Much of this letter is opposite of what we know as fact. For instance:
*   *U-530* did carry cargo - that is fact;
*   Silver or uranium on board – probably not but there was cargo;
*   *U-530* did indeed meet with a Japanese submarine in the central Atlantic – that is fact.

The first and obvious one might draw is that **WERMUTH** is a liar. That is absolutely NOT the case. Over the years that I have dealt with German veterans and officers of the war, I have found that their honor and honesty was always above reproach. So why the discrepancy? Keep reading.

Otto Wermuth

Ludwigstr.4

7080 Aalen/Wttbg.

Herrn   den 13.7.90

Harry Cooper

SHARKHUNTERS

P.O.Box 1539

www.sharkhunters.com

Hernando, Fl 3344?

Sehr geehrter Herr Cooper,

ich darf mich zuerst für die Zusendung Ihrer
KTB-Ausgaben und die Auszeichnung,Ehrenmitglied
zu sein,recht herzlich bedanken.
Zur Beantwortung Ihrer Frage kann ich ganz eindeu-
tig und wahrheitsgemäss feststellen:

"U 530" hatte auf seiner letzten Feindfahrt von
19.2.45 auslaufend aus Kiel bis 10.7.45 einlaufend
in argentinischen Mar del Plata keine Zuladung,
also weder Silber noch Uran an Bord.

"U 530" hatte in dieser Zeit auch kein Treffen
mit dem japanischen I-52.

Ich hoffe Ihnen mit dieser Aussage gedient zu
haben und verbleibe

                        mit freundlichen Grüssen

                        [signature] Otto Wermuth

Based on our experience and knowledge of the German officer Corps, it is inconceivable that **WERMUTH** was telling a deliberate lie. However, we have also learned that when a German military man, especially an officer, swore an oath – nothing would drag it out of him or change his comments. Therefore, based on this and also from the interviews conducted with Captain **WERMUTH** by S.E.I.G. Agent **PIZZARRO**, we must conclude that he had sworn an oath not to divulge anything of that last patrol and would take it with him to the grave, as so many did.

If you will remember the interview conducted by **PIZZARRO** (look back to page 251 this book) and you note that when the questions were getting to be more than **WERMUTH** wanted to deal with – as **PIZZARRO** said:
"Wermuth smiled and said no more."

That smile and silence speaks volumes. We had similar experience when tracking down details pertaining to *Operation "URSULA"*, the secret combat operations of the U-Bootwaffe in the Spanish Civil War in 1936. Nobody would say anything until **PETER HANSEN (251-LIFE-1987)** gave us the entire story, naming the Skippers, crew and mission. We then reported all these details in our KTB Magazine and with that issue in his hand, Captain **MATTIAS BRÜNIG (1943-LIFE-1991)** showed this to a friend of his who had been awarded the Spanish Cross in Gold. His friend had always refused to tell **BRÜNIG** how he earned this medal until he was show the article in our KTB Magazine. He smiled and said that as long as it was now known, he could confirm the story.

The same is most likely true with **WERMUTH**. If he swore an oath which we believe he did, nothing was going to make him reveal what he swore to keep secret. Certain facts are true and his denial does not change things, but it also does not make **WERMUTH** a liar. He swore an oath and he kept it, in the tradition of the utmost honor of a German officer.

We have already read the content of the surrender document signed by the proper personal on the surrender of *U-530* and her crew when they came into Mar del Plata. You see the actual document itself on the next page.

/3

U B E R G E B U N G S A K T E

www.sharkhunters.com

In Mar del Plata, den 10 Juli, übergibt der Kommandant des deutschen Unterseeboots "U 530", Oberleutnant zur See OTTO WERMUTH, be-
dingungslos dem Kommandanten der argentinischen Kriegsmarine, Fre-
gattenkapitän JULIO C. MALLEA das Schiff unterseinem Befehl und die
Besatzung desselben nach anliegender Liste.

Del oberleutnant zur See, OTTO WERMUTH, bestätigt, dass dasUn-
terseeboot "U 530", dessen Besatzung ausgeschifft worden ist, sich
im schwimmsicherem Zustande befindet; dass der einzigste Explosiv-
stoff an Bord, sich in einem Torpedogegecntskopf befindet, dessen Ge
fechtspistole entfernt worden ist und dass sich kein Element oder
Vorrichtung im Boot befindet, um das Schiff zu versenken oder ganz
oder teilweise zu beschädigen.

Diese Akte, mit einliengender Besatzungsliste, wird in vier
Exemplaren in spanischer und deutscher Sprache angefestigt.

Der sapnische Text wird als der einzig Gültige angesehen.-Er
wird von den argentinischen und deutschen Kommandanten unterzeichnet

Mar del Plata, den 10 Juli,1945.

Fdo: OTTO WERMUTH			Fdo: JULIO C. MALLEA
Oberleutnant zur See-Otto		Fregattenkapitän Julio C.Mallea
Wermuth-Kommandant des			Kommandant der argentinischen
"U 530"					erseebootsdivision.-

Facts and Conclusions

After reading our previous book "***Hitler in Argentina***" it is impossible to believe the tired old propaganda that Hitler and his wife Eva Braun committed suicide in the Führerbunker in Berlin. Only a fool could still believe that tired, old and worn out story.

The Foundation for the Escapes

Even the most die-hard, concrete-headed (**PETER HANSEN**'s favorite term) has to realize, after reading this book, that not only Adolf Hitler and Eva Braun-Hitler escaped to South America, but so did Martin Bormann and thousands of others – all thanks to the foundation that was laid over the past one hundred years with the secret alliance that Germany had with various South American countries.

Anyone who cannot see this most likely still lays out cookies and milk on Christmas Eve for a fat guy in a red suit that will squeeze his 60 inch girth down a 4 inch chimney while carrying a bag full of toys.

About the Author

Born and raised in Chicago and the western suburbs, Harry Cooper joined the US Air Force right out of high school. After six months intensive training is special weapons (hydrogen bombs) at Lowry Air Force Base (Denver) he was mis-assigned to Chanute Air Force only 100 miles from his home. To his very good luck, he was assigned to the base swimming pool as a lifeguard, working one day on and one day off, making it easy to go home every second day. When the summer ended, he was transferred to an active base and was assigned to the 98th Bomb Wing at Lincoln Air Force Base just outside Lincoln, Nebraska.

After spending two and a half years working with special weapons and since he always wanted to be a fighter pilot, he applied for Officer Candidate School as he neared his 21st birthday. He was the only one of 30 who passed the tough two-day long battery of tests and he was assigned an OCS class. His pilot's physical gave him a clean slate to fly, but luck was not with him. The Air Force was so overloaded with pilots from World War II and Korea that Air Cadets was shut down. He could be an officer but not a pilot. That is not what he wanted.

He was then honorably discharged from the Air Force and went to college where he earned his BS in Business Administration and began his career in the Chicago area. Since he could not enter aerial combat, he chose the next best thing – he went into auto racing! He first tried his hand at drag

racing and while driving for a friend, he was Class Champion 11 times out of 22 – pretty good. But the following year, he drove his own car and out of the next 26 weeks, he was Class Champion 26 times and Little Stock Eliminator four times, setting some national records along the way.

Then his heart turned to the oval tracks and after three successful years at the short tracks around Chicago, where he was a racing news sportscaster on the "*Motorsports International*" television show, he moved up to the big tracks (photo prev. page) racing against A. J. Foyt, the Unser Brothers, Johnny Rutherford and other great racers. He was a Feature Editor at *Stock Car Racing Magazine* during his racing years doing '*behind the wheel*' racing reports as well as monthly columns for major American and Australian racing magazines and was an executive for a Chicago firm.

Things changed drastically for him in 1976. His crew chief left for a job in the normal world, his assistant crew chief quit to open his own auto parts store and his best crew member quit to join the Air Force. While running the 1976 Texas 500 in the lead pack, his engine blew! On the

way back to Chicago, the engine in the transporter truck blew. It was not a good sign. The final straw was when he got to the office the next day and found that his superior had left the company and his new boss was a corporate executive for whom Harry had no respect. Time for a change!

It really was time for a major change so Harry sold everything, bought a 30-foot sailing yacht and went to live the quiet life in the Florida Keys and the Bahamas. This was to change his life and in fact, the history of the War At Sea itself. It was there he became interested in the U-Bootwaffe.

While cruising in the southern Bahamas, Harry stopped at a strange island that had been a working plantation during the war years. There were the ruins of a mansion atop a hill, the remains of a barracks building and a radio shack nearby. The caretaker told him that a few German U-Boats had stopped there for fresh water during the war. That put the hook in Harry and once he returned to Chicago, he began to intensively research the U-Boat portion of WW II and has become the world's preeminent expert on the subject.

Returning to the business world, he became Regional Vice President for a major company in Chicago but founded Sharkhunters in 1983. By mid-1987, he realized that it would be impossible to keep a regular job and then spend all the time necessary to contact the veterans, dig in the files, visit the veterans to interview them and all the other tasks necessary to preserving this history honestly. He made a tough decision.

On a Friday in July, he turned in the keys to his six offices around Illinois and quit his high-paying executive job, just two weeks after getting a nice raise in salary. His wife of just two years was most surprised with this decision and even more surprised (maybe even shocked) to learn that they were moving to Florida to do this research full time and at no salary. She was not convinced at all, since they were to have their first child in less than four months and now there was no insurance, no security - but this had to be done!

Fortunately, it succeeded and Sharkhunters has the great distinction of being the only real source for the history of the WW II U-Bootwaffe.

Harry is a LIFE member of the Adventurer's Club in Chicago (former Editor of the newsletter), member of the Chicago Press Club and the International Press Club of Chicago. He wrote more than a dozen books, helped produce several television productions and escorted dozens of history tours around the world.

Harry is listed in "*Who's Who in America*" as well as in "*Who's Who of American Business Leaders*" and in 2006 was nominated as "*Man of the Year*" by the American Biographical Institute. He spent twelve years with the United States Coast Guard (Aux.) achieving the position of Flotilla Commander with a rank similar to a full Lieutenant. With this research, Harry has met and become friends with most of the surviving Skippers, many of the officers and crewmen from the U-Bootwaffe as well as
American sub vets and world leaders from the US, the former Soviet Union and modern day Russia.

About Sharkhunters

Founded in February 1983, Sharkhunters International is the first, the best and the only accurate and official source of published history on the U-Bootwaffe. The reason is simple; the data not only comes from official files and documents but it also comes from the memories of those who lived this war. The top Skippers, many of the officers and crewmen of the U-Bootwaffe were participating Members as were a great many Allied personnel including the four *Medal of Honor* American submarine Skippers of the war.

Fluckey	O'Kane	Ramage	Street
(2169-1992)	(1540-1990)	(948-1989)	(2448-1992)

Many other great men were Members of Sharkhunters including these;

Kretschmer	Topp	Hardegen	Hess
(122-1985)	(118-19985)	(102-1985)	(125-1985)

RONALD REAGAN (1858-1991) was a Sharkhunters Member from 1991 until his passing.

Let us send a complimentary copy of our **KTB** Magazine for your inspection. Send an email to us at **sharkhunters@earthlink.net**, tell us your name (first & last); by return email, you'll be reading our **KTB** Magazine.

Sharkhunters '*Patrols*' and '*Expeditions*'

In addition to publishing the most historically accurate information on the history of the U-Bootwaffe and the men who fought the war on both sides, Sharkhunters also organizes tours to many historic places for our Members. For instance:

Bunker Patrol from Berlin east to Warsaw.

Destroyed HQ of the OKW   Abandoned fortress in Poland

Gun bunker overlooking the Baltic   Wolfsschanze (Wolf's Lair)

Sharkhunters does not merely use files and documents in our research but we go to the places where this history took place. We videotape, shoot still photos and we walk in the footsteps of history. During this '*Patrol*' we slept in the SS officers' barracks at Hitler's Wolfsschanze, the (Wolf's Lair), where the assassination attempt was made on Hitler in 1944. Sharkhunters was there.

The Southern Redoubt/Fortress Area

The Allies feared the leaders of the Reich would make a desperate last ditch stand in the Bavarian Alps at the Obersalzberg with its bunkers, tunnels and fortifications, some of which are still undiscovered today.

 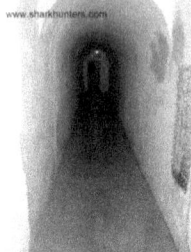 

| Coal bunkers | Hitler's tunnel | Göring's bunker entrance |

Go to our website www.sharkhunters.com and click Previous Tours

Northern Germany

At the U-Boat Memorial   **The Skipper at the Periscope**

With the veterans   **At the submarine *U-995***

What the Allies Called the "Ratline"

Thousands of important men of the Third Reich escaped Germany in various ways but almost all of them departed from places like Villagarcia in Spain aboard tramp steamers, large wooden sailing ships and in some cases, by U-Boat. To replenish fresh water and food (pigs, goats & turtles) they could stop at Trindade.

Ready to leave the ship by chopper

Northern plateau; radio tower #2

Ruins on the southern plateau where radio tower #1 was built.

Special thanks to the Brazilian Navy for their tremendous help in making this expedition possible. Their ships, their personnel and their Navy were absolutely top notch. We could not have made this exploration to Trindade without them. Obrigado!

The Relocated Third Reich in Argentina

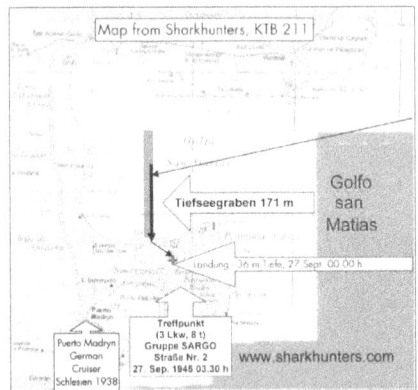

The Reich knew Golfo San Mathias very well before, during and after World War Two

Singing the old German military songs in a quiet restaurant in a little town deep in the Argentine wilderness

Sharkhunters goes where the history was made. We talk to the people who made this history; we talk to those who watched it happen; we talk to children of the people involved and we shoot our own photographs for the most accurate details possible. Much more information is released in the 2nd book in the Hitler Escape Series entitled "*The Secret Alliance*". It is the story of the long relationship between Germany and Argentina.

The Reich Moves to South America
And our Sharkhunters "*Patrols*" follow them.....

.....to an island in the southern Atlantic vacated by Brazil in 1939 for the use of the Kriegsmarine in the early stages of the war then again at the end of the war for two years after, including this radio facility built in 1939.

1939 German photo

2009 photo by the author

Who lived here in Argentina?

In this manor house?

In this eerie hotel?

We know the answers to these questions because our Sharkhunters groups have been here. You may join Sharkhunters for any of our expeditions; check the website for details. You may also read all about the move by the leaders of the Reich to this area in our book "*Hitler in Argentina*" which is also available from Sharkhunters. Check the website for details and click on "*Previous Tours*". Our web address is below on every page.

What Else From Sharkhunters?

We do more here at Sharkhunters – much more. Log onto our website at
www.sharkhunters.com and see all that is featured there – such as:

- Books – many more books are listed;
- DVDs – almost 200 different titles covering:
    Combat action on land – tanks, artillery, infantry,
    aerial combat – much from gun cameras,
    submarine warfare of several countries,
    personal interviews with many WW II veterans,
    great films by Sharkhunters Member **LENI RIEFENSTAHL,**
    different looks at life before the war as well as during
    training films to fly various USAAF fighters and bombers,
    much more………….take a moment to check them out

- Hand signed, limited edition fine art prints
- Hand signed photographs of veterans
- CDs of music of the war years – German, Russian etc.
- CDs of interviews with WW II U-Boat Skippers
- History Tours to places of great interest.
Many of the places Sharkhunters visits are not open to the general public.

Naturally you will read all the details on becoming a Member of
Sharkhunters – receiving a free hand signed photo of a veteran,
our **KTB** Magazine ten times annually, discounts on any items
offered by Sharkhunters and you will see all about our:
Sharkhunters '*Patrols*'…..you can join us in Germany,
France, Austria, Argentina, Chile and any of the other
fascinating places we go AND into places off limits to
everyone else. Check the website.

Other Great Books from Sharkhunters

"Hitler In Argentina"

"*Hitler in Argentina*" relates the historically accurate escape of Hitler, Eva Braun, Martin Bormann and many other high ranking figures of the Third Reich with top secret Abwehr and Kriegsmarine charts as well as files from the OSS, FBI and various other Intel organizations.

This book is the faithful transcription of a letter from a man, a Sharkhunters Member, who was a World War Two German agent and a smuggler of "*special*" people. He even had a code name. This was Don Angel Alcazar de Velasco and he told us how he helped Hitler's second in command, Martin Bormann, safely to Argentina - and how he met with Hitler again in 1952.

He reported that the dead "*Hitler*" was a double and that he personally saw the real Hitler forcibly drugged by orders of Martin Bormann and removed from the Führerbunker. We checked him out thoroughly and found him to be exactly who he said he was. This information, combined with hundreds of files from the United States National Archives, from other Intelligence Agencies and from "*Spooks*" of various countries makes this story absolutely factual.

Through our further research and personal visits by Sharkhunters Founder and President Harry Cooper has further proved this to be accurate. In 2008 and again in 2009 Cooper was at the estate where Hitler lived in Patagonia from 1945 until 1955 then to the hotels he frequented in Cordoba until his passing in the early 1960's.

Order this book today and learn real history.

Other Great Books from Sharkhunters

"Hitler and the Secret Alliance"

"We shall never forget, nor be able to repay, the immense debt of gratitude we owe to our comrades of the German Army."

This was part of a speech made by General Juan Perón – on 4 April **1952**! What was the connection between the Third Reich and the Argentine strongman? It's in this book.

The European conflict of World War Two ended in early May 1945, but not all Germans remained to suffer their fate at the hands of the victorious and in many cases, the brutal Allies. There were thousands of high ranking Party members, SS officers, spies, agents, scientists, engineers and all manner of the elite of the Reich who escaped the crumbled Europe in favor of a fresh start in South America, primarily Argentina.

In this book, researcher Michael Ivinheim reveals what his exhaustive researcher has discovered about the *"Black Boats"* that figure prominently into the history – not the **END** of the Third Reich but the *RELOCATION* of the Third Reich. This book tears away the veil of secrecy of the history of what really happened to the Third Reich.

This book will open your eyes!

Order this book as a companion to *"Hitler in Argentina."*

Other Great Books from Sharkhunters

"U-BOAT!" (volume I)

In the **"U-BOAT!"** series, each and every volume is jam-packed with the combat memories of the men who fought the Battle of the Atlantic from all sides. You will read history and see photos available nowhere else.

"The pages of **"U-BOAT!"** (vol. I) are fascinating reading. They tell the gripping stories of the war at sea in the words of those who lived and died in submarines and from those who hunted submarines. That old enemies have become friends is the real story of this book. None could have thought that many decades ago that this book could be published or that such mortal enemies would relate the grim stories of the war in a book written together.

I found these stories of great interest and recommend them to those who would like to know how the war was fought at sea. It should be remembered the life of Britain and Germany depended on the outcome of the U-Boat conflict. This book reveals how this battle took place scene by scene, and the courage and bravery of the men who participated on both sides. I recommend its reading as a reminder never to get enveloped in such a conflict again."

Admiral **Frank Kelso**, CNO and Sharkhunters Member.

Read memories of Kretschmer, Dönitz, Topp, Hardegen and many other Skippers and crews. You won't find this history anywhere else.

Other Great Books from Sharkhunters

"U-BOAT!" (volume II)

"**U-BOAT!**" (vol. II) continues the fascinating tale of the German U-Bootwaffe in World War Two as well as some stories from the American side – and sadly, one of the most barbaric acts of atrocity perpetrated in any war.

These stories come directly from the memories of the men who fought in this greatest of all conflicts and there is no better or more accurate history than that which comes directly from the warriors who made this history. This book is their story and is an extension of "**U-BOAT!**" (vol. I). Come with us on a journey into the greatest conflict the world has ever known.

You'll read wartime memories from:

- Dönitz
- Thäter *U-466*
- Wattenberg *U-162*
- *AVISO GRILLE*
- Italian submarine *FINZI*
- Clandestine supply in the Caribbean to U-Boats?
- *HMS VALIANT*
- The Enemy Below
- The "*Rot Teufelboot*"
- Radiostation Atlantik
- Operation *URSULA*
  Combat long before 1939

- End of *SS SANDEMITRO*
- R-Boats across Europe
- Death of *AWA MARU*
- *SURCOUF* –French giant
- The Type IX U-Boat
- Former Mortal Enemies
- USN "*Armed Guard*"
- *U-DEUTSCHLAND*
- WW I, the Royal Navy and the German Navy
- Pirates - Uncle Sam's Navy
- *SS JEAN NICOLETTE*
  Butchery on the high seas

Other Great Books from Sharkhunters
"U-BOAT!" (volume III)

"U-BOAT!" (vol. III) continues the fascinating tale of the German U-Bootwaffe in World War Two as well as some stories from the American side with more first-person memories of the war at sea.

This book is their continuing story and is an extension of "U-BOAT!" (vol. I and vol. II). Come with us on a journey into the greatest conflict the world has ever known.

In this book you will read wartime memories from great warriors including:

- The code for Fähnrich
- Erich Topp *U-552*
- Harry Cooper
- *U-DEUTSCHLAND*
- Werner Hartenstein *U-156*
- French Submarine History
- American U-Boat Captive
- A Brit in USN Submarines
- Fregettenkapitän Norden
- Paukenschlag off Capetown
- Axis Sally
- Sink the *RIO GRANDE*
- *SS BARKDULL*
- "*Silent*" Otto Kretschmer
- Sinking of the *BERTA*
- Italian Navy Submarines
- Antarctica
- Shinjo Uchino and *I-8*
- The "*Drumbeater*"
- Helmut Schmoeckel *U-802*

- The mysterious voyage of *U-977* and the so-called 66 days marching submerged
- Cape Fear
- loss of the aircraft carrier *USS BLOCK ISLAND*
- the "*Tethered Goats*" meant to draw kamikaze pilots to a needless death

"With the reminiscences of Topp, Kretschmer, Dönitz, Hardegen and others who fought against us with some who were on our side, we are getting the accurate picture of the men who bore the burden and gave it their all."

Captain **Edward L. Beach**
Sharkhunters Member #**1163-1989**

Other Great Books from Sharkhunters
"U-BOAT!" (volume IV)

"**U-BOAT!**" (vol. IV) continues the fascinating tale of the German U-Bootwaffe in World War Two as well as some stories from the American side with more first-person memories of the war at sea.

This book is their continuing story and is an extension of "**U-BOAT!**" (vols. I, II and III). Come with us on a journey into the greatest conflict the world has ever known.

In this book you will read wartime memories from more great warriors including:

- *U-234* and her living cargo of scientists and high rank Luftwaffe personnel
- Newfoundland as an "*Aircraft carrier*" and *HMCS CARIBOU*
- Reinhard Hardegen *U-123*
- The Golden Gate in '48
- New England's U-Boat War
- Monsunboote
- The 212 Class submarine
- The "*Slender Thread*" of German and Japanese cooperation in the war
- Shelling of Lago refinery on the island Aruba by *U-156*
- Werner Hartenstein *U-156*

- Gerhard Thäter and *U-466*; through Gibraltar TWICE!
- Midgets and Chariots – the story of the Italian small boat special operations men
- Was it really such a "*Happy Time*"?
  "*Silent*" Otto Kretschmer gives us his impression of this time

Other Great Books from Sharkhunters
"U-BOAT!" (volume V)

"**U-BOAT!**" (vol. V) continues the fascinating tale of the German U-Bootwaffe in World War Two as well as some stories from the American side with more first-person memories of the war at sea.

This book is their continuing story and is an extension of "**U-BOAT!**" (vols. I, II, III and IV). Come with us on a journey into the greatest conflict the world has ever known.

In this book you will read wartime memories from great warriors including:

- POW's from *U-66* aboard *USS BLOCK ISLAND*
- Aboard *U-764*; coward?
- Death of *U-654*
- *SS BENJAMIN BOURNE*
- Capture of *HMS SEAL*
- *"Battle of Bowmanville"*
- *U-960* in September 1943
- Helmut Witte *U-159*
- Jürgen Oesten *U-861*
- Art Jacobson, Merchant
- Günther Gräser
- Skipper of *U-81* and *U-513*
- Could the V-2 win the war?
- Eisenhower's Starvation Camps – more than one million starved to death
- More Secrets of *U-234*
- Aboard *USS GRAYLING*

- U-Boat operations off Aruba and Curacao
- *USS QUEENFISH* attacks and sinks *AWA MARU*
- Last Patrol of *U-3030*
- The Type IX U-Boat

Helmut Witte

"Rise and Fall of the U-Bootwaffe"

Germany was designing and building U-Boats in secret long before the outbreak of the Second World War. They had false companies set up in other European countries under cooperation between Krupp's Germania Werft and the German Navy, not yet called the Kriegsmarine. Various world navies placed orders with these shell companies for submarines and the German submarine industry learned.

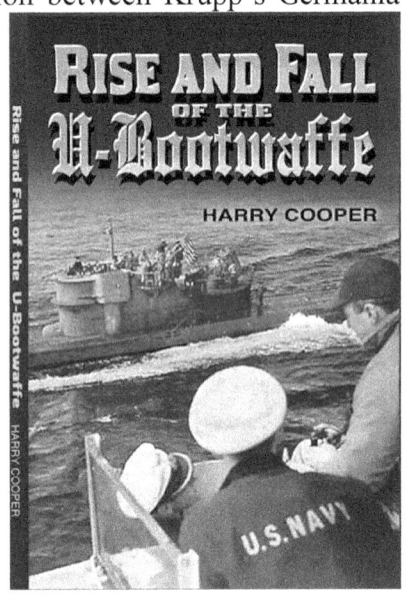

German U-Boats were in combat and sinking ships some three years before World War Two began! In this book you will read the actual oath these U-Bootfahrer swore for their secret missions – and you will walk through the modified *U-234* with her secret cargo of scientists, technicians, a Luftwaffe general with his staff as well as high tech weaponry...........and uranium.

Ursula Dönitz Hessler

Insights by Großadmiral Karl Dönitz are in this book as well as Germany's aid to Generalissimo Franco in the Spanish Civil War during the operation named for the daughter of Dönitz.

Why was Germany vigorously involved in building U-Boats in contravention to the edicts of the brutal Treaty of Versailles? How was it kept secret from the rest of the world? Why did Germany enter World War Two so poorly prepared for submarine warfare and what contributed to her loss? The answers are in this book.

Other Great Books from Sharkhunters
"When Eagles Soared!" (vol I & 2)

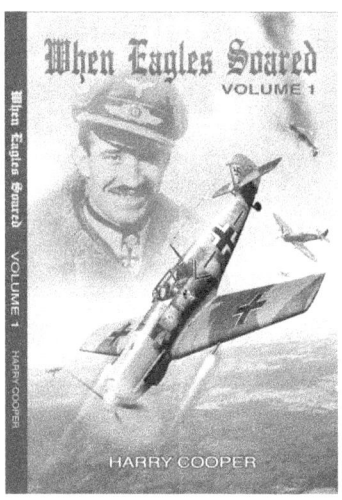

These were the *"Golden Knights"* of the skies in World War Two. They slipped the chains of gravity and soared high above the earth on their wings and dreams. Some returned covered in glory – many did not return at all.

There books contain first person memories of Luftwaffe pilots, American pilots, Royal Air Force and Royal Navy pilots – fliers of many nations are included here as well as some technological insights into the planes, the powerplants and the weaponry they carried.

Some memories will make you ache to turn back the clock to those days of glory – some will bring a tear to your eye for a brave flier who did not return while a few will make you all but collapse with laughter!

There are stories of the war that you've never read; hundreds of photos many of which you have never seen; stories from the greatest fighter pilots of all time and really funny memories of some very strange planes.

Strap on your parachute and helmet, climb into your P-38, your Me 109, your La-5 or whatever is your favorite warbird and fly along with us on this mission back into military aviation history and memories.

These men will never come our way again; this kind of man vs. man combat in the skies has faded into history forever. Relive it in this book.

Other Great Books from Sharkhunters

"Kassel 1939"
"The First Warrior's Convention of Greater Germany"

Germany and Austria had just reunited during the *"Anschluß"* forming "Großdeutschland" or Greater Germany and there was great pride in this accomplishment. The city of Kassel hosted the first Greater German Reich Warriors' gathering on the weekend of 2 – 4 June 1939. Hundreds of thousands of soldiers came from all parts of the Reich on more than 120 special trains and hundreds of thousands citizens swelled the group to more than half a million. Kettles of one thousand liters each dished out three hundred sixty thousand meals daily – this was a demonstration of power!

Germany was destroyed – devastated, broken and helpless under the victorious Allied powers after World War One and Germany was allowed only a token military. By 1939 however, Germans held their head up proudly – they had their dignity back!

Return with us now to a time when national pride and patriotism was at its zenith in Germany as well as in many other nations. The Reich was forged in a fire never before witnessed in the civilized world.

This book is a compilation of 100 rare photos of this massive event that haven't been seen since the end of World War Two. One of our European Members found these extremely rare photos and sent them to us for this book. It is pure history!

Other Great Books from Sharkhunters
"Rare U-BOAT Types"

The U-Bootwaffe of the Kriegsmarine had the largest submarine Force ever in history, before or since World War Two.

The Types VII and Type IX with all of their variants are well known, and there were hundreds of these Types built. They cruised the world's oceans with great success and will be the subject of other books in the near future.

In this book we look at U-Boats that were produced in limited numbers as well as boats that the Kriegsmarine thought about, planned, built and experimented with, including some that were far advanced for their time. They were quickly scooped up by the victorious Allies and went to the USA, to England and to the Soviet Union for testing and evaluation.

This book tells about those rare Types and included photos of the boats and the Skippers, some never seen before, as well as Turmabzeichen (conning tower emblems) along with the dates of launch, commissioning, their final fates as well as any ships they sank during their career.

This book gives details of the rare U-Boats Types like no other before. We know of no other book that gives all this history.

Keep checking our website www.sharkhunters.com as we are coming out with a few new books each year............facts and history that you can't get anywhere else. This all came from the veterans themselves.

Send an email to sharkhunters@earthink.net with your name and we will send the current issue of our **KTB** Magazine to you by return email at no charge or obligation.

DVDs of History

In addition to great books of history, Sharkhunters has also made available DVDs of history. Many of our DVDs come from the veterans themselves. Go to **www.sharkhunters.com** then click **DVDs** for full information and in many cases, for short clips of the DVD.

DVD-4   DVD-5   DVD-6

DVD-8   DVD-11   DVD-12   DVD-14

DVD-15   DVD-16   DVD-17   DVD-18

More Great DVDs of History

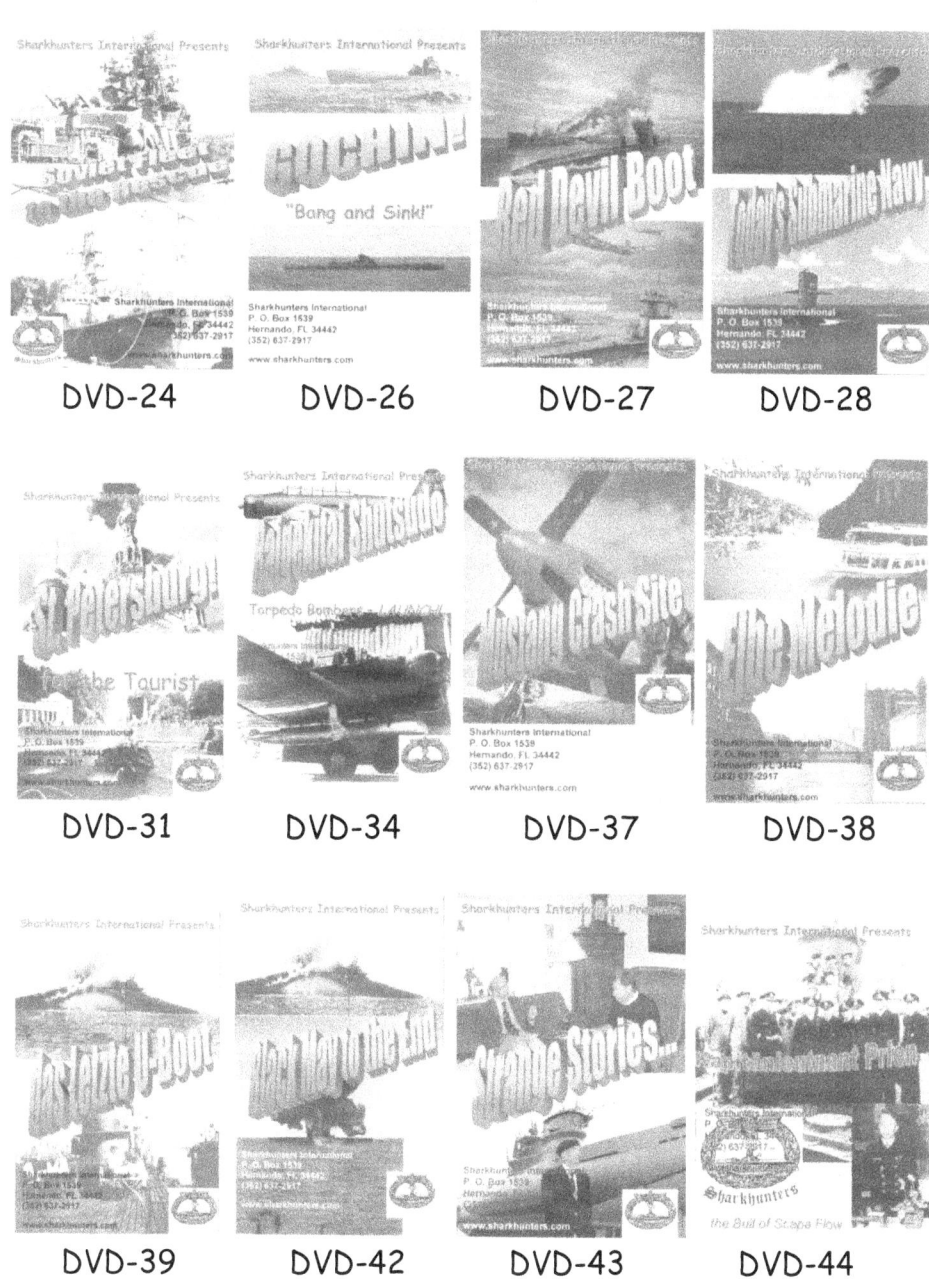

| DVD-24 | DVD-26 | DVD-27 | DVD-28 |

| DVD-31 | DVD-34 | DVD-37 | DVD-38 |

| DVD-39 | DVD-42 | DVD-43 | DVD-44 |

More Great DVDs of History
You Can't Find Anywhere Else

DVD-4   The story of *U-995* in the Kriegsmarine and Norwegian Navy

DVD-5   The lost bunker with three Type XXI boats still inside

DVD-6   Günther Prien and his triumphant entry into Berlin

DVD-8   **KARL-FRIEDERICH MERTEN** and *U-68*

DVD-11 Castles of the SS

DVD-12 Tunnels of the Third Reich

DVD-14 Triumph of the Will

DVD-15 U-Boats in Combat

DVD-16 Combat at Sea

DVD-17 Dive and Discovery of "*U-WHO*"?

DVD-18 Visit the Soviet Union 1991

DVD-24 Soviet Fleet to the Rescue

DVD-26 *GOCHIN!* Ride along aboard *I.10* on her 4th war patrol

DVD-27 Red Devil Boot – Ride along with **ERICH TOPP** and *U-552*

DVD-28 Today's Submarine Navy; run to the recruiter

DVD-31 St. Petersburg for the Tourist; a magnificent city

DVD-34 Raigekitai Shutsudo

DVD-37 Mustang Crash Site. The war ends in a Florida swamp

DVD-38 Elbe Melodie – beautiful German tourism film

DVD-39 Das Letzte U-Boot; the story of *U-234*

DVD-42 Black May to the End; Hans-Georg Hess tells of the end

DVD-43 Strange Stories; more from Hans-Georg Hess

DVD-44 Kapitänleutnant Prien; story of the "*Bull of Scapa Flow*"

DVD-46 Interview with **HANS GÖBELER** of the crew of *U-505*

DVD-47 Interview with **GERD RICHTER** of the crew of *U-81*

DVD-48 Interview with **DETLEV ZIMMERMANN** of *U-315*

DVD-49 Champagne in the Combat Boot; riotously funny!

DVD-50 1994 Interview with **ERICH TOPP** (*U-57, U-552*)

DVD-52 1994 Interview **REINHARD HARDEGEN** (*U-147, U-123*)

DVD-53 Secrets of the Third Reich

DVD-54 1994 Interview with **GERD THÄTER** (*U-466, U-3506*)

DVD-56 1994 Interview with **OTTO KRETSCHMER** (*U-23, U-99*)

DVD-58 1994 Interview with **HANS-GEORG HESS** (*U-995*)

More Great DVDs of History
Check the website for full details

DVD-46

DVD-47

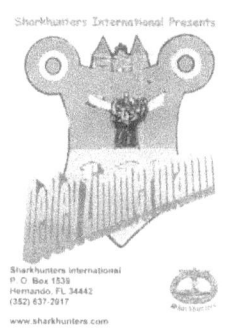
DVD-48

DVD-49

DVD-50

DVD-52

DVD-53

DVD-54

DVD-56

DVD-58

DVD-59

DVD-60

More Great DVDs of History
Rare – and Full of Action

| DVD-63 | DVD-64 | DVD-65 | DVD-66 |

| DVD-68 | DVD-69 | DVD-70 | DVD-72 |

| DVD-73 | DVD-74 | DVD-76 | DVD-78 |

More Great DVDs of History
And Your Satisfaction is Guaranteed!

DVD-59   The Red Baron; story of von Richtofen

DVD-60   Interview with **JÜRGEN OESTEN**

DVD-63   Wreck of "*U-WHO?*" Revisited

DVD-64   2000 Interview with **WILHELM GRAP** (*U-506*)

DVD-65   Germany Special

DVD-66   2000 Interview with **JÜRGEN OESTEN**

DVD-68   2000 Interview with **GÜNTHER HEINRICH** (*U-960*)

DVD-69   Katoh Hayabusa Sentatoi

DVD-70   2000 Interview **HELMUT SCHMOECKEL** (*U-802*)

DVD-72   2000 Interview **GERD THÄTER** (*U-466, U-3506*)

DVD-73   Capture of *U-505* on the high seas

DVD-74   2000 Interview with **HANS-GEORG HESS** (*U-995*)

DVD-76   2000 Interview **HORST von SCHROETER** (*U-123*)

DVD-78   2000 Interview with **KURT DIGGINS** (*U-458*)

DVD-80   2000 Interview with **VOLKMAR KÖNIG** (*U-99*)

DVD-81   Rover Boys Express; shot down over Japan

DVD-82   2000 Interview with **HARRY COOPER**

DVD-85   Germany by Rail; a wonderful touristic trip

DVD-86   Westernfront! Pure combat action

DVD-87   Corregidor Sogogeki; All our assault on Corregidor

DVD-88   Sensuikan Ito Go

DVD-89   die Grauen Wolfe; More combat at sea

DVD-92   Rhine Cruise; another great touristic look to Germany

DVD-93   Song of My Comrades; Japanese submariners

DVD-94   Eva Braun Home Movies – in color

DVD-98   der Rote Faden; the Red Thread Around Hamburg

DVD-100 Wehrmacht in Combat – 1; pure combat action

DVD-101 Wehrmacht in Combat – 2; more incredible combat

More Great DVDs of History
Check the website for special prices

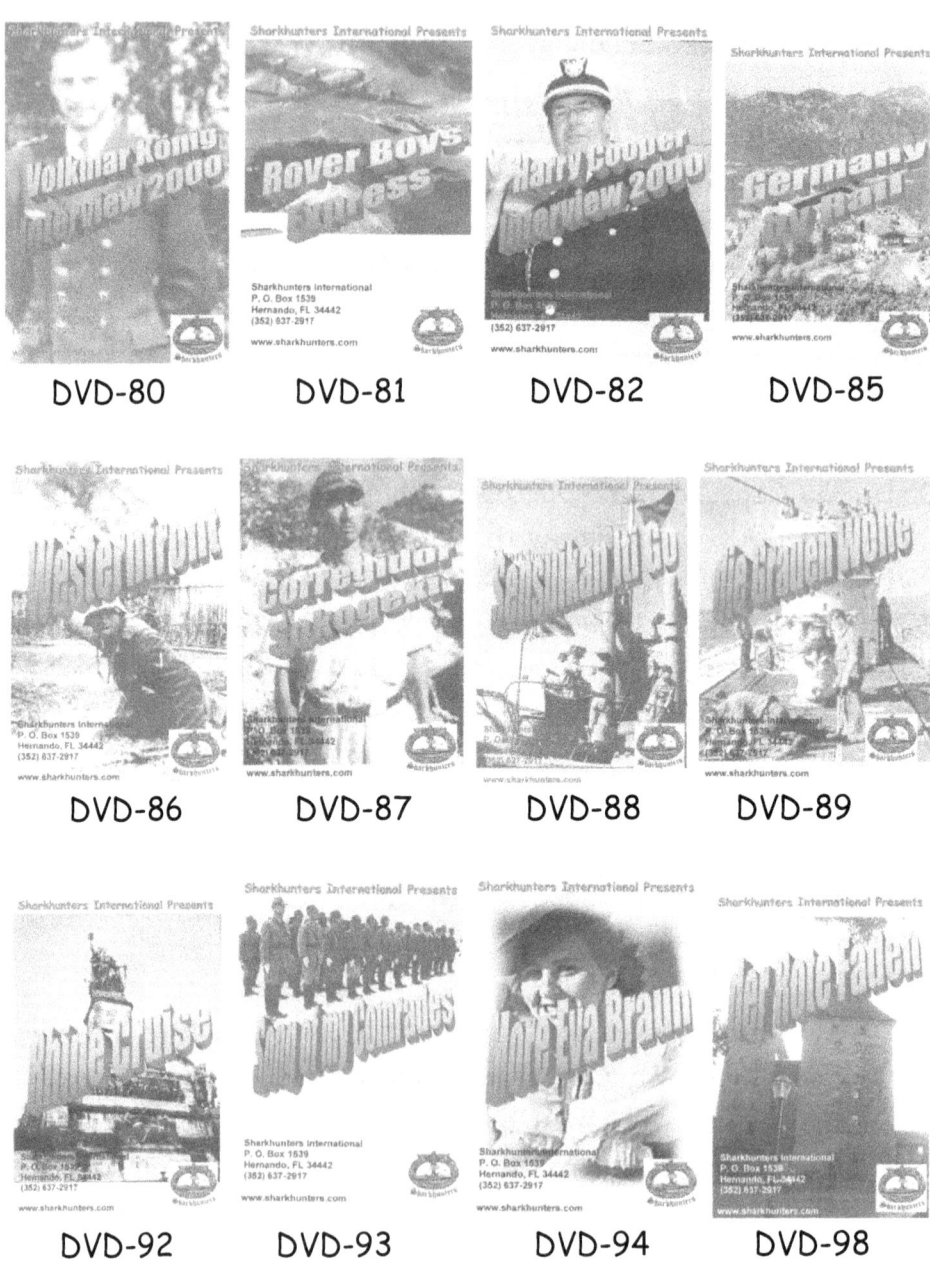

| DVD-80 | DVD-81 | DVD-82 | DVD-85 |

| DVD-86 | DVD-87 | DVD-88 | DVD-89 |

| DVD-92 | DVD-93 | DVD-94 | DVD-98 |

More Great DVDs of History
Check the website for special prices

DVD-100   DVD-101   DVD-103   DVD-104

DVD-105   DVD-106   DVD-107   DVD-108

The next four are from **LENI RIEFENSTAHL (3157-1993)**

DVD-110   DVD-111   DVD-112   DVD-113

More Great DVDs of History
Check the website for special prices

DVD-114   DVD-115   DVD-116   DVD-117

DVD-118   DVD-120   DVD-121   DVD-122

DVD-123   DVD-126   DVD-127   DVD-129

Go to www.sharkhunters.com for more

More Great DVDs of History
Pure History Available Nowhere Else

DVD-103 WW II, the Beginning (1939 – 1941)
DVD-104 Barbarossa; the Invasion of the Soviet Union
DVD-105 Kampf in Sewastopol! The Crimean Campaign
DVD-106 Only the Elders; Soviet Fighter Pilots
DVD-107 Soviet Dive Bombers
DVD-108 Soviet Torpedo Bombers
DVD-110 das Blaue Licht; from **LENI RIEFENSTAHL**
DVD-111 SOS Iceberg; in English from **LENI RIEFENSTAHL**
DVD-112 Victory of Faith; from **LENI RIEFENSTAHL**
DVD-113 Olympia I; from **LENI RIEFENSTAHL**
DVD-114 Day of Freedom; from **LENI RIEFENSTAHL**
DVD-115 Olympia II; from **LENI RIEFENSTAHL**
DVD-116 History of the Reich; great history
DVD-117 Vlassov; the Soviet general with the Reich
DVD-118 the Winter War; Finland turns back the Red Army
DVD-120 Vichy; many French hated the British & Americans
DVD-121 Interview with SS Soldier; right to the point
DVD-122 Tiefland; from **LENI RIEFENSTAHL**
DVD-123 Prelude to War
DVD-126 die Goldene Stadt; Prague was beautiful
DVD-127 Doctor of Stalingrad; post-war Prison Camp
DVD-129 Firebombing of Dresden; an atrocity
DVD-130 Geburtstag der Führer; Hitler's Birthdays
DVD-131 Interview with Wolf Hess
DVD-132 SS Division Viking; how it was formed and fought
DVD-133 History of the SS
DVD-135 Blitzkrieg; STUKA dive bombers and tanks in action
DVD-136 Birth of a Nation; birth of the Klu Klux Klan

More Great DVDs of History
Check the website for special prices

DVD-130   DVD-131   DVD-132   DVD-133

DVD-135   DVD-136   DVD-137   DVD-138

DVD-139   DVD-140   DVD-141   DVD-142

Check the website for complete description of each DVD

More Great DVDs of History
Pure History Available Nowhere Else

| DVD-143 | DVD-144 | DVD-145 | DVD-146 |

| DVD-147 | DVD-148 | DVD-149 | DVD-150 |

| DVD-151 | DVD-152 | DVD-153 | DVD-154 |

More Great DVDs of History
Satisfaction Guaranteed or Full Refund

DVD-156

DVD-157

DVD-158

DVD-159

DVD-161

DVD-162

DVD-163

DVD-164

DVD-165

DVD-166

DVD-167

DVD-168

More Great DVDs of History
So real you hear the guns; smell the powder

DVD-137   German Folk Life; how it was in the early war years

DVD-138   Hitler Junge Quex; Early Reich History

DVD-139   Fortress Europe; hard fought combat

DVD-140   Nürnberg! The Beginning

DVD-141   Advances in Russia I; Barbarossa

DVD-142   Advance in Russia II; Barbarossa

DVD-143   Third Reich in Color; great color films of the time

DVD-144   Despair! German civilians were not well treated

DVD-145   Shattered Dreams; the end of the war was bitter

DVD-146   Personal Wars; personal films from various soldiers

DVD-147   Legion Condor; the famed fighting force in Spain

DVD-148   Reich Classics; German orchestras

DVD-149   Krieg in Farben I; the war in color

DVD-150   Krieg in Farben II; more of the war in color

DVD-151   Hitler's First Speech

DVD-152   Franco's Italians; more soldiers in Spain

DVD-153   Italian Air Force; combat not usually seen

DVD-154   Operation Drumbeat

DVD-156   Top Secret 212 Class; film taken out of Germany

DVD-157   Weltfeind; the enemy of the world – the USSR

DVD-158   Adolf Hitler – Dead or Alive; propaganda

DVD-159   Party Rally Nürnberg; a very early rally

DVD-161   Learn to Fly the P 47; USAAF film

DVD-162   Learn to Fly the B 25 and the B 26; USAAF film

DVD-163   Learn to Fly the P 40 and the P 38; USAAF film

DVD-164   Fly with the Nickel Air Force

DVD-165   Battle for Seeloh Heights; at doorsteps of Berlin

DVD-166   Starvation Camp Lager X; an Eisenhower Camp

More Great DVDs of History
Pure History Available Nowhere Else

DVD-169   DVD-170   DVD-172   DVD-173

DVD-167   Battle of the River plate; GRAF SPEE

DVD-168   Kamikaze

DVD-169   *USS BARB*; last patrols

DVD-170   Anti-Communist Russians in WW II

DVD-172   92nd Bomb Group I; actual combat films

DVD-173   92nd Bomb Group II; actual combat films

We are constantly adding great historical DVDs to our list – combat footage, interviews with veterans and much more. Please keep checking back to our website and check out our unique DVDs.

Sharkhunters offers many great CDs as well. Some are music of marching bands, others are speeches and yet others are – interesting. Go to our website and click on CDs to see them all.

Check our website www.sharkhunters.com often. We are constantly adding new DVDs and CDs. Don't miss seeing our new additions.

We are constantly adding more books to our list as well. Look at the website to see when new books are released.

NOTES

Use this page for your notes and observations.

CPSIA information can be obtained
at www.ICGtesting.com
Printed in the USA
LVHW04s0014150918
590043LV00002B/67/P